GRID COMPUTING

TECHNIQUES AND FUTURE PROSPECTS

COMPUTER SCIENCE, TECHNOLOGY AND APPLICATIONS

Additional books in this series can be found on Nova's website
under the Series tab.

Additional e-books in this series can be found on Nova's website
under the e-book tab.

COMPUTER SCIENCE, TECHNOLOGY AND APPLICATIONS

GRID COMPUTING

TECHNIQUES
AND FUTURE PROSPECTS

JORGE G. BARBOSA
AND
INÊS DUTRA
EDITORS

New York

NOTICE TO THE READER

Library of Congress Cataloging-in-Publication Data

Grid computing (2015)
  Grid computing : techniques and future prospects / editors, Jorge G. Barbosa and Injs Dutra, Department of Informatics Engineering of Faculdade de Engenharia da Universidade do Porto (FEUP), and other.
      pages cm. -- (Computer science, technology and applications)
  Includes index.
  ISBN 978-1-63117-704-0 (hardcover)
  1. Computational grids (Computer systems) I. Barbosa, Jorge G. II. Dutra, Injs. III. Title.
  QA76.9.C58G75525 2014
  004'.36--dc23
                        2015005441

Published by Nova Science Publishers, Inc. †New York

CONTENTS

PREFACE

In the past two decades, grid computing have fostered advances in several scientific domains by making resources available to a wide community and bridging scientific gaps.

Grid infrastructures have been harnessing computational resources all around the world allowing all kinds of parallelism to be explored. Other approaches to parallel and distributed computing still exist like the use of dedicated high-performance (HPC) infrastructures, and the use of clouds for computing and storage, but grid computing continues to be the predominant technology used for scientific computing in Europe, through the European Grid Infrastructure (EGI) and the European Middleware Initiative (EMI). Currently, there is a trend towards the use of cloud technologies for computing and storage. In Europe, this trend is being followed by taking advantage of all the experience gained on building grid infrastructures and the technologies developed around them (resource management orchestration, unified job description languages, security, user interfaces, programming models, and scheduling policies, among others). As a result, the European Grid Infrastructure Federated Cloud is being built on top of the grid infrastructure already available. After almost two decades of the development of grid software and components and the emergence of competing technologies, now is the time to discuss current trends and to assess future prospects.

When organizing this book, we considered contributions that would review the current grid computing scenario as well as contributions that would summarize the main tools and technologies used so far. We invited colleagues that had made contributions in the past and were very fortunate to have a positive answer from most of them. The chapters in this book provide reviews for the following topics: a) performance prediction for parallel and distributed computing systems, b) resource sharing on computational grids, c) economic models for resource management, and d) programming frameworks. The chapters address grid issues such as a) the challenges of designing efficient job schedulers for production grids, b) scalability analysis of bag-of-tasks applications, c) the energy efficiency of resource reservation-based scheduling, and d) the development of parallel applications using the grid environment. Additionally, the following tools are presented: a) a programming framework based on the concept of a pluggable grid service that avoids explicit calls to grid services in scientific code and b) a desktop grid framework that runs on top of a cloud and can be deployed on the fly.

The authors were each invited to contribute a chapter to this book, which were carefully revised and selected based on their originality and the value of their contribution to the discussion of grid computing issues and future prospects. The book comprises seven chapters, organized as follows.

In Chapter 1, Seneviratne et al. present a review of performance prediction systems for parallel and distributed computing systems. Such systems are a key feature for enabling optimized resource usage decisions by users and Resource Management Systems. A taxonomy covers four different perspectives, namely, the prediction approach, the resource type, the resource level and the grid-enabled job model. The contribution of this chapter is a taxonomy of performance prediction systems that allows for the identification of approaches and issues not yet fully explored by researchers.

In Chapter 2, Barbosa et al. discuss the limitations, with respect to energy, of the advanced static reservation of nodes for a workflow job and present the advantages of resource sharing. Challenges for grid resource managers, with the intent of achieving energy-efficient resource sharing, are devised. Moreover, a review of economic models for resource management and pricing is also presented, along with a case study.

In Chapter 3, Klusáček and Tóth discuss the challenges involved in the design of efficient job schedulers for production grids. The authors demonstrate that efficient job scheduling is a very complex problem when realistic scenarios are considered, in contrast to the popular belief that the entire problem can be solved by evaluating a scheduling algorithm using a simple system model. Based on their experience with real systems, they enumerate several aspects of the problem that must be carefully modeled and evaluated to obtain realistic and useful results.

In Chapter 4, Silva and Senger present a study of the scalability of bag-of-tasks (BoT) applications executing on master-slave and hierarchical platforms. Examples of BoT applications include Monte Carlo simulations, massive searches, image manipulation applications and data mining applications. They conclude that, in general, scalability depends on both the communication model and the characteristics of the application with respect to input and output files.

In Chapter 5, Atanassov et al. discuss the development of parallel applications using the grid environment. Two strategies are addressed, namely, the batch execution of a large number of jobs in a coordinated manner and parallel jobs that require MPI and/or OpenMP. Particular attention is given to tools that speedup job execution, such as the Job Track Service (JTS), as well as several techniques for the Map Reduce processing model.

In Chapter 6, Medeiros et al. present a review of current programming frameworks that enable the execution of scientific applications on grid platforms and discuss the requirements for future programming frameworks that target computational grids. Additionally, a programming framework is introduced based on the concept of a pluggable grid service that provides seamless access to computational grids using aspect-oriented techniques. The authors identify issues of critical importance to enable seamless access to heterogeneous resources, preferably requiring the same programming effort as that required to build traditional desktop applications.

In Chapter 7, Kacsuk et al. discuss the usage of desktop grids in the era of cloud computing. The authors also demonstrate how virtualization and cloud computing make the BOINC desktop grid more generic and how they can be deployed on a time scale of a few minutes in the cloud. The authors have developed a Generic BOINC Application Client (GBAC) that eliminates the need for porting applications to BOINC. The integration of the cloud with BOINC systems solves the tail problem in volunteer desktop grids, and as a result, an increasing number of user communities have begun to adopt the EDGeS@home BOINC desktop grid.

We would like to thank all authors of this book for their contributions and for their efforts in addressing the reviewers' comments and revising their manuscripts to improve the quality of the book.

We hope readers enjoy!

Jorge G. Barbosa
Departamento de Engenharia Informática
Faculdade de Engenharia da Universidade do Porto
Porto, Portugal

Inês Dutra
Departamento de Ciência dos Computadores
Faculdade de Ciências da Universidade do Porto
Porto, Portugal

In: Grid Computing: Techniques and Future Prospects
Editors: J. G. Barbosa and I. Dutra, pp. 1-44

ISBN: 978-1-63117-704-0
© 2015 Nova Science Publishers, Inc.

Chapter 1

A TAXONOMY OF PERFORMANCE PREDICTION SYSTEMS FOR PARALLEL AND DISTRIBUTED COMPUTING SYSTEMS

Sena Seneviratne[1,*], David C. Levy[1] and Rajkumar Buyya[2]
[1]Computer Engineering Lab., School of Electrical and Information Engineering,
The University of Sydney, Australia
[2]Cloud Computing and Distributed Systems Lab.,
Department of Computing and Information Systems,
The University of Melbourne, Australia

Abstract

As Distributed Computing Systems (DCSs) such as Clusters, Parallel Systems, distributed database systems, Peer-to-Peer Desktop Systems, Grids and Clouds are congregations of geographically distributed heterogeneous resources, the efficient scheduling/ utilization of the resources requires the support of sound Performance Prediction Systems (PPS). The performance prediction of DCS resources is helpful for both Resource Management Systems and users to make optimized resource usage decisions. In this chapter we focus on the taxonomy for the Grid PPS architecture. The taxonomy is used to categorize and identify approaches which are followed in the implementation of the existing PPSs of DCSs such as Clusters, Parallel Systems, Peer-to-Peer Desktop Systems and Grids. The taxonomy and the survey results are used to identify approaches and issues that have not been fully explored in research.

Keywords: Performance Prediction System, Cloud Computing, Cluster Computing, Grid Computing, Resource Management Systems

---

* E-mail address: ssen2304@uni.sydney.edu.au (Corresponding author)

1. Introduction

As Grids are ever-changing loosely-coupled congregations of dynamic and heterogeneous resources, the efficient scheduling and allocation of resources requires the support of a sound Performance Prediction System (PPS) [1]. The performance prediction is helpful for both Resource Management System (RMS) and grid users to make optimized resource usage decisions to meet QoS requirements committed in a Service Level Agreement (SLA) [2]. For instance, if the PPS predicts a job task's future load profiles (runtimes) on the nodes of a Grid, the RMS can use such information to schedule a set of job tasks in a time optimal way. Alternatively, if the PPS can predict the cost profile of a job task on the nodes of a Grid, then an affordable set of nodes can be selected to execute a set of job tasks satisfying the user's budgetary requirements which were specified through the SLA [3].

The requirements of the PPS for a Grid span over all of the grid resources in several dimensions. They consist of the fundamentally important Application Level Prediction (ALP), namely the requirement of forecasting of the runtime of a job task on a specific machine for the given input volume, prediction of the availability of a machine and its resources for a particular duration of time, prediction of disk storage resources, prediction of network bandwidth resources, prediction of overheads of grid resources, prediction of the resultant execution time of the workflow, prediction of the reliability of grid resources, prediction of the availability of a number of nodes on a cluster/grid and so forth [2]. Therefore, the performance prediction in Grids needs to consider different approaches.

In recent times, different avenues for grid performance prediction are being explored as different research communities introduce novel approaches to perform prediction. The numerous approaches yield several different performance prediction models. Each model addresses a different performance prediction problem. Tables 1 and 2 compare a range of features of existing models, which can be used to enhance the efficiency of scheduling in grid environments.

Downey [4], eNANOS [5], DIMEMAS [6], Grid Performance Prediction System [7], Modelling Workloads for Grid Systems [8], QBETS [9], Smith et al. [10], Li et al. [11], Minh & Wolters [12] and GAMMA [13] focus on performance prediction of job (bag of tasks) runtime or queue time either on a cluster or parallel computers with a batch queue system, but their models can be modified to address the prediction requirements in both grid and cloud environments. In this chapter we survey and discuss about their suitability to the grid environment. However the taxonomy and performance prediction models/ algorithms discussed in this chapter are applicable to cloud computing environments such as Inter Clouds which are distributed geographically [14-15].

The prediction approaches can be divided into two main categories. They are the prediction approaches that are based on (1) Analytical models (e.g., PACE and LaPIe) and (2) Prediction models trained from historical execution (Machine Learning models) (e.g., Smith's, Li's). An analysis of a wide range of prediction approaches is given in section 4.

This chapter surveys through numerous PPSs that are currently available and presents taxonomy to classify them. The taxonomy covers on four different perspectives: (a) the prediction approach, (b) the resource type, (c) the resource level, (d) the job model, and they are mapped in tables 1 and 2 to selected PPSs that are designed for both clusters and grids. The main objective of this chapter is to provide a basis for categorizing the existing performance prediction models for identifying future development areas such as invention of new metrics, common standards for workloads and more efficient prediction algorithms. This chapter provides the reader with an understanding of the essential concepts of this research area and helps them identify outstanding issues for further investigation.

This chapter consists of three major parts. The first part focuses on the general challenges for the developers of the PPSs. The second part introduces a taxonomy which separates existing PPSs. The third part includes the survey of all existing PPSs. The sections of the chapter are organised as follows. Section 2 introduces the background and related work, section 3 discusses the current challenges for PPS developers and section 4 gives a description of various taxonomies for PPSs. Section 5 includes the complete survey of the existing PPSs, section 6 includes the analysis of the survey and discussion and section 7 presents a conclusion and suggestions for future work.

2. Background and Related Work

In a grid system design the RMS contains the most fundamental and essential components for its management of a Grid [3]. As a fundamental requirement, a RMS needs to have the support of sound PPS. Therefore, it is required to design or select a PPS which serves the requirement of a particular RMS [16].

In designing a large scale distributed computer system, efficient application performance and efficient system performance may require two different treatments. For instance it may not be possible for the same scheduler to optimise application performance and resource performance. One solution to this is to have two RMSs which use an application scheduler such as AppLes in conjunction with a resource scheduler such as Globus to form a two-layer RMS [17]. This suggests that there should be two different PPSs connected to application and resource schedulers respectively. Further, due to the diverse nature and large scale of the Grid, the resultant grid RMS is most likely an interconnection of various RMSs and each one of them needs the service of a suitable PPS. For example, the computational, data intensive and service oriented applications would require different RMS-PPS pairs and so on. Therefore, each RMS needs to have a PPS which serves its specialised requirements. Further, as the scale of the Grid grows, there can be an interconnection of various RMSs that cooperate with one another within a common framework.

A handful of efforts have been reported for conducting surveys on Grid PPS:

Venugopal [18] has conducted a lengthy study on various taxonomies of data grids, namely *Data Grid Organization, Data Transport, Data Replication and Storage, and Resource Allocation and Scheduling*. The Data Transport, Data Replication and Storage and Resource Allocation and Scheduling Taxonomies reflect the need to have the services of sound PPSs for the prediction of network bandwidth, resources such as data storage facilities and suitable computational resources for processing data on them respectively.

The CoreGRID [19] has analysed early PPSs using a well organized template that is used to describe the prediction models and solutions. The template contains (1) Name and small description of the model, (2) Authors, (3) Scope, (4) Estimated values, (5) Predictor inputs, (6) Classes of applications or jobs, (6) Classes of resources, (7) Prediction method, (8) Prediction quality, (9) Scheduling policies, (10) Software tools, (11) Availability, (12) Architecture, (13) Support of technologies, (14) Publications, and (15) Links. Nevertheless, they consider one of the best ways to have good performance on the Grid is through performance guarantees (e.g., SLAs).

They emphasise the fact that as the requirements of PPSs for the Grid span over all of the Grid resources, the prediction of resource availability needs to consider different approaches. Therefore, if a scheduler needs to have predicted levels of several different resources, which have to be done using an integrated infrastructure and this provides access to different PPSs. Also, they suggest the PPS developers identify new performance metrics which are relevant for the Grid. They reached valuable conclusions such as the importance of the usage of data mining and AI techniques in learning prediction systems and the need for better predictors for workflow and MPI applications. They also found the necessity to have better predictors for bandwidth and data transfer rates.

Krauter [20] provides several taxonomies for RMSs with classification by *Machine Organization within the Grid, Resource Model, Dissemination Protocols, Namespace Organization, Data Store Organization, Resource Discovery, QoS Support, Scheduler Organization, Scheduler Policy, State Estimation and Scheduling Approach.* They provide a description of scheduling on the Grid in relation to their State Estimation (prediction) taxonomy which is relevant to our study.

Except for CoreGRID's effort [19], in the previous surveys, Venugopal et al. [2006], and Krauter et al. [2002] focus respectively on the Data Grids and RMSs and their interests in the PPSs are secondary. The CoreGrid survey provides the reader an abundance of information about early PPSs, however they do not classify the PPSs in terms of different levels of the resources, nor do they sufficiently identify the prediction approaches along the lines of analytical methodology, machine learning and spatio-temporal correlation, nor have they classified PPSs according to their ability to use historical information as training samples, manually or through automated means. In our survey, not only do we address a large number of PPSs, but also classify them using a number of taxonomies that is defined using the above mentioned concepts, aiming to expose the missing links of the PPSs with respect to different levels of resources and applications and to motivate the researchers to invent novel prediction methods.

3. Challenges

One of the basic challenges arises due to the heterogeneous nature presented in the grid. This happens due to the underlying differences in the diverse type of applications, resources and different standards of grid environments. For example, the input or output data for embarrassingly distributed application is different from that of MPI application, and the data intensive applications require accessing distributed replicas which are stored across the globe.

The historical data profiles of a particular grid can be archived and would be of great help for the forecasting of future profiles. However, past experience indicates their effectiveness depends on the cleverness of their usage. Once the data is transformed into information, the next challenge is to exploit them effectively and efficiently using one of the prediction approaches. The truth is that none of the listed prediction approaches are proven near 100% successful in solving the performance prediction problem. Further, it is evident that some approaches can be better used to meet a given objective than others. For example, prediction of runtimes of parallel batch job tasks in a homogeneous cluster by Modelling Workloads for

Grid Systems [8]. Therefore, at this point in time, it is essential to ponder over combining several approaches to produce the best results.

In the past, the input and output point valued parameters might have been acceptable for prediction of performance of a short job task. However, a grid job/ application consists of long job tasks and therefore such parameters may produce inaccurate results, since they can only represent a certain point of time. Therefore it is appropriate to design relevant grid performance metrics [21].

Therefore, for the success of the PPSs, it is necessary to address diverse and different levels of problems which require the answers in terms of the nature of the Grid and they can be listed as follows [19].

1. Prediction of diverse parameters such as runtime, queue time, job resource requirement, resource load, communication time of MPIs, data transfer time.
2. Prediction of possible errors in the prediction of grid resources in the system. If we can collect information on possible prediction errors, then it is possible to make statistical corrections for the prediction errors of grid resources.
3. Standardization of application performance models. Though NASA has categorised the applications into different application types, still there is no common way to express application performance model [22].
4. There is not a standard grid workload format.
5. The PPS should be able to predict even if the input information is incomplete.
6. The PPS should be extendable for a large scope of applications and resources. In the present context and also due to the factors 3, 4 and 8, there is no single PPS to address the prediction problem of such a wide spectrum of prediction metrics and therefore it is preferable that the several prediction models may be incorporated into a single giant prediction system.
7. If possible, new performance metrics should be proposed to suit the grid. In traditional parallel computing, response time and system utilization are a suitable. However in the Grid we need to reconsider such traditional metrics, because the Grid is dynamic and therefore common metrics like peak performance, throughput and point load average may be outdated or not relevant.
8. The grid environments themselves need to have single standards to be able to streamline above 3 and 4. If there is single standard, the comparison of different prediction metrics from different PPSs becomes easy. The Computational Grids, Data Grids, Service Grids etc. can be streamlined under such a single standard. Currently there are different types of grid standards, and therefore interfacing them with a certain PPS requires different strenuous adjustments to the PPS.
9. The PPS should be able to predict the quality of service.
10. The PPS should be able to predict the overheads of the system.
11. The PPS should be able to predict the availability of the required data storage.

4. The Taxonomy

Various resource types and target applications motivate the architecture of PPS. Thus PPSs have been categorized into four different taxonomies, namely prediction approach, resource type, resource level, and job model.

Taxonomy of Prediction Approach

The full scale simulation of activities of the grid environments has been successfully done. For example MicroGrid [23] which allows the execution of Globus applications using a virtual grid environment; SimGrid [24] which is used for simulation of "C" language application scheduling; GridSim [25] that facilitate the simulations of different classes of heterogeneous resources, users, applications, resource brokers, and schedulers in a single VO [19].

While the above effort is suitable for the representation, understanding, and analysis of the grid performance for the performance prediction of the Grid, these methods have some inherent difficulties. The main problem is that the prediction of grid commodities such as resources and services or cost needs to be done online. Predictions need to be calculated within a short period of time ($< 30s$) because in the ever-changing dynamic grid environment, the status and cost of the grid commodities are being continuously updated [19]. None of the above simulators meets these basic criteria and therefore in their current status they are not suitable for the performance prediction of the Grid.

There are two main categories of prediction methods and they are,

1.   Analytical prediction models
2.   Prediction models trained from historical executions.

Analytical Prediction Models

In both PACE [26] and TPM [21, 27] the characteristic behaviour of the job task is represented by either its code or its CPU /Disk load profile. The characteristic behaviour of the hardware environment is represented by the algorithms which mainly models the internal workings of the runnable queue and the processors. These two models belong to the school of analytical models which is developed after studying the characteristics grid application and its hardware environment. Apart from these models there are other analytical models such as LaPIe [28] which use the pLogP model to predict the overall communication time of a MPI application and the GAMMA model [13], which selects the most suitable cluster for a particular embarrassingly distributed application. The analytical models can be based on different algorithms and principles, and therefore, there can be numerous analytical models with each one having a potential for further development.

Prediction Models Trained from Historical Executions

Learning from historic information or trace data to make future predictions using time series algorithms has always been a traditionally popular area of study [29]. Previous research by Wolski et. al. shows that the CPU load is strongly correlated over time, and therefore the history-based load prediction schemes are feasible [30]. This means that modelling the relationship of the historical data is of help in making accurate predictions [31-33].

Dinda conducted a complete analysis of statistical properties of host loads through a variety of load measurements collected over a wide range of time-shared machines from single PCs to clusters [31]. One of his key findings is that while load varies in complex ways, it shows high epochal behaviour. This means the pattern of change of load remains relatively constant for a relatively long period of time. The existence of epochs is significant for modelling future loads. He also found that the load does not exhibit seasonality [31]. This means that the load profile does not contain dominant underlying periodic signals on top of which are layered other signals.

Another key observation of Dinda is that the load exhibits a high degree of self-similarity with Hurst Parameter [34] ranging from 0.63 to 0.97 with a strong bias towards the top of that range. This result indicates that load varies in complex ways on all time scales and has long-range dependence and the load is difficult to model and predict [31].

Dinda carried out a thorough statistical analysis on the load traces and found that there is an opportunity to use prediction algorithms even under heavily loaded conditions. According to Dinda [35], time series analysis tools such as autocorrelation and periodogram show that the past load values have a strong influence on future values, and therefore load prediction, which is based on historical loads, is feasible and the linear time series models may be used in prediction [36].

The statistical analysis can be used on historical data to understand their behaviour. For example, Modelling workloads for grid systems [8] and Queue wait time prediction in space shared environments [4] are based on the statistical analysis of historical information. The workload modelling is introduced to make use of the collected workload traces for analysis and simulation in an analytical and manageable way [36-37]. For example, the modeller has full knowledge of the workload characteristics and therefore it is easy to know which workload parameters are correlated with each other [38]. Also, it is possible to change model parameters, one at a time, in order to investigate the influence of each one, while keeping the other parameters constant, enabling the measurement of system sensitivity against different parameters. Further, a model is not affected by policies and constraints that are particular to the site where a trace was recorded. However, the models have their own problems because it's difficult to say to what degree they represent the real workloads that the system will encounter in practice [37].

Artificial intelligent techniques can be used to dynamically model historical information as it provides the basis required for the current and future behaviour of a system. For example, according to Kurowski et al. [7] mean, min, max, standard deviation, error values are calculated for each workload category. The category is decided by a template which consists of command, command argument, number of processors, maximum memory usage, host name, queue name, user name etc. Such categories with specific parameters are entered into a knowledge database as rules which are used to generate predictions for new jobs. Kurowski et al. [7] have designed their prediction system, namely the Grid Performance Prediction System (GPRES), which is based on the architecture of the expert systems.

Data mining rules can be used on historical information to find similar datasets. For example, Li [39] uses Distance Function to categorize similar jobs and resources. The Genetic Search Algorithm is used to search for certain weights of the nearest neighbours from the historical archives [39]. After extracting the sets of information of nearby jobs, the Instance

Based Learning (IBL) prediction algorithm [40] is used for the prediction of runtimes and queue times. The details of the algorithm are found in the relevant literature [11].

The prediction models, which are based on Machine Learning, can be further divided into two major types. They are:

1. The Spatial Temporal Correlation Models (STC),
2. The models that analyse data as independent data tuples (datasets) (IDT).

    For example, Smith's usage of static templates to categorize data and Genetic Algorithm to search the best match and Li's use of nearest neighbours on the independent historical load profiles to categorise similar datasets (i.e., jobs with a certain similarity) [11] and Also the Reinforcement Learning (RI) prediction models.

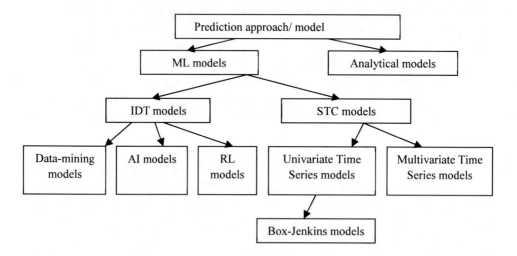

Figure 1. Prediction approach taxonomy.

Figure 1 graphically presents the constituents of the Prediction approach. Another classification among the ML models is with respect to the selection of attributes/ data that would serve as training samples. The attributes/ data can be manually or automatically selected. The attributes/ data can be automatically selected, with the use of additional algorithms to select, transform, and filter.

Resource Type

There are different types of fundamental resources that are utilized by the grid users. They are (1) CPU (Processor time), (2) Memory, (3) Disk (Access cost), and (4) Network bandwidth per CPU. The performance prediction of each fundamental resource type can be done separately as each one has different characteristics and behaviour and each resource serves a different purpose.

Other complex resource types include PC nodes, Network bandwidth and Disk storage units. A cluster can be considered as a single resource type which consists of many fundamental resource types.

The resources can be shared in two different ways, either time-shared, or space-shared. An example of a time shared resource is the manner in which the CPU in a desktop PC shares its job tasks. In this case, a few similar priority job tasks are running in round-robin fashion during their allocated time slots or time slices. In contrast, the space-shared CPU can only be allocated to a single job task at a time. The next job task may be allocated to the next available CPU. A good example of this is a Cluster computing system where a number of CPUs is managed in a space-shared manner. The Network bandwidth and Disk storage are space-shared resources [2].

As the resources can be shared in two different ways, the collected historical information differs and, therefore, the performance prediction strategies need to be different. For example, for a time-shared system, the collection of historical information is based on the load average metric because it is the future load average that needs to be predicted. In contrast, for a space-shared system it is important to predict the number of free CPUs.

The resources can be either homogeneous or heterogeneous. For example, a cluster can have identical PC-nodes which give it the homogeneous character. Also, the resource can be centralised or distributed. For example, the Grid is a loosely connected distributed heterogeneous resource. Further, the resource can be shared or dedicated. For example, a cluster of nodes, which is permanently available for HPC tasks, can be considered as a dedicated resource. On the other hand, the Grid contains a collection of PCs that are temporarily borrowed from a third party for its use and therefore considered as a shared resource. Table 2 contains the details of the PPSs which can be performed on each of the above resources.

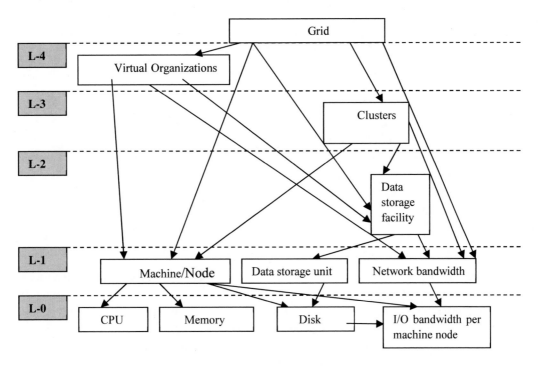

Figure 2. Resource hierarchy.

For a particular resource, the resource consumption can be interpreted in several metrics. Therefore, it is important to measure these resources with relevant metrics that are easy to predict. For example, the CPU resource for a certain job task can be measured as (1) through CPU time share allocated to a certain job task within the elapsed second or (2) as the load average of the job task. In the OS kernel, the load average is calculated by adding the number of tasks in the CPU's queue and the number of running tasks. Therefore, it measures the load on a CPU by supplying crucial information for a prospective user who needs to decide to which nodes to submit.

Resource Level

Figure 2 shows the different levels of predictability on the Grid. The most fundamental resources such as CPU, Memory, Disk space and I/O bandwidth per machine node are on the ground level (L-0). Level-1 (L-1) contains Machine/ Node, Network bandwidth and a Disk storage unit. Level-2 (L-2) contains the Data storage facility. Level-3 (L-3) contains the clusters and the queue. Level-4 (L-4) contains virtual organizations and the Grid. Some of the cluster PPSs (Table 2) which can be easily modified to predict on machine/ node resources at level-0 are considered to be level-0 predictors. Please read section 6 for more details.

Level 0

CPU: CPU, which is available for a new job task (of a parallel application), can be predicted on a single node by using Dinda [31], Smith et al. [10], ASKALON [41], OpenSeries & StreamMiner [42], DIMEMAS [6], eNANOS [5], MWGS [8], GPRES [7], Li et al. [11], PACE [26], PPSKel [43], FREERIDE-G [44], Minh & Wolters [12], FAST [45], Prediction of Variance [46], AWP [47], or TPM [21]. This value is important because then the user knows how much further the CPU can be loaded.

Memory: Memory, which is available for new applications, can be predicted on a single node by using PACE [26], FAST [45] or OpenSeries and StreamMiner [42]. This value is necessary; otherwise the new application would crash without sufficient memory.

Disk: In FREERIDE-G project [44] the disk space access cost (time) or the data retrieval time is predicted by running the Performance Prediction Frame Work on each PC node.

I/O Bandwidth per Node: Both Network I/Os and Disk I/Os inherit I/O Bandwidth per node. (please see next level).

Level 1

At this level, there are 3 main resource components that can be predicted either using the parameters of the level-0 or directly.

Machine/ Node: The availability of a machine/ node can be predicted directly using historically collected information as the service provider expresses the time intervals in the day that the machine is available for Grid users. NWS [30] or OpenSeries & StreamMiner [42] predicts the availability of PC nodes. Also the availability of machine/ node can be forecast after performing L-0 level predictions on CPU, memory, or disk (access cost) resources.

Network Bandwidth: Available bandwidth can be predicted by using NWS [30], Faerman et al. [48], PACE [26], EDG ROS [49], FREERIDE-G [44], FAST [50], Vazhkudai & Schopf [51] or PDTT [52].

Data storage unit: In typical data grids, a large amount of replica data is stored in different Hierarchical Storage Management (HSM) systems with access latencies ranging from seconds to hours [53]. The access latency consists of two major components and they are network access cost and storage access cost. In EDG ROS, the prediction of storage access cost is performed by CrossGrid data access estimator [49]. If the data storage consists of individual machines/ nodes, then after predicting the disk space access cost of each machine at level-0, the total data storage access cost can be calculated.

Level 2

At this level, there is a single resource component that can be predicted either using the parameters of the level-0 and level-1 or directly.

Data storage facility: The prediction of the access cost of the Data storage facility can be done through the prediction of individual data storage units at level-1. If a data storage unit consists of several individual machines/ nodes, after predicting the disk space access cost of each machine at level-0, the total data storage access time can be calculated.

Level 3

At this level there are four cluster resource components that can be predicted either using the predicted information of level-0, level-1 and level-2 or directly.

Cluster (Parallel application's total runtime): DIMEMAS [6] can predict the communication and computational times of a MPI parallel application. Smith et al. [10], eNANOS [5], Li et al. [11], Minh & Wolters [12] or PQR2 [54] predict the parallel job's runtime. Also MWGS [8] or GPRES [7] predict the parallel job's runtime.

Cluster (Parallel application's required number of nodes): The MWGS [8] or RBSP [55] predicts a parallel application's required number of nodes. The suitability of a parallel application to a particular cluster of nodes can be predicted using the GAMMA Model [13] therefore, it also belongs to level-3.

Cluster (Available memory): PQR2 or eNANOS predict the available memory.

Cluster (Queue wait time): In the available PPSs, the queue waiting time is defined for a space-shared cluster of nodes and therefore it belongs to level-3. Downey [4], Smith [1999], ASKALON [41], Li et al. [11], QBETS [9] or eNANOS [5] predicts the queue waiting time. Also, MWGS or GPRES predict the queue wait time.

Level 4

The suitability of a particular VO and the requirements of a particular grid need to be predicted using the predicted information of the levels below them (level-0-level-3). Sanjay & Vadhiya [56] or HIPM [57] predicts the MPI parallel job's runtime on a Grid. GIPSY predicts the parameter sweep applications runtime on a Grid. LaPIe [58] can predict the total communication time of a MPI parallel application on a Grid.

Job Model

Large HPC applications (or jobs) need to be grid-enabled for deployment on a Grid. New codes may be written in distributable form, but older applications that were not written for the Grid must be grid-enabled, often by being split into multiple tasks with a grid wrapper provided for each task [59]. Figure 3 shows the different levels of predictability in grid enabled job model taxonomy. At the ground level, there are grid enabled CPU bound tasks (or computational tasks), grid enabled Disk bound tasks (tasks with disk IO components) and inter task data. In the next upper level, grid enabled job tasks are related to either HPC or High Throughput Computing (HTC). The next level contains jobs and MPI parallel applications/ workflows.

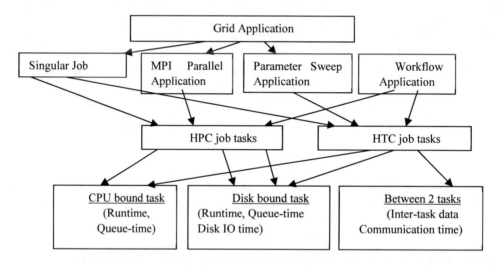

Figure 3. Grid Enabled Job model.

Also, the Grid applications may consist of various groups of jobs with complex inter-task communications, therefore it is necessary to identify them through a Data Flow Graph (DFG). Such identification helps the development of generalized prediction algorithms for a particular group of MPI parallel applications or workflows. The grid enabled parallel applications are categorized into four main patterns of DFGs, in accordance with the NAS Grid Benchmarks (NGB) [22]. They are Embarrassingly Distributed (ED), Helical Chain (HC), Visualization Pipe (VP) and Mixed Bag (MB) [22]. The NGB suite is based on NAS Parallel Benchmarks (NPB) which was originally designed to provide an objective measure of the capabilities of hardware and software systems to solve computationally intensive Fluid Dynamics problems relevant to NASA.

At the lowest level, for the prediction of runtime of a CPU bound job task, the PPSs namely Dinda [60], Smith [10], ASKALON [41], MWGS [8], GPRES [7], eNANOS [5], OpenSeries & StreamMiner [61], PACE [1], PPSkel [43], FAST [45], AWP [47], Li [11], Minh & Wolters [12] or TPM [27, 62] can be used.

For an application that requires data transfer via the network, the PPSs, namely Faerman et al. [48] or Vazhkudai and Schopf [51], PDTT [52] or FAST [45] can be used to predict the data transfer rate. Either FREERIDE-G or EDG ROS can also be used for this purpose.

The performance prediction of a MPI parallel application/ workflow involves both computational and communication times. Therefore, it is preferable to predict the combined computational and communication time of a task rather than predicting individual components. DIMEMAS [6] or ASKALON [41] can be used for the prediction of computational and communication time of a MPI parallel application or a workflow. The MWGS [8] and GPRES [7] predict the total runtime of the parallel application.

The RBSP [55] predicts the cluster size for the MPI parallel application and the GAMMA model [13] can be used to predict the suitability of any parallel application/ workflow to a cluster.

At the highest level, HIPM [57] or Sanjay & Vadhiyar [56] can be used for the prediction of computational and communication time of a MPI parallel application on the Grid. Also LaPIe [58] predicts the total communication time of a MPI parallel application on a Grid.

5. The Survey

This section includes a description of existing PPSs that have been proposed by researchers for various computing platforms such as clusters, grids, parallel and distributed systems, peer-to-peer (p2p) and distributed databases. In the next section 6, the taxonomy that is explained in the previous section 4 is used to classify these existing PPSs. Table 1 and 2 provide the summary of the analysis of the survey that is conducted using these taxonomies.

The PPSs for the survey are selected based on several criteria. Firstly, the survey should be concise and include a sufficient number of PPSs to demonstrate how the taxonomy can be applied effectively. Secondly, the selections of different resource types are considered for prediction. Thirdly, the selected PPSs are fairly recent work or performance prediction models that are currently in use, so that the survey creates an insight into the latest development in research.

Descriptions of the Prediction Models

Descriptions of the Analytical Models

PACE (Clusters & Grids): The PACE toolkit [26] for the performance evaluation and prediction is developed by adapting the standard methodology of the software engineering performance analysis to provide a representation of the whole system in terms of three modular components, namely the software execution module, parallelization module and the hardware module. These three modules are fed through the evaluation engine which runs the simulation of the application on a faster time scale to make required predictions. The runtime, memory and bandwidth of the future application are the major prediction metrics that can be calculated through simulation by PACE.

Prediction quality: The average runtime prediction error is 7%.

The Task Profiling Model (TPM) (Clusters & Grids): The Task Profiling Model for Load Profile Prediction is proposed [27, 62], which forecasts the load profiles of job tasks of individual machines based on current and immediate past information. The Free Load Profile

(FLP) or footprint of a job task on a load free node is a necessary input to the proposed Performance Prediction Model. TPM predicts the load profile (runtime) of future job tasks on the nodes of a Grid. Also, it predicts the load profiles of all currently running job tasks on each node, thereby giving an opportunity for the scheduler to protect the user set time limits of currently running job tasks. The predictions are performed by the software agents running on the nodes of a Grid. The predicted data, thus obtained, aids in choosing the most suitable set of computers for the deployment of the tasks in time-optimal manner.

Prediction quality: The average runtime prediction error is below 7%.

DIMEMAS (Single Machines/ Clusters): The DIMEMAS [6] simulator reconstructs and predicts the total runtime which is the computation and communication time for a MPI application on a cluster. The inputs are the trace-file of the previous run of the application (a set of computation bursts and calls to the MPI primitives), description of the architecture and the model for the collective MPI primitives [19].

Prediction quality: The average prediction error versus the measured value ranges between 8% and 17%.

LaPIe (Clusters and Grids): The LaPIe [58] predicts the overall time of a collective communication. It first subdivides the Grid network into homogenous subnets or logical clusters to handle each cluster individually and later aggregate them to form the Grid. The pLogP model is used to construct the prediction models. It consists of the communication latency –L, the message gap according to the message size –g(m) and the number of processes –P. It first establishes the performance models for a number of different communication strategies in order to select the better performing strategy for each different logical cluster. Thereafter, the best communication strategy is selected in each logical cluster. Through the analysis of the inter-clusters and intra-cluster performance predictions, it is capable of defining a communication schedule that minimises the overall execution time.

Prediction quality: The average prediction error is 5-10% for real communication experiments with varying message sizes (0- 1 MB), number of processes (1-50) and for different network infrastructures such as Fast Ethernet, Giga Ethernet and Myrinet.

ASKALON (Single Machines/ Clusters): In the ASKALON [41], G-prophet performs the job execution and waiting time based on the minimum training set and the historical information. The execution times and different input data sizes to the job task are measured from previous job runs on a machine. If the job task with the same input data size is submitted to a similar machine, then the future execution time is predicted using the background load and memory. However, if the job task is submitted to a machine with different characteristics (e.g., different CPU speed) then the new execution time on the new machine is estimated and the future execution time is predicted using the background load and memory. Mathematical models have been used in making adjustments and predictions to the execution times.

Prediction quality: The average runtime prediction error is 10%.

GAMMA (Clusters): In the GAMMA model [13], for a particular parallel application and for a set of available clusters, a set of Γ factors and the total functioning costs are calculated. The cluster with the least functioning cost and that best satisfies the condition $\Gamma > 1$ is selected for the deployment of the parallel application. This model is integrated into ISS VIOLA metascheduling environment. The cluster with the highest Γ factor and the least cost may be selected for the MPI parallel application.

Prediction quality: They have experimentally demonstrated the ability to select the most suitable cluster for a particular parallel application.

Performance Prediction with Skeletons (PPSkel) (Clusters and Grids): Sodhi et al. [43] have proposed a methodology that runs the scaled down simulation of the actual distributed system. The scaled down job tasks are automatically generated by using execution traces of CPU usage, and message exchanges. Their procedure is summarised as follows,

- a. Record job task's execution trace
- b. Compress execution trace into an execution signature
- c. Generate performance skeleton program from the execution signature

The scaled down simulation is run on a particular node where the prediction of runtime needs to be performed. The evaluation of the model is done using NAS grid benchmark programs. They have successfully tested the model for both CPU bound and MPI applications.

Prediction quality: For all benchmark programs throughout the time range 0.5s- 10s, the average error is 6.7%

Performance Prediction Model for FREERIDE-G (Grids): Glimcher and Agrawal [44] have developed an analytical prediction model for Grid-based data mining applications. Frame work for Rapid Implementation of Data-mining Engines in the Grid (FREERIDE-G) middleware supports the high level interface for developing data mining and scientific data processing applications that involve data stored in remote repositories. Its prediction model helps to achieve the following two tasks:

(a) Choosing the best one among multiple replicas of data

(b) Finding the best computing resources for processing data.

This is achieved by predicting (a) data retrieval and communication times and (b) data processing times and selecting the replica and computing configuration pair where the data processing can be performed with minimum cost (time).

Prediction quality: System performs within 5-12% when execution time is dominated by data processing time and within 4-7% when execution time is dominated by remote data retrieval time.

Fast Agent's System Timer (FAST) (Grids): FAST [45] is a software package allowing client jobs to get an accurate forecast of communication and computation time and memory use which uses LDAP for reading and searching static data. It also uses NWS for dynamically monitoring network and hosts. The FAST dynamically acquires the CPU speed, available memory, BW, Latency, topology etc and depends on its well-targeted API library which depends on linear algebraic algorithms to perform shortened calculations and combine static and dynamic data for the purpose of forecasting. The forecasts can be summarised as follows:

fast_comm_time(data_description, source, dest): The time needed to transfer the data from its location to the host on which the computation will be done.

fast_comp_time(host, problem, data_description): The time needed for the computation on a given host.

fast_comp_size(host, problem, data_description): memory space required for the problem.

fast_get_time(host, problem, data_description, localization): This function aggregates the results of others functions and forecasts the time needed to execute the given problem on a host for the data described by data_description, taking the prior localization of data and the time to get them on a host.

Prediction quality: Average prediction error is 10%

Prediction of the QoS (Grids): Carvalho et al. [63] make an effort to predict the Quality of Service of a peer-to-peer desktop grid by determining the amount of resources available to a particular grid consumer at a certain future time t_p. Their model can be briefly explained as follows. In a peer-to-peer grid, the two peers are considered, namely donating peer P_d and consumer peer P_c. When P_d and P_c interact, the resource balance with P_d goes down to a minimum of zero and this guarantees that it provides a defence against whitewash attack. In contrast, the resource balance with P_c goes up, proportionally to the amount of resources donated by P_d.

When the P_c submits a bag of tasks to the Grid, it needs to gather information from each peer of the Grid. The goal is to predict the amount of resources P_c is able to obtain from the Grid by the future time t_p. The prediction has to be performed with information gathered just prior to the submission of the tasks. Therefore, it is assumed that the balance of resource of P_c and each of the P_d s (all the other peers of the grid and P_c) do not change between the time of submission and t_p.

The error is defined as (ER-OR). The ER is the ratio between the estimated and requested amount of resources. The OR is the ratio between the obtained and requested amount of resources.

Prediction quality: Mean prediction error, how much of resource a peer will get from grid 7.2%

EDG Replica Optimization Service (**ROS**) (Grids): The task of the ROS [49] is to select the best replica with respect to network and storage access latencies because the best replica must be accessed by an application programme. In Data Grids, a large amount of data is stored across the world in different storage systems with access latencies ranging from seconds to hours. Therefore, the data access prediction needs to be done through the cost-estimation service which consists of estimation of the access costs of the network and storage systems.

For example, if a replica is a single file,

$$\textit{File transfer } \cos t = access \cos t \textit{ of the network } + access \cos t \textit{ of the storage} \qquad (1)$$

For estimating the access cost of the network, the EDG Network Cost-Estimation Service is used and for the access cost of the storage, the CrossGrid Data Access Estimator is used.

Prediction quality: The average estimated access cost error 6.9%

Descriptions of ML Models: STC

Wolski (Distributed resources, clusters and grids)**:** According to Wolski et. al., the Network Weather Service[1] (NWS) [30] provides one-step-ahead predictions for any time-series fed to its prediction module. Its prediction strategies include running average, sliding window average, last measurement, adaptive window average, adaptive window media, media filter, a-trimmed mean, stochastic gradient and autoregressive strategies. Its predicted values include CPU availability, TCP end-to-end throughput and TCP end-to-end latency.

Prediction quality: The CPU availability is predicted with an absolute mean error of less than 10%. The mean-based predictors are better for throughput time series. The median based predictors are better for latency time series. It is shown that mean percentage errors are less than 2.5%. The best methods have the mean percentage errors less than 0.8%.

Dinda (Clusters and grids)**:** On a typical shared unreserved host, Dinda [31] estimates the runtime of a computer-bound task, given the task's CPU demand and AR(16) time series prediction of the load on the host. A prediction is presented to the application/ scheduler as a confidence interval that neatly expresses the error associated with the measurement and the prediction processes-error that must be captured to make statistically valid decisions.

Prediction quality: Almost 90% of the tasks are completed in their computed confidence intervals. The target confidence interval of 95% has been used.

Modelling Workloads for Grid Systems (MWGS) (Parallel Computers with Batch Queue Systems)**:** Song et al. [8] use the statistical analysis and Markov-chain to predict estimation of the arrival time of a job, parallelism of a job (number of nodes) and user estimated job runtime. In their strategy, they first classify workload traces similar to Smith and then further model the workloads using Markov-chains. A Markov chain matrix has been created for each user group to model its individual behaviour and thus to predict the work loads of future jobs.

Prediction quality: The Standard Workloads are used to create the corresponding Markov chains. Thereafter using those Markov chains new workload traces are created (forecast). The KS test [64] revealed high degree of similarity. Then the model is compared with Lublin/ Feitelson model and it is found they are almost similar [65].

Prediction of Variance (Grids)**:** Yang et al. [66] have previously developed one-step-ahead tendency based time predictor for the prediction of CPU load as a point value. They use NWS one-step-ahead predictor for this purpose. They [46] further improved that time series based predictor to predict both mean and variance over some future time interval.

Prediction quality: 3 metrics are used to successfully compare the predictor with others. Please refer to the cited literature for details.

Prediction of Data Transfer Time (PDTT) (Data Grids)**:** Yang et al. [52] have predicted the data transfer times using predicted means and variances in the shared networks. They use NWS one-step-ahead predictor for this purpose. They predict the effective bandwidth using the following formulae

---

[1] Wolski's NWS project provides a multifaceted prediction approach for short tasks.

$$EffectiveBW = BWMean + TF * BWSD \qquad (2)$$

where *BWMean* is the predicted mean in end-to-end bandwidth that the data will encounter during the transfer, *BWSD* is the predicted variance in end-to-end bandwidth that the data will encounter during the transfer, and *TF* is a per link *Tuning Factor* used to scale the impact of the *BWSD* on the effective bandwidth. In fact *TF* regulates the *EffectiveBW*. For example, if the variance becomes higher for a particular link, *TF* becomes lower and helps reduce the *EffectiveBW* for that link.

Prediction quality: 3 metrics are used to successfully compare PDTT with others. Please refer to the cited literature for details.

Adaptive Workload Prediction in Confidence Window (AWP) (Grids): Wu et al. [47] have proposed a prediction methodology, Adaptive HModel (AHModel), which is based on Auto-Regression. HModel uses a fixed historical data interval as an input to predict the load n time steps ahead, within a confidence window. However, in the AHModel, the historical data interval is calculated to minimise the mean square error in the work load, before predicting the load over certain look ahead span n time steps. In other words, when the load fluctuates rapidly, the AHModel changes the historical data interval to improve the prediction accuracy.

They also use a Kalman filter to reduce the measurement errors and thereby improve the prediction accuracy. A Savitzky-Golay filter is used to smooth the spikes of the workload data in several steps of the prediction process.

Prediction quality: Mean Squared pred. error is 0.04- 0.73 as the confidence window increases from 10-50 steps.

QBETS (Parallel Computers with Batch Queue Systems): Nurmi et al. [9] have named their method as Queue Bounds Estimation from Time Series (QBETS). They consist of four main strategies: (a) Percentile estimation; (b) Change point (of history data profile) Detection; (c) Similar job clustering; and (d) Machine availability interference.

They focus on space-shared batch job tasks and propose a user friendly metric to express queue wait times. According to them, the queue delay is represented to the potential users as quantified confidence bounds rather than as a specific point value prediction, because then the users can feel the probability that the job will fall outside the range. They use two metrics, namely correctness and accuracy to explain the delay. The correct prediction should be one that is greater than or equal to a job's actual queuing delay and therefore the correct predictor should be one for which the total fraction of correct predictions is greater than or equal to the success probability specified by the target percentage. The RMS error is only calculated for over-predictions as a measure of accuracy.

The other important fact is that instead of inferring from a job execution model the amount of time the job tasks will wait, a job wait time inference is made from the online actual job wait time data itself. They use time series based methods for the prediction of confidence bounds.

Prediction quality: The system predicts bounds correctly for 95% or more individual job wait times. Non-parametric Binomial percentile estimator is more effective than others.

Descriptions of ML Models: Usage of Independent Data Tuples (IDT)

Downey (Clusters): Downey's statistical approach [4] predicts a job queue time in space shared environments. It is found that for cluster jobs up to 12 hours, the cumulative distribution function (CDF) of lifetimes for jobs is nearly uniform on a logarithmic x-axis [4]. Using this approximation, Downey simplifies the calculation of distribution of job lifetimes conditioned on the current age of a process. He derives formulae to calculate the median/ mean remaining lifetime of a job as a function of its current age.

For example, if there are p processes running with ages a_i, and cluster size n_i he predicts the mean/ median value of $Q(n')$ which is the time until n' additional nodes become available. This calculation is straightforward because if one knows the age of a process and number of nodes, then using the above mentioned information he can calculate the remaining lifetime of the process [4].

Prediction quality: The average time saving per job is 13.5 minutes (Average job duration is 78 minutes). The coefficient of correlation between predicted queue times and the actual queue times from the simulated schedules is between 0.65 and 0.72.

Smith (Single Machine/ Cluster): In previous work by Smith et al. [10, 67] the historical runtimes of similar applications are used to predict the future runtime of the job in the parallel computer systems.

Smith et al. [67] use a rich search technique to determine the application characteristics that yield the best definition of similarity for the purpose of making predictions. According to them, the job tasks may be judged as similar because they are submitted by the same user, at the same time, on the same computer, with the same arguments, on the same number of nodes, and so on. They use a genetic algorithm and a greedy search, looking for similar templates [68]. Eventually, they find that their technique provides more accurate runtime estimates than the techniques of other researchers. For example, they achieve mean errors that are 14 to 49 percent lower than those obtained by Gibbons [69], and 23 to 60 percent lower than those by Harchol-Balter and Downey [70].

Prediction quality: The mean prediction errors are between 40% and 59% of mean application runtimes.

Krishnaswamy [71] and Ali [72] further improve on Smith's work by introducing new techniques for data definition and search.

Li's data mining method (Clusters): Li et al. [11] present a new prediction technique for the prediction of a job task's queue wait time and runtime using the Instance Based Learning (IBL) techniques [40]. They use data mining algorithms, namely K-Nearest Neighbour and Genetic Search to find similar datasets in a history database. Li categorizes similar jobs using a distance function [73] and makes improvements on Smith et al. [10]. After extracting sets of information from nearby jobs, Instance Based Learning Algorithm is used for the prediction.

Prediction quality: The majority of jobs have relative error between -0.5 and 0.5 with the largest percentage centred around 0.

eNANOS (Clusters): eNANOS [5] prediction service uses a set of predictors which are based on statistical techniques and data mining techniques. Similar to the predictions of Smith, eNANOS classifies the historical information of job tasks according to static templates (user, group, number of processors etc.). Therefore, the prediction of runtime and memory is done using the statistical estimators namely mean, median, linear regression and standard deviation.

The prediction of runtime can also be calculated using the clustering algorithms of the K-Nearest Neighbours, K-Means and X-Means and the above mentioned statistical estimators. In this case, instead of using a set of static templates like Smith et al. [67], for a certain job task, a set of job task typologies are created for each ß seconds using the above mentioned clustering algorithms. Thereafter, a set of predictors, based on the statistical techniques, is used on each topological group to make the predictions.

The queue waiting times are predicted using data mining algorithms of decision trees [5].

Prediction quality: In the evaluation of e-NANOS for parallel jobs, it has been compared with other RMSs and schedulers such as IBM backfilling scheduler. This system has shown a remarkable improvement in reducing runtime.

OpenSeries and StreamMiner (Desktop grids): OpenSeries and StreamMiner framework [61] which is interfaced with the Weka 3.4 data mining library, uses data mining techniques such as Various classifiers, Decision trees, Bayesian and Support Vector Machines and AI techniques such as Fuzzy rules and Genetic algorithms for the prediction of machine loads, percentage of free virtual memory (memory load) and availability of machines.

Prediction quality: The workload and memory is predicted as a value between 0%-20%, 20%-40% and so on. In the first 2 cases Mean Squared Error is below 0.5 and for the availability of machines MSE is below 0.1.

GPRES (Clusters): The GPRES model [7] proposes a similar approach as it groups similar jobs based on static or dynamic templates for the prediction of job's runtime, queue time and total runtime. The mean, min, max, standard deviation and error values of predicted parameters are calculated for each group. Thereafter, the groups with specific parameters are inserted into the knowledge database as rules. The reasoning system (e.g., expert systems) selects rules from the Knowledge Database and generates the requested predictions.

Prediction quality: The average runtime error is 25%. The average total runtime error is 35%.

Faerman (Collection of distributed resources): Faerman et al. [48] use linear regression for prediction and combine NWS measurements with instrumentation data obtained from previous application executions to predict the data transfer performance of an application.

Prediction quality: The reported Normalized Mean Absolute Errors for file transfer throughputs using Adaptive Regression Modelling (AdRM) are less than 12%.

Vazhkudai and Schopf (Data Grids): Vazhkudai and Schopf [51] have performed the prediction of large data transfer for efficient access of databases. The recent increase of usage of distributed databases provides an environment for the researches to share, replicate and manage access of copies of large datasets. It is important to know which replica can be accessed most efficiently. Therefore, fetching data from one of the several replica locations requires an accurate prediction of end-to-end data transfer. The large data transfers can be predicted using univariate and multivariate regression techniques. The multivariate predictors are combined with GridFTP logs, disk throughput observations and network throughput data.

Prediction quality: The univariate predictors have an error of at most 25%. When the multivariate predictors are combined with GridFTP logs, disk throughput observations and network throughput data, it provides gains up to 9% of that of univariate predictor.

PQR2 (Clusters): This machine learning prediction methodology [54] is based on PQR which is an algorithm that generates a binary tree that can combine a variety of classifiers. Matsunaga et al. [54] have further developed PQR [74] by allowing the leaves of the tree to select the best training regression algorithm from a pool of known methods. Although any regression algorithm can be placed on the pool when the fast predictions are required, the preference should be given for the parametric methods and therefore Linear-regression and Support Vector Machine (SVM) are used.

The PPS is developed to predict application's runtime, memory and disk space on a cluster using a considerable large number of applications and system specific attributes.

Prediction quality: PQR2 proved the best and required a few minutes for training /create a new model and few milliseconds to produce a single prediction. Please refer to the cited literature for details.

Sanjay and Vadhiyar (Grids): Sanjay and Vadhiyar [56, 75] have developed a PPS which is suitable for tightly coupled parallel applications that are run on non-dedicated computer systems where the background load can change during the application execution. Their prediction system periodically measures the loads on the processors and network links during the executions. The total runtime which is computational and communicational is predicted using a single equation.

Prediction quality: In general, the average prediction error is below 30%.

Minh and Wolters (backfilling parallel systems): Minh and Wolters [12] have improved the previous method by Li by dividing the historical jobs into big, medium, and small groups and have determined required parameters for each group to predict a job's runtime on a backfilling parallel system. The parameters include a template to categorise jobs, historical database size (N), the number of nearest neighbour jobs K, the factor α, and the factor β. During the training of the model the genetic algorithm is used to find the parameters.

Prediction quality: Comparing with Li, they reduced underestimated jobs by 20%, mean absolute error by 6.25% and Weighted absolute error by 17.5%.

Hybrid Intelligent Prediction Model (HIPM) (Grids): Duan et al. [57] propose a hybrid intelligent method for performance modelling and prediction of the execution time of the workflow activity on the Grid. They combine the functionality of the neural and Bayesian networks using the methods used by Petri, to achieve high accuracy in prediction of runtimes of the workflow activities with almost negligible training times. The training time of the predictor is very low due to the introduction of the Bayesian networks. They have shown that the combined Bayesian-Radial Basis Function-Neural Network (Bayesian-RBF-NN) predictor is better than the normal RBF-NN or SVM or REP Tree.

Prediction quality: The average accuracy is 91.5%

Regression-Based Scalability Prediction (RBSP) (Clusters): Barnes et al. [55] propose a multivariate regression to predict the ideal number of machines required for parallel application. The number of machines depends on the application, input variables, and machines under consideration. They propose three different techniques and they are as follows:

a. Total execution time (TOT)
b. Maximum per-processor computation (Max)
c. Global critical path (GCP)

Prediction quality: Median prediction error is less than 13%.

Grid Information Prediction System (GIPSY) (Grids): Verboven et al. [76] focus only on a particular class of applications, namely the parameter sweep, when developing their PPS. They select any of the following statistical/ML methods for modelling the final engine for the prediction of runtime. They are Polynomial approach [77], Radial basis functions [78], Kriging methods [79],Neural networks [80], Support vector machines [81], Nearest neighbour predictions [40] and Techniques of Iverson [82].

Prediction quality: The predictor helped the normal scheduler to improve its efficiency by 13.74%.

RL Based Scheduling Strategies (RLSS) (Grids): Costa et. al.[83] had further improved the multi-agent Reinforcement Learning (RL) algorithm which was proposed by Galstyan et. al. [84]. In Galstyan's, the resource selection is done firstly using greedy by calculating the highest score of each resource and then among the resources with equal low scores the selection is done randomly. Modified Galstyan's [83] is better than the normal Galstyan's et. al. [84] because now it is able to select the best resource which has the best efficiency with a high confident level of 85%.

Also they had improved the Multiple Queues with Duplication (MQD) Algorithm which was proposed by Lee and Zomaya [85] by modifying the MQD resource evaluation function by enabling it to use RL to compute relations of performance among resources which is entirely new feature in MQD.

They had modified Gridbus Broker to contain a new parameter which would contain the RL calculated resource performance and this helps them to select the best resource.

Prediction quality: The two improved scheduling strategies had made significant gains compared with the standard scheduling algorithm based on round-robin. Please see the literature for detailed results[83].

6. Analysis of the Survey

Introduction

In this section, we investigate the results of the survey. We also analyse the results of the existing prediction solutions in terms of their exploitation in grid scheduling. In the analysis of about 33 different PPSs, which are tabulated in the Tables 1 and 2, it is understood that the accurate estimation of the prediction information in the heterogeneous grid environment is a complex and challenging task.

In the survey, the majority of PPSs (18 of them) predict a job task's runtime or CPU resource. Eight PPSs predict the parallel job's queue waiting time on a cluster. Seven PPSs predict the parallel job's runtime on a cluster. A single PPS (DIMEMAS) predicts MPI parallel job's combined computational and communicational time on a cluster. Two PPSs predict the available cluster memory. Two PPSs predict MPI parallel job's combined computational and communicational time on a Grid. Eight PPSs predict only the communication time between two points. One PPS predicts the total communication time on the Grid (LaPIe). Three PPSs predict the node memory. Four PPSs predict the availability of a PC or available number of PCs. One PPS predicts the suitability of a parallel application to a cluster (GAMMA model).

Also, there is a prediction effort on Quality of Service of the resources [63]. The statuses of the current resource balance of the nodes are assumed to be the future resource balance of the nodes. Therefore this methodology can be further improved by using the historical resource balance values to predict the future resource balance of the node.

Meeting the Challenges

Appropriate Performance Metrics for the Grid:

It is necessary to introduce the metrics that are relevant to the behaviour of grid-enabled applications. In the survey, there is a handful of PPSs which introduce novel metrics. For example, instead of predicting the CPU load at a certain point in time, Yang et al. [46] have predicted the average CPU load over a certain time interval and variation of CPU load over some future time interval. They have used a set of stochastic scheduling algorithms to evaluate such predictions of future availability and variability when making resource mapping decisions.

Yang et al. [52] have proposed a Tuned Conservative Scheduling Technique that uses predicted mean and variance over the duration of the data transfer. They predict the effective bandwidth over the time interval of the data transfer using the equation (6). *TF* regulates the predicted *EffectiveBW*.

Instead of predicting a point load value ahead of n steps, Wu et al. [47] predict the load profile across the n time steps within a certain confidence window. Also, its AHModel predictor considers the fluctuations in the historical loads and changes the historical interval (w time steps) accordingly. The Mean Square Error of prediction is calculated over n and w steps, and therefore this prediction model is much relevant to the Grid.

Seneviratne and Levy [21, 27, 62] use TPM to forecast the new metric individual load profiles of the future job tasks. The profiles include CPU and Disk IO intervals. The inputs to the model are the new metrics Free Load Profiles and Disk I/O maps of the currently running job tasks.

The GAMMA model [13] computes the GAMMA factor which is directly related to the efficiency of a MPI parallel application on a cluster, and helps predict the most suitable cluster for a particular MPI parallel application.

LaPIe [58] predicts using a novel metric, namely total communication time of a bag of MPI tasks or workflow on the Grid.

Also, it is relevant to include a new metric that is used by the QBETS [9] project to report the delay times on the queue. Instead of producing the average delay of recorded queue waiting times, they use the probability of past queue wait times reaching the confidence level (95%) of the predicted queue wait time to inform the clients about the prospective delays that one may have to experience. If the queue wait time exceeds its predicted value, it is considered to be an incorrect result. For example, the information that there is a 75% chance that the job task will execute within 17 minutes tells the client more about what kind of delay his job task will experience, than the information that the expected wait time of a particular job task is 30 minutes.

Prediction of the Network Bandwidth

The prediction of network bandwidth has been achieved by fewer PPSs than that of job task's run time. Faerman et al. [48] have implemented the prediction of data transfer using the linear regression at resource level L-1. NWS predicts TCP end-to-end bandwidth, latency and connection time [30] at resource level L-1. NWS uses auto-regressive methods which predict the next step or data set of the collected series of data samples [30]. Therefore, for an application with long communication times, this method alone cannot provide successful predictions. Vazhkudai and Schopf [51] use multivariate regression predictors, while Yang et al. [52] predict means and variance of the network bandwidth over a certain future time interval. The latter effort is better for the Grid job tasks than the first because it predicts the result over a period of time. Since the development of NWS, there has been a good effort to predict the communication time. PACE [1] predicts the communication time of a certain job task at resource level L-1. Also, it is encouraging to see how LaPIe [58] predicts the total communication time of a bag of MPI tasks or a workflow at resource level L-4 with a reasonable accuracy. One of the major drawbacks with LaPIe is that it focuses on limited scenarios where there is no background network traffic. Also, FAST [45] predicts communication time without considering the background congestion. However, the univariate and multivariate regression predictors and methods used in NWS, take into account the history of network traffic when predicting the future BW.

Prediction of Multiple Metrics:

There are integrated PPSs which predict multiple parameters and they focus on predicting several diverse parameters. For example, GPRES, eNANOS, and PACE belong to this category. When the classes of applications which require prediction solutions become large, a larger number of multiple parameters may be predicted. This is applicable for grids containing heterogeneous resources where a wide range of various applications can be run. As they do not specialise in a particular resource type, their prediction accuracy may be low. However, where a grid scheduler needs to use several parameters for scheduling, it would have to use multiple Performance Prediction solutions to provide the required parameters.

Prediction of Data Access:

The prediction of data access time or the time required to access replicated data from any location on the Grid, consists mainly of the access time of the storage system and access time through the network. Through experience with data grids, it is known that Hierarchical

Storage Management (HSM) systems are the main bottleneck rather than network links [53]. Therefore, the prediction of the access times for the HSM systems is critical to the effectiveness of the user application for reading data efficiently. In the survey, there are two PPSs for the prediction of data access. They are EDG Replica Optimization Service [49] and Prediction Model for FREERID-G [44].

Taxonomy

Resource Type and Resource Level Taxonomies:

There are many resource types which are required to be predicted for efficient and effective scheduling in the grid and each resource type consists of several levels. Therefore, if required, the prediction can be conducted at all the levels of a certain resource. In the resource level tree of Figure 2, the predictions which are conducted at a lower level can be transferred to a higher level without the loss of information because the nodes of the lower level are dependencies of the higher level. For example, the Level-0 predicted usage values of CPU, Memory and Disk can be used to predict the availability of a machine/ node which is at Level-1. In contrast, the prediction information such as CPU capacity or Memory capacity may not be directly derived from the value predicted at Level-1. Similarly, if you predict the required number of nodes or a suitable cluster (at level-3) for a parallel application, this value cannot be transferred down the tree to extract the predicted CPU capacity, Memory capacity or Disk access cost of a particular node. The reason is that the information is tightly entangled at the upper levels of the tree and therefore accurately separating them is either extremely difficult or impossible [31, 62].

It is important that the parameter at the lowest level is fundamental and thus not a combination of any other basic parameters. Therefore, it is independent of any other metrics and it can be measured directly. Also, its characteristics and runtime environmental details can be easily understood and measured (e.g., a CPU resource). Therefore, the overall result is directly related to this fundamental resource. For this reason, the accuracy of prediction of the parameter at the lower level is better than that of higher levels (e.g., Dinda, PACE, PPSKel and TPM). Therefore, more predictors are developed to predict at the lowest level of the tree and transfer the results to the top level.

A resource at the higher level depends on the several types of metrics at the lowest level, and therefore its behaviour becomes complex. This makes it difficult to analyse or predict its behaviour. For example, a cluster of heterogenous nodes depends on its numerous CPUs, Memories, Disk access capabilities, and BWs which are at the lowest level of the tree (Figure 2). Therefore, it is harder to analyse or predict the behaviour of a cluster of heterogeneous nodes which is multi-dependant than a CPU or a memory.

If you compare the parameters of Table 2 and the prediction quality from each prediction method in section 4, you find that at the higher levels of the resource tree (Figure 2), it is difficult to make predictions accurately, and for this reason there are only a few predictors available for making predictions at the highest levels for the Grid. For example, at level-4, only Sanjay and Vadhiyar, or HIPM is capable of prediction of total runtime which is an aggregate of the computational and communication times of a MPI parallel application or a workflow.

At level-1 NWS, Faerman, EDG ROS, FREERIDE-G, FAST, Vazhkudai and Schopf, PDTT or PACE can predict the communication time between two points. NWS or OpenSeries and StreamMiner predict the availability of a machine/ node. EDG ROS or FREERIDE-G can predict the data storage access time.

At level-0, there are 18 PPSs (Dinda, OpenSeries and StreamMiner, DIMEMAS ASKALON, PACE, TPM, AWP, PPSKel, FREERIDE-G, RLSS, Prediction of Variance, and FAST, *Smith, Li, Minh and Wolters, eNANOS, GPRES and MWGS*) for the prediction of CPU resource or job task's runtime. The last six PPSs are originally developed for the clusters to predict job runtime (at level-3), however they can be easily modified to predict the CPU resource at level-0. Also, available memory on a node can be predicted by either PACE or OpenSeries and StreamMiner.

Unlike a homogeneous cluster of nodes, a Grid is made of heterogeneous resources; therefore it is better to perform prediction at the lowest level because the prediction of independent resource is easy. If we try to predict a resource at a higher level, a collection of heterogeneous resources (e.g., Cluster of heterogeneous nodes) are going to behave in more complex manner with several dependencies; therefore prediction is going to be complex. However, if the relevant application's historical data, its characteristics and its runtime environmental characteristics are not accessible to the predictor at the lowest level, the higher level prediction may be chosen.

Prediction Approach Taxonomy:

Table 1 classifies the PPSs according to the nature of their basic design, i.e., whether they belong to Analytical or ML category. The ML category has two major subdivisions and they are STC family and the group of predictors that analyses individual data sets (tuples). There are 11 analytical models, 8 ML-STC models and 14 ML-Independent Data Tuple models.

The PACE, TPM, DIMEMAS, ASKALON, PPSkel, FREEDRID-G, FAST, EDG ROS, LaPIe, GAMMA and the Prediction of QoS are the analytical models. Among the analytical PPSs, the PACE uses the job tasks' source code and machine's hardware configuration to simulate the predictions. Although exposing the source code is not a popular option in the competitive IT world, this model is capable of making multiple predictions with good accuracy. For example, to predict a grid job task's runtime, memory, disk access cost and communication time with an error less than 8%, is a remarkable achievement [26]. The TPM has more in common with the prediction models that use source code and machine hardware configurations as inputs rather than history based predictors. This first category of models is not popular in the industry as exposing source code is a poor business practice. Therefore the TPM which uses FLPs instead of source code to reflect the behaviour of both CPU and disk loads could be a useful option. The other novel analytical approach is GAMMA that forecasts the level-3 resource, the suitability of a parallel application to a cluster. The novel procedure of LaPIe also attracts the attention of the reader, because it focuses only on network BW metric.

In the ML category, the automation of the collection of the training data is vital to the efficiency and effectiveness of the predictor because, for the industrial scale predictors where there are hundreds of tuples or data sets, it is not possible to collect them manually. The automation process includes extraction of data from the same prediction system or similar prediction systems and populates the real-time database with them by using awk or purl script or another software package. For parametric ML methods such as linear regression, the training data is used to calculate the model parameters and thereafter stored training data may be deleted. Usually, the process of training takes a few minutes and critics who do not want ML predictors to be part of PPSs for the Grid, point out this fact often. The positive side is that ML models are comparatively faster than analytical ones. However, for non-parametric ML methods, such as K-NN, a collection of data sets is continuously used for the prediction.

The prediction approach should be applied at the most suitable level of the resource tree (Figure 2). For example, for a cluster, job runtime and queue time can be predicted at level-3, by using Smith et al. [10, 67] or Li et al. [11] or PQR2 [54]. However we cannot apply the same strategy for a virtual organization or a Grid at the level-4 because they are a collection of heterogeneous resources (nodes). In a similar effort to predict the job runtime on a Grid, Sanjay and Vadhiyar [56] measure inputs at the level-0, therefore this method belongs to the level-0 as much as to the level-4. Therefore for a Grid we need to apply these methods at level-0 to separately predict job task's runtime on each node.

The only exception to this is that when HIPM [57] makes an effort to predict the job runtime on the Grid at the level-4. It measures the inputs at the level-4, for example its inputs are Activity type, Activity name, Arguments, Queue time, Execution time, Number of processors etc. The problem is that the Grid is dynamic and heterogenous collection of resources (nodes), therefore considering it as a single entity may be simplistic because unlike a cluster, the Grid is a very complex system.

Prediction Models and Grid Scheduling

In this section, the existing performance prediction solutions are investigated in terms of their application in grid scheduling. To this end, firstly the models and their usability for grid scheduling are studied. Secondly the availability of software is investigated.

Applicability

The requirements of the PPSs result from the heterogeneity and dynamic nature of the grids. The main requirements that must be taken into consideration during the analysis of models applicability are listed below.

1. Prediction of important parameters. (such as runtime, queue waiting time job resource requirement, resource load, communication time, data transfer time.)
2. Information about errors.
3. Performance guarantees and /or small prediction errors.
4. Performance prediction based on incomplete and/or imprecise information.
5. Large scope of handled applications and resources.

The parameters predicted by PPSs which are included in the survey are presented in the 4th column, under predicted metrics of Table 2. The information, the number of PPS solutions that support the particular parameters is summarised in section 6.

If a scheduler needs to use multiple parameters for scheduling, it would have to employ multiple performance prediction solutions to obtain required predicted parameters. In section 6 under Prediction of Multiple Metrics, this solution has been discussed. Similar conclusions have been made based on the analysis of different classes of applications and their input parameters handled by the considered solutions.

There are prediction solutions which are more generic and provide predictions of great number of parameters for a wide class of applications. For an example, GPRES, eNANOS [5, 7]. However generic solutions that take general input parameters from available data archives can be relatively poor when compared with specialised performance prediction models which require more detailed description of application and resources. Those latter prediction models include DIMEMAS and Gamma [86-87].

Availability of Software

In addition to requirements concerning performance prediction models themselves, there are other practical issues such as that influence the usability of particular solution. They are

1. Software availability
2. Availability of easy to use and generic interface.
3. Ability to integrate with common resource management and grid technologies.

There are a few proficient software packages available such as NWS [30], the Intelligent Grid Scheduling System (ISS) which implements the Gamma model [87] and Grid-Prophet which implements ASKOLON [41]. But most of them are not sufficiently mature to satisfy the customer's/ user's specific needs. This is a major hurdle in taking advantage from available PPS. Therefore the above mentioned problems need to be discussed with the software creators because the licensing rights for versioning and maintaining of each PPS software belong to them.

7. Conclusion

In this chapter, taxonomy is proposed to characterize and categorize various aspects of PPSs that can support the preparation of efficient and effective application schedules for the Grid. The taxonomy covers four different perspectives: (a) the prediction approach, (b) the resource type, (c) the resource level and (d) the grid enabled job model. A survey is also conducted where the taxonomy is mapped in Tables 1 and 2 to selected PPSs that are designed for both clusters and grids. The prediction approach taxonomy is used to identify certain characteristics of machine learning and analytical models and their critical parameters are mapped in Table 1. The application model taxonomy separates various levels of a grid enabled application and it is mapped in the last column of Table 1. The resource type and resource level taxonomies have been used to identify the PPSs that are implemented at various levels of the same resource (Table 2). The survey is helpful to us to analyse the gap between what is already available in existing PPSs and what is still required so that we can identify the research requirements which can be implemented in future projects.

When one compares the identified expectations in section 3 with the survey results of the PPSs, there are only few achievements of which one can be proud. Dinda, PACE, TPM, DIMEMAS, ASKALON, OpenSeries and StreamMiner, PPSkel, AWP, RLSS or FAST make the predictions of CPU resource at the level-0 and can be considered as the most reliable.

Prediction of a parallel job's runtime and queue waiting time (level-3) on a cluster can be achieved by several predictors. It is not possible to use the same methodology on a Virtual Organization or a Grid (level-4) because of their heterogeneity. However, it is explained that the predictors which predict the job's runtime on a cluster can be modified to predict a job task's runtime on a node (level-0) and therefore, there are 18 predictors (level-0) to forecast CPU resource on a node of the Grid. Also it is evident from the survey and taxonomies that the prediction on a Grid, should preferably be done at the lowest level of the tree (Figure 2). Thereafter the prediction results of each node can be transferred from the lowest level to the highest level of the resource tree (Figure 2).

The usage of regression based techniques for the prediction of data transfer times has become a fair trend. Yang et al. [52] is based on the NWS [30] predictor, making predictions over a certain time duration, making it more relevant than others [51] for the Grid. Steffenel [58] has taken a different approach for predicting the most suitable BW for a MPI parallel application on the Grid. His methodology namely LaPIe [58] helps to select the scheduling strategy to minimise the overall communication time on the Grid.

Although a few new performance metrics are proposed by some PPSs, the same old metrics are used by many PPSs because their underlying algorithms are not changed to capture some of the vital characteristics of Grid applications. In contrast, in the TPM, the metric the Free Load Profile captures total behaviour of the job tasks. Yang et al. [46, 52], AWP, GAMMA and LaPIe can be identified as other initial contributors in this area.

The other major problem is the lack of global standards for the Grid. Under such common standards, both application performance model and workload formats can be categorised. Currently, NASA grid bench marks have introduced some application types and this may be a good starting point [22].

The other important need is to have a single framework which addresses the prediction of several different parameters. Currently, there are few PPSs which have a limited capability of doing so (e.g., GPRES, eNANOS, and PACE). However, the major problem that would arise from such a massive integration is that the bigger the framework the more complex and slower it will be, because at this point of time such a single framework has to be developed by integrating several different PPSs.

Also the prediction of required data storage for a certain application requires the assistance of PPSs.

None of the PPSs has made an effort to perform the prediction when their required input information is incomplete. There are no reliable PPSs for the prediction of overheads of the Grid. Therefore, these three areas still remain wide open for the researchers who explore further and evaluate how influential their results would be for the completion of good grid schedules.

Acknowledgments

We thank Srikumar Venugopal, Anton Beloglazov, Nikolay Grozev and Adel Nadjaran Toosi for their valuable comments which have enriched the content of this chapter.

Table 1. Classification of Performance Prediction Approaches

Performance prediction model	Category of the predict model					Input metrics/training data	Res. type	Class of job (time / space shared)
	Machine learning model				Analytical model			
	STC	IDT	Selection of data (Man. / Auto.)					
			Man.	Auto.				
Downey [4]		Yes		Yes		Jobs' historical runtimes, queue times, cluster size and details of their processors are collected from the similar sites to plot the distribution of total allocation time of jobs in log space.	Queue	Parallel jobs (space)
Dinda [31]	Yes			Yes		(1) Historical host load data is automatically stored. (2) Free load runtime of the new job task needs to be recorded.	CPU	short j. tasks (100ms-10s) (time)
NWS [30]	Yes			Yes		Historical values of CPU usage, Memory usage, TCP end-to-end bandwidth and latency, and connection time are stored automatically.	CPU availability, BW	parallel j tasks (time)
Faerman [48]	Yes			Yes		Historical information of data transfer. NWS measurements such as TCP end-to-end bandwidth and latency and the connection time are automatically stored.	BW	Appli. with data transfer infor. (time)
Vazhkudai & Schopf [51]	Yes			Yes		GridFTP logs, disk throughput observations and network throughput data are automatically stored.	BW	Appli. with data transfer infor. (time)
Smith [67]		Yes		Yes		Sets of template attributes and their profiles of historical workload are automatically stored.	CPU, Queue	Parallel job (space)
DIMEMAS [6]					Yes	Sets of computation bursts and calls to MPI primitives. Descript. of application architecture.	CPU & BW	MPI parallel jobs (space)

Performance prediction model	Category of the predict model					Input metrics/training data	Res. type	Class of job (time / space shared)
	Machine learning model				Analytical model			
	STC	IDT	Selection of data (Man. / Auto.)					
			Man.	Auto.				
Predict. of Variance [66]	Yes			Yes		CPU load time series is automatically and online stored on each node.	CPU	Parallel jobs (time)
LaPIe [58]					Yes	Communication latency, message gap according to message size and number of processors.	BW	MPI parallel jobs (time)
ASKALON[41]		Yes		Yes		Job tasks' historical information such as, job task names, runtimes, input parameter sizes, processor speeds are automatically stored from previous actual runs. If the historical information is not available then it is manually supplied from one of the identical machines.	CPU, CPU (total) & Queue	Parallel jobs (time)
Li [11]		Yes		Yes		The profiles of historical workloads are automatically stored.	CPU, Queue	Parallel jobs (space)
PDTT [52]	Yes			Yes		Network bandwidth time series is automatically and online recorded at constant width time intervals.	BW	Data intensive appli. (time)
eNANOS [5]		Yes		Yes		Statistical and data mining predictors need the same inputs: job name, user name, group name, no. of processors, job & script names automatically stored as load profiles.	CPU, Memory, Queue	MPI parallel jobs (space)

Table 1. Continued

Performance prediction model	Category of the predict model					Input metrics/training data	Res. type	Class of job (time / space shared)
	Machine learning model				Analytical model			
	STC	IDT	Selection of data (Man./ Auto.)					
			Man.	Auto.				
OpenSeries & StreamMiner [61]		Yes		Yes		Historical values of workload such as CPU idleness, percentage of free virtual memory, machine availability (switched on or off) and user presence indicator (logged on or off). The attribute selection process which has 3 phases can be semi-automated.	CPU, Memory & CPU availability	Parallel jobs (time)
GPRES[7]		Yes		Yes		Historic jobs are categorised according to static or dynamic template attributes. Then the mean of values estimated parameters are calculated for each category. Categories with specific set of values fed to knowledge database as rules & this can be automated.	CPU, Queue	Parallel jobs (space)
MWGS [8]	Yes			Yes		User-name, submission time, job ID, number of nodes requested, user-predicted job runtime, actual job runtime are the input to generate two Markov chains for the runtimes & num of nodes. Data collection & generation process can be automated.	Queue, No. of nodes, CPU (total)	Parallel jobs (space)
GAMMA [13]					Yes	Computational and network traffic information of the application and the cluster and costing parameters	Cluster	Parallel job (space)
PACE [26]					Yes	Software code of the applications and machine and environmental details.	CPU, Mem, BW, Queue	MPI parallel job (space/ time)

Performance prediction model	Category of the predict model — Machine learning model: STC	IDT	Selection of data (Manual/Automated): Man.	Auto.	Analytical model	Input metrics/training data	Res. type	Class of job (time / space shared)
TPM [21]					Yes	FLPs of the job tasks and machine environmental details. Disk IO maps of the job tasks.	CPU, Disk	Parallel job (space/ time)
PPSkel [43]					Yes	The records of execution activities of the CPU usage, Memory consumption and MPI message exchanges are taken from the same program.	CPU, BW Mem.,	MPI parallel jobs (time)
EDG ROS [49]					Yes	Characteristic details of CPU, network and storage.	Disk, BW	Remote data processing appli. (time)
Sanjay & Vadhiyar [56]		Yes		Yes		Available CPUs & Available BWs are automatically measured for all processors and links at periodic intervals. The calculated coefficients are used in the total runtime equation.	CPU & BW	MPI parallel jobs (time)
PQR2 [54]		Yes		Yes		Application and system-specific attributes such as cluster name, CPU clock, amount of memory, location of data, CPU speed, memory speed, disk speed, number of threads. The data sets can be collected automatically.	CPU, Mem, Disk	MPI parallel jobs (space)
QBETS [9]	Yes					Historical data profiles of similar jobs. The data is collected online: collection can be automated.	Queue	Parallel jobs (space)

Table 1. Continued

Performance prediction model	Category of the predict model					Input metrics/training data	Res. type	Class of job (time / space shared)
	Machine learning model				Analytical model			
	STC	IDT	Selection of data (Manual/Automated)					
			Man.	Auto.				
FREERIDE-G [44]					Yes	No. of storage nodes, dataset size, network bandwidth, execution speed, disk speed, no. of computing nodes, & the corresponding values of the outputs.	Disk, BW, CPU	Remote data processing appli. (space)
Minh & Wolters [12]		Yes		Yes		Original inputs: user_name, group_name, queue_name, job_name, Intermediate parameters: historical database size (N), no of nearest neighbour jobs K, the factor α and β. Training parameters: user_name, group_name, queue_name, job_name, point_of_separate, N, K, α, β. The traces are collected automatically and training parameters are calculated automatically.	CPU	Parallel jobs (space)
HIPM [57]		Yes		Yes		Data/ Activities of the workflow application, such as type (e.g., metric multiplication), name, arguments, problem size, preparation time, user name, grid site, submission time, queue time, external load, processors, execution time can be automatically collected and the predictor can be trained fast using Bayesian network.	CPU & BW	Workflow job (time)

Performance prediction model	Category of the predict model					Input metrics/training data	Res. type	Class of job (time / space shared)
	Machine learning model				Analytical model			
	STC	IDT	Selection of data (Manual/Automated)					
			Man.	Auto.				
RBSP [55]		Yes		Yes		Job's input variables, number of machines under consideration are inputs to the regression equation. The collection of the training data can be automated.	Cluster	MPI Parallel jobs (time)
AWP [47]	Yes			Yes		Historical workload points are collected online	CPU	Parallel jobs(time)
FAST [45]					Yes	Dynamically collected data such as CPU speed, workload, BW, available memory, batch system.	CPU, Memory, BW	Parallel jobs (space)
GIPSY [76]		Yes		Yes		(a) Initial Training sample selection can be automated. (b) Selection of the model may be automated subjected to the condition. The selected models can be run until the predicted runtime error converges, and then the most suitable model will be selected..	CPU	Parameter sweep jobs (space)
Prediction of the QoS [63]					Yes	The current measurement of the balance of resources of all the nodes (CPU, Mem etc).	CPU, memory	Parallel jobs (space)
RLSS [83]		Yes		Yes		Training sample selection can be automated.	CPU	Parallel jobs (space)

Table 2. The Classification of the Resource Types

Prediction model	Res. type	Res. level	Predicted metrics	Centralized/ Decentralised	Homogeneous/ Heterogeneous	Dedicated/ Shared
Downey [4]	Queue	L-3	Queue time	Centralized	Homo	Dedicated
Dinda [31]	CPU	L-0 L-0	Host load, Job task's runtime	both	both	both
NWS [30]	CPU availability, BW	L-1, L-1, L-1	CPU availability, TCP end-to-end throughput, TCP end-to-end latency.	Decentralised	Hetero	Shared
Faerman [48]	BW	L-1	Data transfer rate.	Decentralised	Hetero	Shared
Vazhkudai [51] and Schopf	BW	L-1	Data transfer rate.	Decentralised	Hetero	Shared
Smith [67]	CPU & Queue	L-3, L-3	Job's runtime, Queue time	Centralized	Homo	Dedicated
DIMEMAS [6]	CPU & BW	L-3	Job's runtime	Centralized	Homo	Dedicated
Prediction of Variance [66]	CPU	L-0	CPU load mean & variance over a time	Decentralised	Hetero	Shared
LaPIe [58]	BW	L-4	MPI job's communication makes span	Decentralised	Hetero	Shared
ASKALON [41]	CPU, CPU (total) & Queue	L-0 L-3 L-3	Job task's runtime, Job's runtime, Queue time.	Centralized	Hetero	Dedicated
Li [11]	CPU, Queue	L-3 L-3	Job's runtime, Queue time.	Centralized	Homo	Dedicated
PDTT [52]	BW	L-1	Data transfer time between 2 nodes	Decentralised	Hetero	Shared
eNANOS[5]	CPU, Memory, Queue	L-3, L-3, L-3	Job's runtime, Memory, Queue time	Centralized	Homo	Dedicated
OpenSeries & StreamMiner [61]	CPU, Memory, CPU availability	L-0 L-0 L-1	Idle % of CPU, Memory, Availability of PCs	Decentralised	Hetero	Shared

Prediction model	Res. type	Res. level	Predicted metrics	Centralized/decentralised	Homogeneous/Heterogeneous	Dedicated/Shared
GPRES [7]	CPU, Queue	L-3 L-3	Job's runtime, Queue time	Centralized	Homo	Dedicated
MWGS [8]	Queue, No. of nodes, CPU (total)	L-3 L-3 L-3	The arrival time of job, No. of nodes, Job's runtime	Centralized	Homo-	Dedicated
GAMMA Model [13]	Cluster	L-3	1. For each cluster Γ (γ_a / γ_m) 2. Total usage cost.	Centralized	Homo-	Dedicated
PACE [26]	CPU, Memory, BW, Queue	L-0, L-0, L-1, L-3	Job task's runtime, Memory, Communication. Time, Queue time.	Decentralised	Hetero	Shared
TPM [21]	CPU, Disk	L-0 L-0	Load profiles of future Job tasks. Disk access time	Decentralised	Hetero	Shared
PPSke [43]	CPU, BW, Memory,	L-0, L-0, L-0	MPI Job task's runtime (CPU, communication and memory).	Decentralised	Hetero	Shared
EDG ROS [49]	Disk, BW	L-1 L-1	Data retrieval time & communi. Time	Decentralised	Hetero	Shared
Sanjay & Vadhiyar [56]	CPU & BW	L-4	Job's runtime	Decentralised	Hetero	Shared
PQR2 [54]	CPU, Memory, Disk	L-3, L-3, L-3,	Job's runtime, Memory, Disk space	Decentralised	Hetero	Shared
QBETS [9]	Queue	L-3	Probability of past queue wait times reaching the confidence level (95%) of the predicted queue wait times and the RMS error of job tasks that delays less than the predicted value	Centralized	Homo	Dedicated

Table 2. Continued

Prediction model	Res. type	Res. level	Predicted metrics	Centralized/ decentralised	Homogeneous/ Heterogeneous	Dedicated/ Shared
FREERIDE-G [44]	Disk, BW, CPU	L-0, L-1, L-0,	Data retrieval time, commun. time, & data processing time.	Decentralised	Hetero	Shared
Minh & Wolters [12]	CPU	L-3	Job's runtime	Centralized	Homo	Dedicated
HIPM [57]	CPU & BW	L-4	Job's runtime	Decentralised	Hetero	Shared
RBSP [55]	Cluster	L-3	No of machines	Centralized	Homo	Dedicated
AWP [47]	CPU	L-0	Load profile	Decentralised	Hetero	Shared
FAST [45]	CPU, Memory, BW	L-0, L-0, L-1	Processing runtime, Memory, Communication time	Decentralised	Hetero	Shared
GIPSY [76]	CPU	L-4	Job's runtime	Decentralised	Hetero	Shared
Prediction. of QoS [63]	CPU, Mem etc	L-0, L-0	Future available balance of resources (CPU, Mem etc)	Decentralised	Hetero	Shared
RLSS [83]	CPU	L-0	Job's runtime	Decentralised	Hetero	Shared

References

[1]   Jarvis S. A., Spooner D. P., Keung H. N. L. C., Cao J., Saini S.,Nudd G. R.: Performance Prediction and its use in Parallel and Distributed Computing Systems, Future Generation Computer Systems (FGCS), vol. 22, Aug. 2006, pp. 745–754.

[2]   Nadeem F., Prodan R.,Fahringer T.: Characterizing, Modeling and Predicting Dynamic Resource Availability in a Large Scale Multi-Purpose Grid, presented at the 8th Int'l Symp. on Cluster Computing and the Grid (CCGRID '08), Lyon, France, 2008.

[3]   Abramson D., Buyya R.,Giddy J.: A Computational Economy for Grid Computing and its Implementation in the Nimrod-G Resource Broker, Future Generation Computer Systems (FGCS), vol. 18, Oct. 2002, pp. 1061-1074.

[4]   Downey A. B.: Predicting Queue Times on Space-sharing Parallel Computers, in 11th Int'l Symp. on Parallel Processing, Geneva, Switzerland, 1997, pp. 209-218.

[5]   Rodero I., Guim F., Corbalán J.,Labarta J.: eNANOS: Coordinated scheduling in grid environments, presented at the Parallel Computing: Current & Future Issues of High-End Computing, Parco 2005, 2005.

[6]   Badia R. M., Escale F., Gabriel E., Gimenez J. , Keller R., Labarta J.,Muller M. S.: Performance Prediction in a Grid Environment, presented at the Int'l Conf. on Grid Computing, First European Across Grids Conference, Santiago de Compostela, Spain, 2003.

[7]   Kurowski K., Oleksiak A., Nabrzyski J., Kwiecien A., Wojtkiewicz M., Dyczkowski M., Guim F., Corbalan J.,Labarta J.: Multi-criteria Grid Resource Management using Performance Prediction Techniques., in CoreGrid Integration Workshop, Pisa, Itally, Nov. 2005.

[8]   Song B., Ernemann C.,Yahyapour R.: Parallel Computer Workload Modelling with Markov Chains, presented at the Int'l Conf. on Job Schdeduling Strategies for Parallel Processing, NY, USA, 2004.

[9]   Nurmi D. C., Brevik J.,Wolski R.: QBETS: queue bounds estimation from time series., presented at the SIGMETRICS '07. Int'l Conf. on Measurement & Modeling of Computer Systems, San Diego, CA, USA, June 2007.

[10] Smith W., Foster I.,Taylor V.: Predicting Application Run Times with Historical Information, Parallel and Distributed Computing, vol. 64, Sept. 2004, pp. 1007-1016.

[11] Li H., Groep D.,Wolters L.: Mining Performance Data for Metascheduling Decision Support in the Grid, Future Generation Computer Systems, vol. 23, 2007, pp. 92–99.

[12] Minh T. N.,Wolters L.: Using Historical Data to Predict Application Runtimes on Backfilling Parallel Systems, presented at the 18th Euromicro Conf. on Parallel, Distributed and Network-based Processing (PDP '10), Pisa, Italy, 2010.

[13] Gruber R., Volgers P., Vita A. D., Stengel M.,Tran T. M.: Parameterisation to tailor commodity clusters to applications, Future Generation Computer Systems, vol. 19, 2003, pp. 111-120.

[14] Grozev N.,Buyya R.: Inter-Cloud Architectures and Application Brokering: Taxonomy and Survey, Software: Practice and Experience, vol. 44, March 2014, pp. 369-390.

[15] Buyya R., Ranjan R.,Calheiros R. N.: InterCloud: Utility-Oriented Federation of Cloud Computing Environments for Scaling of Application Services, in 10th ICA3PP, Busan, South Korea, 2010, pp. 13-31.

[16] Foster I.: Globus Toolkit Version 4: Software for Service-Oriented Systems, Computer Science and Technology, vol. 21, July 2006, pp. 513-520.

[17] Berman F., Wolski R., Casanova H., Cirne W., Dail H., Faerman M., Figueira S., Hayes J., Obertelli G., Schopf J., Shao G., Smallen S., Spring N., Su A.,Zagorodnov D.: Adaptive Computing on the Grid Using AppLeS, IEEE Transactions on Parallel and Distributed Systems, vol. 14, April 2003, pp. 369-382.

[18] Venugopal S., Buyya R.,Ramamohanarao K.: A Taxonomy of Data Grids for Distributed Data Sharing, Management, and Processing, ACM Computing Surveys,, vol. 38, Article 3, March 2006.

[19] CoreGrid: Review of Performance Prediction Models and Solutions, Institute on Resource Management and Scheduling D.RMS.06, Sept. 1, 2006, 2006.

[20] Krauter K., Buyya R.,Maheswaran M.: A Taxonomy and Survey of Grid Resource Management Systems for Distributed Computing, Software Practice and Experience, vol. 32, Feb. 2002, pp. 135-164.

[21] Seneviratne S.,Levy D.: Task Profiling Model for Load Profile Prediction, Future Generation Computer Systems, vol. 27, 2011, pp. 245-255.

[22] Van der Wijngaart R. F.,Frumkin M. A.: Evaluating the Information Power Grid using NAS Grid Benchmarks, in 18th Int'l Symp. on Parallel and Distributed Processing, Santa Fe, New Mexico, USA, 2004, p. (CDROM) pp. 275.

[23] Song H., Liu X., Jakobson D., Bhagwan R., Zhang X., Taura K.,Chien A.: The MicroGrid: A scientific tool for modelling computational Grids, in IEEE Int'l Conf. on Supercomputing (SC2000), Dallas, TX, Nov. 2000.

[24] Casanova H.: Simgrid: A toolkit for the simulation of application scheduling, presented at the IEEE/ACM Int'l Symp. on Cluster Computing & the Grid (CCGrid), Brisbane, Australia, May 2001.

[25] Buyya R.,Murshed M.: Gridsim: a toolkit for the modelling and simulation of distributed resource management & scheduling for Grid computing, Concurrency and Computation Practice and Experience, vol. 14, 2002, pp. 1175-1220.

[26] Nudd G. R., Kerbyson D. J., Panaefstathiou E, Perry S. C., Harper J. S.,EWilcox D. V.: Pace-A Toolset for the Performance Prediction of Parallel and Distributed Systems, High Performance Computing Applications, vol. 14, Fall 2000, pp. 228-252.

[27] Seneviratne S.,Levy D.: Enhanced Host Load Prediction by Division of User Load Signal for Grid Computing, presented at the 6th Int'l Conf. on Algorithms and Architectures for Parallel Processing (ICA3PP 2005), Melbourne, Australia, 2005.

[28] Steffenel L. A.: LaPle: Communications Collectives Adaptées aux Grilles de Calcul, PhD, INPG, Grenoble, France, 2005.

[29] Lendasse A., Bodt E. D., Wertz V.,Verleysen M.: Nonlinear Financial Time Series Forecasting-Application to the Bel 20 Stock Market Index, Economic and Social Systems, vol. 14, 2000, pp. 81-91.

[30] Wolski R., Spring N.,Hayes J.: The Network Weather Service: A Distributed Resource Performance Forecasting Service for Metacomputing, Future Generation Computing Systems, vol. 15, Oct. 1999, pp. 757-768.

[31] Dinda P. A.: Resource Signal Prediction and its Application to Real time Scheduling Advisors, PhD, School of Computer Science, Carnegie Mellon University, USA, 2000.

[32] Iosup A., Li H., Jan M., Anoep S., Dumitrescu C., Wolters L.,Epema D. H. J.: The Grid Wokloads Achives, Future Generation Computer Systems, vol. 24, 2008, pp. 672-686.

[33] Yang L, Schopf JM,Foster I: Conservative Scheduling: Using Predicted Variance to Improve Scheduling Decisions in Dynamic environments, in ACM/IEEE Int'l Conf. on Supercomputing (SC2003), Phoenix, Arizona, USA, 2003, pp. 31-37.

[34] Beran J.: Statistical Methods for Data with Long-Range Dependence, Statistical Science, vol. 7, 1992, pp. 404-416.

[35] Dinda P. A.: The Statistical Properties of Host Load, Scientific Programming, vol. 7, Aug. 1999, pp. 211-229.

[36] Eacutelteto T., Germain-Renaud C., Bondon P.,Sebag M.: Discovering Piecewise Linear Models of Grid Workload, presented at the 10th IEEE/ACM Int'l Conf. on Cluster, Cloud and Grid Computing (CCGRID '10), Melbourne, Australia, 2010.

[37] Feitelson D. G.: Workload Modelling for Performance Evaluation, School of Computer Science & Engineering, Hebrew University, Jerusalem, Israel 2002.

[38] Downey A. B.,Feitelson D. G.: The Elusive Goal of Workload Characterisation Performance Evaluation Rev., vol. 26, Mar 1999, pp. 14-29.

[39] Li H., Sun J.,Sun B. L.: Financial Distress Prediction based on OR-CBR in the Principle of K-Nearest Neighbors, Expert Systems with Applications, vol. 36, 2009, pp. 643–659.

[40] Atkeson C. G., Moore A. W.,Schaal S. A.: Locally Weighted Learning, Artificial Intelligence Review, vol. 11, 1997, pp. 11-73.

[41] Fahringer T., Jugravu A., Pllana S., Prodan R., Seragiotto C. Jr.,Truong H. L.: ASKALON: A Tool Set for Cluster and Grid Computing, Concurrency and Computation: Practice and Experience, vol. 17, Feb.-April 2005, pp. 143-169.

[42] Andrzejak A., Graupner S.,Plantikow S.: Predicting Resource Demand in Dynamic Utility Computing Environments, in Int'l Conf. on Autonomic and Autonomous Systems (ICAS'06), Santa Clara, USA, July 2006.

[43] Sodhi S., Subhlok J.,Xu Q.: Performance Preidtion with Skeletons, Cluster Computing, vol. 11, 2008, pp. 151-165.

[44] Glimcher L.,Agrawal G.: A Performance Prediction Framework for Grid-based Data Mining Application, presented at the Int'l Parallel and Disributed Processing Symposium (IPDPS), 2007.

[45] Desprez F., Quinson M.,Suter F.: Dynamic Performance Forecasting for Network-Enabled Servers in a Heterogeneous Environment, presented at the Int'l Conf. on Parallel & Distributed Processing Techniques & Applications (PDPTA), Las Vegas, USA, 2002.

[46] Yang L., Schopf J. M.,Foster I.: Conservative Scheduling: Using Predicted Variance to Improve Scheduling Decisions in Dynamic environments, in ACM/IEEE Int'l Conf. on Supercomputing (SC2003), Phoenix, Arizona, USA, Nov. 2003, pp. 31-37.

[47] Wu Y., Hwang K., Yuan Y.,Zheng W.: Adaptive Workload Prediction of Grid Performance in Confidence Windows, IEEE Transactions on Parallel and Distributed Systems, vol. 21, July 2010, pp. 925-938.

[48] Faerman M., Su A., Wolski R.,Berman F.: Adaptive Performance Prediction for Distributed Data-Intensive Applications, in ACM/IEEE Int'l Conf. on Super Computing, Portland, OR, USA, 1999, p. (CDROM) Article No. 36.

[49] Bell W. H., Cameron D. G., Capozza L., Millar P., Stockinger K.,Zini F.: Design of a Replica Optimization Service, EU DataGrid Project, Geneva, Switzerland Technical Report DataGrid-02-TED-021215, Dec. 2002.

[50] Desprez F., Quinson M.,Suter F.: Dynamic Performance Forecasting for Network-Enabled Servers in a Heterogeneous Environment, INRIA 4320, Nov. 2001.

[51] Vazhkudai S.,Schopf J. M.: Using Regression Techniques to Predict Large Data Transfers, High Performance Computing Applications, vol. 17, Summer 2003, pp. 249-268.

[52] Yang L., Schopf J. M.,Foster I.: Improving Parallel Data Transfer Times Using Predicted Variances in Shared Networks, presented at the Fifth IEEE Int'l Symp. on Cluster Computing and the Grid (CCGRID05), Washington, DC, USA., 2005.

[53] Stockinger K., Stockinger H., Dutka L., Slota R., Nikolow D.,Kitowski J.: Access Cost Estimation for Unified Grid Storage Systems, presented at the Fourth Int'l Workshop on Grid Computing (GRID03), Phoenix, AZ, USA., 2003.

[54] Matsunaga A.,Fortes J. A. B.: On the Use of Machine Learning to Predict the Time and Resources Consumed by Applications, presented at the 10th IEEE/ACM Int'l Conf. on Cluster, Cloud and Grid Computing (ccgrid), Melbourne, VIC, Australia, 2010.

[55] Barnes B. J., Rountree B., Lowenthal D. K., Reeves J., Supinski B.,Schulz M.: A regression-based approach to scalability prediction, presented at the 22nd Int'l Conf. on Supercomputing (ICS '08), Kos, Greece, 2008.

[56] Sanjay H. A.,Vadhiyar S.: Performance Modeling of Parallel Applications for Grid Scheduling, Parallel and Distributed Computing,, vol. 68, 2008, pp. 1135-1145.

[57] Duan R., Nadeem F., Wang J., Zhang Y., Prodan R.,Fahringer T.: A Hybrid Intelligent Method for Performance Modeling and Prediction of Workflow Activities in Grids, presented at the 9th IEEE/ACM Int'l Symp. on Cluster Computing and the Grid (CCGRID '09), Shanghai, China, 2009.

[58] Steffenel L. A.,Mounie G.: A Framework for Adaptive Collective Communications for Heterogeneous Hierarchical Computing Systems, Computer and System Sciences, vol. 74, Sept. 2008, pp. 1082-1093.

[59] Karonis N. T., Toonen B.,Foster I.: Mpich-g2: A Grid-enabled Implementation of the Message Passing Interface, Parallel and Distributed Computing, vol. 63, May 2003, pp. 551-563.

[60] Dinda P. A.: Online Prediction of Running time of Tasks, Cluster Computing, vol. 5, July 2002, pp. 225-236.

[61] Andrzejak A., Domingues P.,Silva L.: Predicting Machine Availabilities in Desktop Pools, in IEEE/IFIP Network Operations & Management Symp. (NOMS 2006), Vancouver, Canada, April 2006.

[62] Seneviratne S.: A Framework for Load Profile Prediction for Grid Computing, PhD, Electical & Information Engineering, Sydney University, Sydney, 2009.

[63] Carvalho M., Miceli R., Maciel Jr. P. D., Brasileiro F.,Lopes R.: Predicting the Quality of Service of a Peer-to-Peer Desktop Grid, in 10th IEEE/ACM Int'l Conf. on Cluster, Cloud and Grid Computing (CCGrid), Melbourne, Australia, 2010, pp. 649-654.

[64] Lilliefors H. W.: On the Kolmogorov-smirnov Test for the Exponential Distribution with Mean Unknown., presented at the JASA, 1969.

[65] Lublin U., Feitelson D. G.: The workload on Parallel Supercomputers: Modeling the Characteristics of Rigid Jobs Parallel & Distributed Computers vol. 63, Nov. 2003, pp. 1105–1122.

[66] Yang L., Schopf J. M.,Foster I.: Homeostatic and Tendency-Based CPU Load Predictions, in 17th Int'l Parallel and Distributed Processing Symp. (IPDPS 2003), Los Alamitos, California, USA, 2003, pp. IEEE CD-ROM pp. 9.

[67] Smith W., Taylor V.,Foster I.: Using Runtime Predictions to Estimate Queue Wait Times and Improve Scheduler Performance, in Int'l Workshop on Job Scheduling Strategies for Parallel Processing, San Juan, Puerto Rico, 1999, pp. 202-219.

[68] Goldberg D. E.: Ed., Genetic Algorithm in Search, Optimization and Machine Learning. Boston, MA, USA: Kluwer Academic Publishers, 1989, Pages

[69] Gibbons R.: A Historical Profiler for Use by Parallel Schedulers, Masters Thesis, University of Toronto, Toronto, Canada, 1997.

[70] Harchol-Balter M.,Downey A. B.: Exploiting Process Lifetime Distributions for Dynamic Load Balancing, in ACM SIGMETRICS' 96 Int'l Conf. on Measurement and Modelling of Computer Systems, Philadelphia, PA, USA, 1996, pp. 253-285.

[71] Krishnaswamy S., Zaslasvky A.,Loke S. W.: Estimating Computation Times in Data Intensive E-services, in 4th Int'l Conf. on Web Information Systems Engineering (WISE 2003), Rome, Italy, 2003, pp. 72–80.

[72] Ali A., Anjum A., Bunn J., Cavanaugh R., van Lingen F., McClatchey R., Mehmood M. A., Newman H., Steenberg C., Thomas M.,Willers I.: Predicting the Resource Requirements of a Job Submission, in Int'l Conf. on the Computing in High Energy and Nuclear Physics (CHEP2004), Interlaken, Switzerland, 2004, p. (CDROM) Article no. 273.

[73] Wilson D. R.,Martinez T. R.: Improved Heterogeneous Distance Function, Artificial Intelligence Research, vol. 6, 1997, pp. 1-34.

[74] Gupta C., Mehta A.,Dayal U.: PQR Predicting Query Execution Times for Autonomous Workload Management, presented at the Int'l Conf. of Autonomic Computing, 2008.

[75] Sanjay H. A.,Vadhiyar S.: A Strategy for Scheduling Tightly-Coupled Parallel Applications on Clusters, Concurrency and Computation: Practice & Experience, vol. 21, 2009, pp. 2491-2517.

[76] Verboven S., Hellinckx P., Arickx F.,Broeckhove J.: Runtime Prediction Based Grid Scheduling of Parameter Sweep Jobs, presented at the IEEE Int'l Conf. of Asia-Pacific Services Computing (apscc), Yilan, Taiwan, 2008.

[77] Fan J.,Gijbels I.: Local Polynomial Modelling and its Applications: Chapman & Hall, 1996.

[78] Buhmann M. D.,Buhmann M. D.: Radial Basis Functions. New York, NY, USA: Cambridge University Press, 2003.

[79] Morris M. D.: The Design and Analysis of Computer Experiments. thomas j. santner , brian j. williams , and william i. notz, American Statistical Association, vol. 99, Dec. 2004, pp. 1203–1204.

[80] Hertz J., Krogh A.,Palmer R.: Introduction to the Theory of Neural Computation. Reading, MA: Addison-Wesley, 1991.

[81] Andrew A. M.: An Introduction to Support Vector Machines and Other Kernel-based Learning Methods, Robotica, vol. 18, 2000, pp. 687–689.

[82] Iverson M. A., Zgne F.,Follen G. J.: Run-time Statistical Estimation of Task Execution Times for Heterogeneous Distributed Computing, presented at the HPDC, 1996.

[83] Costa B., Dutra I.,Marta M.: RL-Based Scheduling Strategies in Actual Grid Environments, in International Symposium on Parallel and Distributed Processing with Applications, Los Alamitos, CA, USA, 2008, pp. 572-577.

[84] Galstyan A., Czaijkowski K.,Lerman K.: Resource Allocation in the Grid with Learning Agents, Journal of Grid Computing, vol. 3, June 2005, pp. 91-100.

[85] Lee Y. C.,Zomaya A. Y.: A Grid Scheduling Algorithm for Bag-of-tasks Applications Using Multiple Queues with Duplication, icis-comsar, vol. 5, 2006, p. 10.

[86] Badia R. M., Labarta J., Gimenez J.,Escal´A. F.: DIMEMAS: Predicting MPI Applications Behavior in Grid Environments, in Workshop on Grid Applications and Programming Tools (GGF8), June 2003.

[87] Gruber R., Keller V., Kuonen P., Sawley M. C., Schaeli B., Tolou A., Torruella M.,Tran T. M.: Towards an Intelligent Grid Scheduling System, in 6th Int'l Conf. PPAM 2005, Poznan, Poland, 2005, pp. 751-757.

In: Grid Computing: Techniques and Future Prospects ISBN: 978-1-63117-704-0
Editors: J. G. Barbosa and I. Dutra, pp. 45-70 © 2015 Nova Science Publishers, Inc.

Chapter 2

RESOURCE SHARING FOR SCIENTIFIC WORKFLOWS ON COMPUTATIONAL GRIDS

Jorge G. Barbosa[1],* Christos Michalakelis[2] and Hamid Arabnejad[1]
[1] LIACC, Departamento de Engenharia Informática,
Faculdade de Engenharia, Universidade do Porto, Portugal
[2] Harokopio University of Athens,
Department of Informatics and Telematics, Athens, Greece

Abstract

Many scheduling algorithms for workflow applications target a single application at each time. The degree of parallelism of the application depends on the workflow structure, and for a task parallelism approach, the degree of parallelism will determine the degree of utilization of the resources reserved for the application. As today's computing nodes have several cores and considerable computing power, the single application approach may lead to higher computational costs when considering the energy spent. A plausible alternative is to share resources among applications, avoiding static reservation of resources, so that the energy spent by a job is minimized. In this chapter, we demonstrate the advantage of resource sharing and present a review of algorithms that have been successfully proposed for concurrent workflow scheduling. Challenges for grid resource managers, to accomplish an energy efficient resource sharing, are devised. Moreover, a review of the economic models for resource management and pricing, together with a case study, are also presented.

Keywords: scheduling, grid resource manager, utility model, budget, deadline, Quality of Service

AMS Subject Classification: 68M20

1. Introduction

Grid and HPC resource managers reserve in advance the resources specified by users for their jobs, based on runtime estimations, and assign exclusively those resources to the user

---

*E-mail address: jbarbosa@fe.up.pt; Address: Rua Dr. Roberto Frias, 4200-465 Porto, Portugal (Corresponding author)

application for a given period of time. Users tend to overestimate the required resources to guarantee that their jobs are not stopped before completing the required computations [1]. Therefore, the reservation strategy leads to a waste of resources and to an increase in the energetic running costs of the jobs. Energetic costs are currently a main concern for resource providers as the running costs surpass the installation and acquisition costs of a computer infrastructure. Therefore, energy efficiency in the context of computing has recently become a hot topic for academia and industry. Systems ranging from portable devices to large-scale distributed systems are all constrained to operate within a tight energy budget. To regulate the resource allocation procedure by users, the utility model [2], whereby users are allowed to submit their jobs to different resources based on the computational cost and jobs deadline, is adequate for non-profit grids as well as for market grids. The grid-computing model evolved from the non-profit model whereby users or institutions contribute with resources to form a grid in which resources are geographically distributed, and users from the participating institutions can access a wider range of resources than those available locally. The utility model is useful to regulate the infrastructure usage and to keep operational costs inside a given budget, whatever the profit model used. In this chapter, we analyze the energetic cost for running workflow scientific applications and provide evidence of the drawbacks of the conservative utility model that makes static reservation in advance for user jobs.

The chapter is organized as follows: In section 2, the energetic costs of running jobs using the static reservation model are discussed; section 3 reviews the literature on resource-sharing algorithms and discusses the challenges of grid schedulers to include the resource-sharing model; chapter 4 discusses and reviews economic models of resource management and pricing together with a case study regarding the public grid; section 5 concludes the chapter.

2.   Limitation of Reservation Based Scheduling

Scientific jobs are commonly represented as workflow applications that consist of many tasks, with logical or data dependencies, that can be dispatched to different compute nodes. A typical workflow application can be represented by a Directed Acyclic Graph (DAG), a directed graph with no cycles. In a DAG, an individual task and its dependency is represented by a node and its edges. A dependency ensures that a child node cannot be executed before all its parent tasks finish successfully and transfer the required child input data. The task computation time and communication time are modeled by assigning weight to nodes and edges, respectively. A DAG can be modeled by a tuple $G(V, E)$, where V is the set of v nodes and each node $v_i \in V$ represents an application task, and E is the set of communication edges between tasks. Each edge $e(i, j) \in E$ represents the task-dependency constraint such that task v_i should complete its execution before task v_j can be started. In a given DAG, a task with no predecessors is called an *entry task*, and a task with no successors is called an *exit task*. We assume that the DAG has exactly one entry task v_{entry} and one exit task v_{exit}. If a DAG has multiple entry or exit tasks, a dummy entry or exit task with zero weight and zero communication edges is added to the graph. For a given computing environment with p processors, given that the system may be heterogeneous, the data transfer rates between the processors, i.e., bandwidth, are stored in a matrix B of size

$p \times p$. The communication startup costs of the processors, i.e., the latencies, are given in a p-dimensional vector L. The communication cost of the $edge(i, j)$, which transfers data from task v_i, executed on processor p_m, to task v_j, executed on processor p_n, is defined as follows [13]:

$$c_{i,j} = L_m + \frac{data_{i,j}}{B_{m,n}}. \tag{1}$$

where $data_{i,j}$ is the amount of data to communicate. When both tasks v_i and v_j are scheduled on the same processor, the communication cost is zero.

Tasks may have a different execution time on each processor type. It is common that processors of different generations or of different types may be available, such as multicores and GPUs. Then, computation costs on each processor are represented as a matrix W of size $v \times p$, in which $w_{i,j}$ represents the execution time to complete task v_i on processor p_j. The average execution time is commonly used to compute the priority ranking for the tasks, and for task v_i, it is defined as follows:

$$\overline{w_i} = \sum_{j=1}^{p} \frac{w_{i,j}}{p}. \tag{2}$$

The schedule length of a DAG, also called *Makespan*, denotes the finish time of the last task in the scheduled DAG and is defined by:

$$makespan = max\{AFT(n_{exit})\} \tag{3}$$

where $AFT(n_{exit})$ denotes the *Actual Finish Time* of the exit node. In the case in which there is more than one exit node and no redundant node is added, the *makespan* is the maximum actual finish time of all exit tasks.

Concerning scientific workflows, there is a set of representative applications [3] that are used to evaluate the performance of scheduling algorithms and their implementations. Here, we will consider two applications, namely, *Montage* and *Epigenomics*, to evaluate the level of resource usage and energetic costs of the execution maps generated by state-of-the-art scheduling algorithms.

The *Montage* workflow [4] was created by NASA/IPAC, and it stitches together multiple input images to create custom mosaics of the sky [5]. Figure 1 displays the *Montage* workflow.

Applications represented by a workflow present a level of parallelism that is commonly not constant along all graph levels. This leads to an uneven CPU load along the execution time period. To illustrate this behavior, we present in Figure 2 the CPU load obtained for Montage workflows of 25, 50 and 100 nodes when using 20 processors. We can see that for 25 nodes, only 8 processors are used, and for 50 nodes, there are 6 processors with a utilization rate below 16%. For the Montage with 100 nodes, the usage rate is evenly distributed but with a processor usage rate below 55% for all processors, except for processor 13, which has a usage rate of 98.5%.

Considering the processors usage rate, the main question is to know how many processors should be allocated to each user job that satisfies both user and provider. Attending only to processing time, the user may attempt to select as many processors as possible. This

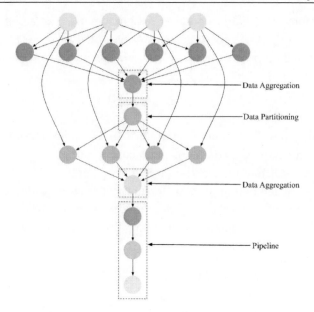

Figure 1. The Montage workflow from [5]. Vertices represent tasks and each color represents tasks of different types.

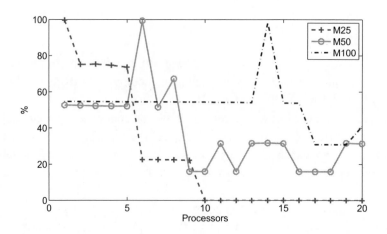

Figure 2. Processor usage rate when executing Montage workflows of size 25, 50 and 100 nodes on 20 homogeneous processors.

may lead to idle processors during the job execution, although these processors may be necessary for other users. From the provider point of view, it may represent higher operational costs and a lower rate of processed jobs.

Operational costs are mainly energetic costs. To estimate the energy consumed in each job execution, we use the high-level energy model described in [6] that uses the CPU usage rate as the only parameter. The authors indicated that the cubic model, represented in equation 4, obtained a mean error estimation below 3% for an AMD Opteron based system.

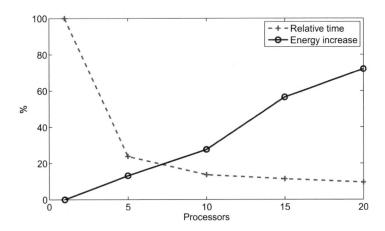

Figure 3. Relative processing time of Montage with 100 nodes when using 1, 5, 10, 15 and 20 homogeneous processors and their relative increase of energetic cost.

Equation 4 represents the power consumed per CPU, where R_{CPU} is the CPU usage rate.

$$P_{total} = 168.3 + 3.529R_{CPU} - 0.05098R_{CPU}^2 + 0.0002705R_{CPU}^3 \qquad (4)$$

The application of the cubic power model to the execution of the Montage workflow with 100 nodes, when running on 1, 5, 10, 15 and 20 homogeneous processors, is displayed in Figure 3.

From Figure 3, we can observe that the execution time decreases significantly when going from 1 processor to 5 processors. This represents a reduction of 76.5% in the execution time, and for 10 processors, the reduction is 86.3%. After that point, the time reduces marginally to 88.6% and 90.5% for 15 and 20 processors, respectively. Concerning energy, we can observe that the most economic execution is using a single processor. All other configurations increase the energetic cost. However, the time obtained for one processor may not be acceptable for the user. The energy spent increases by 13.2%, 27.5%, 56.5% and 70.8% for 5, 10, 15 and 20 processors, respectively. From Figure 3, we can conclude that there are two configurations that are a good compromise between users and providers, that is, using 5 and 10 processors. Using more than 10 processors would reduce just marginally the execution time while increasing substantially the energetic cost of running the job.

The analysis made so far is related to a particular workflow, but that behavior is common to many other workflow applications. The Epigenomics workflow, used for genome sequence processing, is a very regular workflow as indicated in Figure 4.

Figure 5 displays the relative execution time for 1 to 20 processors in relation to the execution time for 1 processor. Again, there is a significant reduction in processing time from 1 to 5 processors and also only marginal improvements are achieved when using more than 10 processors. In terms of energy, again the most energy efficient solution is obtained for 1 processor. For the Epigenomics workflow, the energy spent increases at a lower rate with the number of processors used, obtaining an increase of 49.2% for 20 processors in comparison to 1 processor execution. The same interval of 5 to 10 processors is obtained as the configurations with better compromise between execution time and cost.

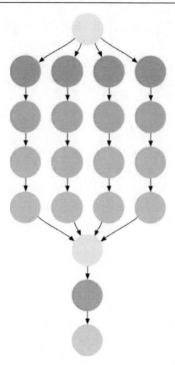

Figure 4. The Epigenomics workflow from [5]. Vertices represent tasks and each color represents different types of tasks.

The results obtained for the applications Montage and Epigenomics indicate that the common reservation policy used by the general Grid schedulers, such as PBS [7], Maui [8] and Moab [9], leave to the user the responsibility of selecting the number of processors for their applications. Due mainly to the aim of reducing the job's processing time, users are pushed to reserve processors without measuring the trade-offs of execution time and cost. Therefore, there is still space for improving actual state-of-the-art schedulers to regulate user requests for resources, reduce running costs and, ultimately, reduce the costs imputed to the users. Next, there are the revised approaches to sharing resources among user jobs without requiring static allocation of resources.

3.   Algorithms for Resource Sharing

Many of the scheduling algorithms address the single application case, such as [10, 11, 13], considering that an application has a set of resources available for the execution, which are commonly reserved in advance. Resource sharing means that more than one application will use the same set of processors, that is, several applications will share the same set of resources.

The common formulation considers time optimization constrained to resource availability. Additionally, a cost constraint may be added so that users can limit the cost of the produced schedules. Considering time and cost, two Quality of Service (QoS) quantities, we call *QoS constrained* scheduling to the formulation, whereby one QoS quantity is opti-

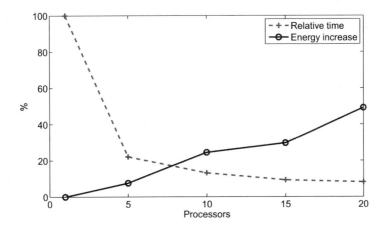

Figure 5. Relative processing time of Epigenomics with 100 nodes when using 1, 5, 10, 15 and 20 homogeneous processors and their relative increase of energetic cost.

mized and the other is a constraint [14]. The other approach that optimizes time and cost, called *QoS optimization* scheduling, is a bi-objective formulation in which the scheduling maps produced are a suitable balance of the QoS quantities [15, 16, 17]. This formulation can produce schedules with shorter makespans, but the cost cannot be limited by the user when submitting the work. In this chapter, we address only the *QoS constrained* scheduling problem.

3.1. Time Optimization and Non-budget Constrained Scheduling

Time optimization scheduling corresponds to the problem formulation that defines the objective function as the minimization of the application finish time. In this section, we review algorithms that do not consider execution costs as a problem constraint. These algorithms are presented in two groups, offline and online scheduling, that correspond to two distinct execution models.

3.1.1. Offline Algorithms for Resource Sharing

The following algorithms have in common the particularity of considering that all applications to be scheduled are available before the execution starts, that is, at compile time. After a schedule is produced and the execution initiated, no other application is considered. This methodology is applied by the most common resource management tools, whereby a user requests a set of nodes to execute his/her jobs exclusively. This approach is named static or offline scheduling [18]. One of the first algorithms was proposed by Iverson et al. [19], in which the performance of the system when several applications compete for the same resources is compared. They present a hierarchical matching and scheduling framework whereby each application makes its own scheduling decisions. No centralized scheduling resource is required so that applications do not need direct knowledge of the other applications. This knowledge is inferred indirectly through load estimates of processor queue lengths. The evaluation compares the average completion time of all submitted applications and does not measure individual metrics.

To address individual performance, several algorithms were proposed with the main concern of achieving fair resource sharing while minimizing the individual completion time of each application. Zhao et al. [20] define Fairness based on the slowdown that each application would experience (the slowdown is the ratio of the expected execution time for the same application when scheduled together with other applications to that when scheduled alone). Two algorithms were proposed, one fairness policy based on finish time and an additional fairness policy based on current time. The procedure is to evaluate the slowdown value of each application after scheduling a task and make a decision regarding which application should be selected to schedule the next task, so that all applications experience the same ratio of slowdown.

N'takpé et al. [21] proposed strategies based on the proportional sharing of resources. The main feature of these strategies is to statically assign to each application a subset of processors proportional to: a) critical path length; b) graph width; and c) work of each application. A weighted proportional sharing was also proposed that represents a better tradeoff between fair resource sharing and makespan reduction of the applications. The strategies were applied to mixed parallel applications, whereby each task could be executed on more than one processor. The results indicated that fairness resource sharing and shortest makespans are not achieved at the same time. The *work based* proportional sharing resulted in the shortest schedules, on average, but was also the least fair with regard to resource usage.

Bittencourt et al. [22] proposed a path clustering heuristic that combines the clustering scheduling technique to generate groups or clusters of tasks and the list scheduling technique to select tasks and processors. Based on this methodology, four algorithms were proposed: a) sequential scheduling, whereby applications are scheduled one after another; b) gap search algorithm, which is similar to the former but searches for spaces between already-scheduled tasks; c) the interleave algorithm, whereby pieces of each application are scheduled in turn; and d) group applications, whereby the applications are joined to form a single graph and then scheduled. The evaluation was made in terms of schedule length and fairness and concluded that interleaving the applications leads to lower average makespan and higher fairness. The results presented lack analysis of the impact of the delay on each application compared with exclusive execution, as only the average makespan is reported.

Casanova et al. [23] extensively evaluated algorithms for concurrent parallel task graphs on a single homogeneous cluster. Applications that have been submitted by different users share a set of resources and are ready to start their execution at the same time. The goal is to optimize user-perceived notions of performance and fairness. The authors proposed three metrics to quantify the quality of a schedule related to performance and fairness among the parallel applications.

Carbajal et al. [24] proposed two algorithms designated multiple workflow grid scheduling, MWGS4 and MWGS2, with four and two stages, respectively. The four-stage version comprises labeling, adaptive allocation, prioritization and parallel machine scheduling. The two-stage version applies only adaptive allocation and parallel machine scheduling. Both algorithms schedule a set of available and ready jobs from a batch of jobs. These strategies were demonstrated to outperform other strategies in terms of mean critical path waiting time and critical path slowdown.

3.1.2.   Online Algorithms for Resource Sharing

Online scheduling algorithms are applied to dynamic systems to which users can submit jobs at any time. Here, we consider the case of time optimization and non-budget constrained.

Yu and Shi proposed a planner-guided strategy, named Rank_Hybd, that dynamically schedules workflow applications that are submitted by different users at different moments in time. In each step, the algorithm reads the ready tasks from all applications and selects the next task to schedule based on their rank. If the ready tasks belong to different applications, the algorithm selects the task with the lowest rank; if the ready tasks belong to the same application, the task with the highest rank is selected. Tasks are ranked using the metric $rank_u$ [11], which represents the length of the longest path from task v_i to the exit node, including the computational cost of v_i, and is expressed as follows:

$$rank_u(v_i) = \overline{w_i} + \max_{v_j \in succ(v_i)} \{\overline{c_{i,j}} + rank_u(v_j)\}, \tag{5}$$

where $succ(v_i)$ is the set of immediate successors of task v_i, $\overline{c_{i,j}}$ is the average communication cost of $edge(i,j)$, and $\overline{w_i}$ is the average computation cost of task v_i. For the exit task, $rank_u(v_{exit}) = 0$.

Rank_Hybd allows the application with the lowest rank (lower makespan) to be scheduled first to reduce its waiting time in the system. However, this strategy does not achieve a great deal of fairness among the applications because it always gives preference to shorter jobs, postponing the longer ones. For instance, if a longer job is being executed and several short jobs are submitted to the system, the scheduler postpones the execution of the longer job to give priority to the shorter ones.

Hsu et al. [26] proposed the online workflow scheduling algorithm (OWM). OWM selects a single ready task from each application, the task with the highest rank ($rank_u$). Then, until there are unfinished applications in the system, it selects the task with the highest priority from the ready list. Then, it calculates the earliest finish time (EFT) for the selected task on each processor and selects the processor that will result in the smallest EFT. If the selected processor is free at that time, the OWM algorithm assigns the selected task to the selected processor; otherwise, the selected task stays in the ready list to be scheduled later. From the results presented in [26], OWM outperforms Rank_Hybd in dynamically scheduling concurrent applications.

Both Rank_Hybd and OWM algorithms use a fairness strategy that selects and schedules tasks from the longer applications first. OWM has a better strategy by filling the ready list with one task from each workflow so that all of the workflows have equal chance to be selected in the current scheduling round. In [18] it was demonstrated that OWM performs worse than Rank_Hybd for higher loaded systems, that is, when the number of applications is higher than the number of processors.

Arabnejad et al. [27] proposed the fairness dynamic workflow scheduling (FDWS) algorithm for online scheduling. As with OWM, it first selects a single task from each concurrent application to form a pool of ready tasks. The same priority rank, $rank_u$ from eq. 5, is used in this step. The second step, which selects from the ready pool one task to be executed, is what makes the major difference to the algorithms Rank_Hybd and OWM. These algorithms did not consider any relative measure among applications to increase fairness in resource sharing. On the contrary, FDWS attributes a new rank to the tasks in the ready pool, based on the execution status of each application to which the tasks belong.

To select tasks from the ready pool, $rank_r$ for task v_i belonging to App_j is computed, as defined by eq. 6, and the task with highest $rank_r$ is selected:

$$rank_r(v_{i,j}) = \frac{1}{PRT(App_j)} \times \frac{1}{|CP(App_j)|}. \tag{6}$$

The $rank_r$ metric considers the percentage of remaining tasks (PRT) of the application and its critical path length ($|CP|$). The PRT gives higher priority to applications that are nearly completed and only have a few tasks to execute. The use of CP length gives higher priority to application graphs with smaller $|CP|$ values, independently of the width of the application graph. The reason for considering CP length instead of the remaining processing time needed to execute all remaining tasks of the application, as in [28], is that a wider graph has a shorter $|CP|$ than other graphs with the same number of tasks, although it also has a lower expected finish time. In [18], it is reported that FDWS generated better solutions more often, with lower distribution for the turnaround time, which is the elapsed time from the submission to the completing execution time of each application.

Ferreira da Silva et al. [29] proposed a workflow fairness control for non-clairvoyant distributed computing platforms. Non-clairvoyant means that the execution time of a task on a given computing resource and resource characteristics are unknown. The fairness control is implemented by prioritizing tasks in workflows in which the unfairness degree is greater than a threshold. The context of this work is slightly different from previous algorithms, and it partially targets the same objective, which is to increase fairness among workflows. The results present average performances from a set of workflows and do not assess individually the workflow executions. Four different applications were evaluated on production conditions, and a reduction in slowdown variability was obtained when compared to the first-come-first-served approach.

3.2. Budget Constrained Scheduling

The algorithms described previously do not take into account the cost factor of executing an application or an available budget to run an application that cannot be exceeded. Here, we consider the *QoS constrained* scheduling problem whereby time is optimized constrained to a budget value.

Processors are rated with a cost per unit of time [30], and the cost of executing task v_i on processor p_j is given by $Cost(n_i, p_j) = w_{i,j}.Price(p_j)$, where $w_{i,j}$ is the estimated execution time and $Price(p_j)$ is the processor price. After assigning a specific processor to execute the task v_i, it is defined $AC(v_i)$ as *Assigned Cost* of task v_i [14]. The total cost of executing an application is defined as $TotalCost = \sum_{v_i \in V} AC(v_i)$.

In this context, the *objective* of the scheduling problem is to determine an assignment of tasks of a given application to processors such that the *Makespan* is minimized, subject to the budget limitation as expressed in equation 7:

$$\sum_{v_i \in V} AC(v_i) \leq BUDGET \tag{7}$$

The $BUDGET$ value must be defined, by the user, in a range that is feasible for the system to run the job.

In the *QoS constrained* scheduling, there is the single application scheduling problem and the concurrent application scheduling problem. Both are revised next.

3.2.1. Single Application Scheduling

Several works have been proposed for scheduling a single application under the QoS constrained scheduling model. The Hybrid Cloud Optimised Cost scheduling algorithm (HCOC)[31] and a cost-based DAG scheduling algorithm called Deadline-MDP (Markov Decision Process) [32] address the problem of minimizing cost while constrained by a deadline.

An Ant Colony Optimization (ACO) algorithm to schedule large-scale workflows with QoS parameters was proposed by [33]. Reliability, time, and cost are three different QoS parameters that are considered in the algorithm. Users are allowed to define QoS constraints to guarantee the quality of the schedule. In [34], a budget constraint workflow scheduling approach was proposed that used genetic algorithms to optimize workflow execution time while meeting the users budget. This solution was extended in [35] by introducing a genetic algorithm approach for constraint-based, two-criteria scheduling (deadline and budget). In [36], the Balanced Time Scheduling (BTS) algorithm was proposed, which estimates the minimum resource capacity needed to execute a workflow by a given deadline. Although the algorithm has some limitations, such as homogeneity in resource type and a fixed number of computing hosts, BTS achieves good performance with workflows having MPI-like parallel tasks.

The algorithms LOSS and GAIN [37] construct a schedule that optimizes time constrained to a budget. Both algorithms use initial assignments made by other heuristic algorithms to meet the time optimization objective; a reassignment strategy is then implemented to reduce cost and meet the second objective, the budget. In the reassignment step, LOSS attempts to reduce the cost, and GAIN attempts to achieve a lower makespan while attending to the budget limitations. Three versions of LOSS and GAIN were proposed. The LOSS algorithms obtained better performance than the GAIN algorithms. All of the versions of the LOSS and GAIN algorithms use a search-based strategy for reassignments; to obtain their goals, the number of iterations needed tends to be high for lower budgets in LOSS strategies and for higher budgets in GAIN strategies.

All the previous algorithms apply guided random search or local search techniques that require considerable processing time to produce good solutions when compared to the following algorithms that are heuristic based and that have a lower time complexity.

A budget-constrained scheduling heuristic called *greedy time-cost distribution* (GreedyTimeCD) was proposed by [38]. The algorithm distributes the overall user-defined budget to the tasks, based on the estimated task average execution costs. The actual costs of allocated tasks and their planned costs are also computed successively at runtime. This is a different approach, which optimizes task scheduling individually. First, a maximum allowed budget is specified for each task, and a processor is then selected that minimizes time within the task budget.

The *Budget-constrained Heterogeneous Earliest Finish Time* (BHEFT) was proposed in [39] for the context of execution for which the environment is characterized by multiple and heterogeneous service providers; BHEFT defines a suitable plan by minimizing the makespan so that the user's budget and deadline constraints are met while accounting for the load on each provider. An adequate solution is one that satisfies both constraints (i.e., budget and deadline); if no plan can be defined, it is considered a mapping failure. Therefore, the metric used by the authors was the planning success rate: the percentage of problems for which a plan was found.

The *Heterogeneous Budget Constrained Scheduling* algorithm (HBCS) was proposed in [14], which minimizes execution time while constrained to a user-defined budget. The algorithm starts by computing two schedules for the application: a schedule that corresponds to the minimum execution time that the scheduler can offer (e.g., produced with PEFT [13]) and the highest cost and an additional schedule that corresponds to the least expensive schedule cost on the target machines. With the least expensive assignment, the user knows the minimum cost and corresponding deadline to execute the job; with the highest cost assignment, the user knows the minimum deadline that can be expected for the job and the maximum cost that should be spent to run the job. With this information, the user is able to verify whether the platform can execute the job before the required deadline and within the associated cost range. If these parameters satisfy the users expectations, he/she specifies the required budget. From the results presented, it was demonstrated that HBCS outperforms LOSS, GAIN, GreedyTimeCD and BHEFT by achieving lower makespans for any given budget.

3.2.2. Concurrent Applications Scheduling

Concerning computational grids, which are dynamic systems, the online execution model is the most relevant. For the problem of online scheduling of concurrent applications with the formulation of *QoS constrained* scheduling, Hamid et al. proposed in [40] adaptations to two state-of-the-art online scheduling algorithms, namely, Rank_Hybd [25] and FDWS [27]. These algorithms are named Budget Rank_Hybd (B-Rank_Hybd) and Budget FDWS (B-FDWS).

Both algorithms first select tasks from all running applications to the ready pool and, afterwards, select a single task from the ready pool to be schedule, as described above in section 3.1.2. B-Rank_Hybd uses $rank_u$ to select the task to be schedule, and B-FDWS selects a task from the ready pool using the priority rank $rank_B$. Each task v_i in the ready pool that belongs to application j is assigned the priority value $rank_B$ defined by equation 8:

$$rank_B(v_{i,j}) = \frac{1}{TP_j} \times \frac{1}{BP_j} \tag{8}$$

The task with highest $rank_B$ is selected to be scheduled. The $rank_B$ value is the product of two factors: a) the inverse of the fraction of the application j that is remaining in the system; and b) the inverse of Budget Proportion. This priority factor gives higher priority to the applications that have a lower percentage of tasks unscheduled and to applications that have higher budgets when compared to the cheapest cost to run the application. The rational for the first factor is to give higher priority to applications that were submitted earlier, so that a longer application with several tasks already executed may have priority over a short and recent application. In addition, the rationale of the budget factor is that the scheduler will first consider tasks that spend more of the budget, and therefore, they will select more expensive and faster processors, resulting in a lower finish time for the application. The fraction of the application j that is remaining in the system is given by equation 9:

$$TP_j = \frac{unscheduled\ number\ of\ tasks}{Total\ number\ of\ tasks} \tag{9}$$

and the Budget Proportion (BP_j), equation 10, expresses the ratio of the Remaining Cheapest Budget (RCB_j) to the Remaining Budget (RB_j):

$$BP_j = \frac{RCB_j}{RB_j} \tag{10}$$

RCB_j is the budget required to execute the remaining task of application j using the cheapest processors, and RB_j is the remaining budget available to complete the execution of application j.

For processor selection, algorithm B-FDWS introduces a quality measure $Q(v_{sel}, p_i)$ to be assigned to each processor p_i when running the selected task v_{sel}, so that the processor with highest Q is selected. The quality measure allows, first, that more processors are considered as affordable and, therefore, selected; second, the selected processor may not be the one that guarantees the earliest finish time. The quality measure that combines time and cost factors for the selected task allowed better performances.

To the best of our knowledge, B-Rank_Hybd and B-FDWS are the first algorithms proposed to dynamically schedule workflow applications in the context of minimizing individual finish time (turnaround time) constrained to a user defined application budget.

3.3.   Challenges for Future Grid Resource Managers

The algorithms described above, B-Rank_Hybd and B-FDWS, can accomplish individual budget constraints for each application but still lack for ensuring an individual deadline that may also be a quality measure for users.

In grid resource management today, users request a fixed amount of CPUs for a period of time; those processors are allocated to the user even if the user application is not able to use all processors; and this reservation policy leads to an overallocation of resources, while many of those resources stay idle and consume energy. As demonstrated in section 2, the CPU usage rate depends on the application graph. It is also demonstrated by Figures 3 and 5 that, for a given graph type and size, there is a range of configurations for which the trade-off of execution time and cost are better balanced. For the case of the Montage and Epigenomics applications, the configurations range from 5 to 10 processors.

The future challenges of grid schedulers, on the one hand, to regulate and motivate adequate resource reservations by users and, on the other hand, to reduce the operational costs of the grid, in particular for non-profit models, are as follows: a) the introduction of credit accounts that users should manage to run jobs in the grid, which, when consumed, may be recharged with costs for the user or users group; b) Quality of Service concerning processing time and cost must be ensured; users may request a minimum set of processors according to the profile of the application they want to run, so that a hard deadline can be guaranteed by the system and, users also may specify a maximum budget they want to spend for that job; and c) the scheduler should guarantee the minimum number of processors to the user job so that the Quality of Service is achieved but may assign more processors if there are free processors and the user budget allows it, resulting in a reduction in the processing time without exceeding the budget.

4.   Economic Models for Resource Management

In a grid computing environment, a service is typically considered access to the system resources, such as a CPU, disk or other resources. The entities that constitute the grid ecosystem are usually independent, a fact that makes decisions regarding resource allocation a challenging problem. Resource management, which is an important aspect of the grid middleware, is a complex undertaking due to different usage policies, cost models, varying load and availability patterns. Traditional models and approaches give emphasis on system-centric resource management, according to which a scheduling component decides which jobs are to be executed at which resource. The corresponding cost functions are driven by system-oriented metrics such as utilization and system throughput [41]. In future grids, however, the technical focus shifts toward business, and requirements are based on a user-centric service provisioning perspective. Consequently, resource management is supposed to follow economic-based approaches, focusing on delivering maximum utility to the individual user of the grid. Decisions should therefore be steered by the user valuation of their results, and price dynamics must be taken under consideration as a key deciding factor in resource use. The use of market-like techniques regulates the supply and demand for resources, provides an incentive for providers, and motivates the users to make trade-offs between deadlines, budgets and the required level of quality of service [42].
An economic basis for resource sharing can provide [43]:

1. Flexibility: Resources can be obtained by users when they need them;

2. Efficiency: Resource price reflects resource value;

3. Scalability: New budget entities and users can be added easily, preserving flexibility and efficiency;

4. Feedback for budget and investment decisions: Prices for resource use and value of resource uses over time can be used to guide management decisions in terms they are familiar with, i.e., money and Net Present Value.

In general, grids need to use dynamic and competitive economic models, as different resource providers and consumers have different objectives, strategies, and requirements, which can change over time. A market-oriented model can be used in solving distributed resource management problems, such as the cost-management problem. This is the problem that grid resource providers face in supporting seamless management of different requests from different users simultaneously. In an economic-based grid computing environment, resource management systems need to provide mechanisms and tools that allow resource consumers (end users) and providers (resource owners) to express their requirements and facilitate the realization of their goals [44, 45]. From the standpoint of the resource consumers, there are the following needs:

1. A utility model, which describes consumer demand for resources and specifies constraints, such as deadlines and budget constraints, along with optimization parameters, as, for example, optimization for time;

2. A broker agent, which supports resource discovery and strategies for application scheduling on distributed resources dynamically at runtime, depending on their availability, capability and cost, along with user-defined QoS requirements. The broker must also dynamically adapt to changes in resource availability at runtime to meet user requirements.

From the resource provider standpoint, the needs include:

1. Tools and mechanisms that support price specification and generation schemes to increase system utilization, and

2. Protocols that support service publication, trading, and accounting.

For the market to be competitive and healthy, coordination mechanisms are required to help reach the equilibrium price - the market price at which the supply of a service equals the quantity demanded, maximizing the social surplus. In general, the price should not be arbitrarily set, but the pricing function must fulfill four essential requirements [46]. As a first requirement, it should be flexible so that it can be easily configured to modify the pricing of resources to determine the level of sharing. Second, the pricing function has to be fair, in the sense that resources should be priced based on actual usage by the users. This means that users who use more resources pay more than users who use fewer resources. The third requirement indicates that the function should be dynamic. The price of each resource is not static and changes depending on the operating condition. Finally, the pricing function needs to be adaptive to changing supply and demand of resources and should compute the relevant prices accordingly. For instance, if demand for a resource is high, the price of the resource should be increased to discourage users from overloading this resource and to maintain equilibrium of supply and demand of resources.

4.1. Pricing the Grid Ecosystem

In the grid environment, as in any other market, the goal is the maximization of both the resource owner and user surplus. Following the principles of competitive market structures, pricing policies should attract users and utilize the consumed resources efficiently, which in turn need to be accounted for and charged. Pricing structures are built upon the following approaches:

- Prepaid Pay and use;

- Use and pay later;

- Pay as you go;

- Grants based.

In general and despite the fact that a fixed price model is a simple pricing scheme, it cannot meet the demand for Quality of Service (QoS), which may vary among the users or with the executed applications and time. Following this, a number of approaches were studied, and corresponding pricing schemes were proposed [44] including, among others:

- Flat price models (the same cost for applications and no QoS like in todays Internet);

- Competitive economic models (e.g., auctions and contract-net);

- Usage timing (peak, off-peak, lunch time like pricing telephone services);

- Usage period and duration (short/long);

- Demand and supply;

- Foresight-based (based on model and predict responses by competitors);

- Loyalty of Customers;

- Historical data;

- Bulk Purchase, etc.

The service items charged and accounted for depend on the resource requirements of the applications (CPU intensive, I/O intensive or a combination). In general, charging is based on the following resources, either individually or in combination of two or more:

- CPU - User time and System time (consumed by and while serving user App, respectively);

- Memory;

- Maximum resident set size - page size;

- Amount of memory used;

- Page faults;

- Storage used;

- Network bandwidth consumption;

- Signals received, context switches;

- Software and Libraries accessed (particularly required for the emerging ASP world).

Table 1. Economic models in grid computing

Economic Model	Characteristics
Commodity market	Resources are priced appropriately, seeking to maintain the equilibrium between supply and demand. There are two types of Commodity market model in general: • flat pricing model (fixed); • supply and demand based pricing model (variable). The supply and demand model is more popular because it has the capability to maintain equilibrium between resource supply and demand by changing price behavior.
Posted Price	Similar to the commodity market model. Their difference is that it advertises special offers, seeking to attract (new) consumers to establish market share or motivate users to consider using cheaper slots.
Double Auction (DA)	Providers are arranged in ascending order and users in descending order, in terms of demand and budget, respectively. If a users request matches with a provider's offer, the trade is performed. There are two types of DA: • Continuous Double Auction (CDA), according to which users post their requirements and budgets, and service providers post their offers at any time during the trading period; • Periodic DA, in which the auction continues for a specific time period as defined by the auctioneer. CDA is the usually employed approach in the grid literature.
English auction	Users are free to increase their bids overtaking others. The auction ends when nobody offers an increase in price. The highest bidder is then declared the winner. Bids can be proposed for a single item (single attribute) or for multiple items (multi attributes).
Bargaining	It is based on the assumption that users seek to obtain a lower access price and higher usage duration, whereas providers like to obtain more profit through bargaining. Users might start with a very low price and providers with a higher price. Bargaining may continue over multiple attributes, such as price, deadline/job execution time, etc.
Proportional share based auction	This is similar to the English auction, except, after the auction process, resources are shared among the participants according to their bids.
Proportional resource share	The percentage of the resource share allocation to the user's application is proportional to the bid value in comparison to the other users' bids.
First price sealed bid auction	A number of users submit their bids only once to obtain a service, without knowing other bids. The highest bidder wins the service at the price that was bid.
Contract net protocol (CNP)	According to this model, a user is called a manager and a provider is called a contractor. The manager declares his/her requirements and invites bids from available contractors. Interested contractors evaluate the demands and respond by submitting their bids. The manager evaluates the bids and selects a contractor to proceed.

Numerous economic models based on microeconomic and macroeconomic principles have been proposed in the literature, and they can be applied over the grid environment [47]. They belong to the following main categories:

- commodity market model;

- posted price model;

- bargaining model;

- tendering/contract-net model;

- auction model;

- bid-based proportional resource sharing model;

- community/coalition/bartering model;

- monopoly and oligopoly.

In a more recent survey [48], a number of market-oriented approaches are presented, evaluating corresponding scenarios, such as the survey performed in which suitable economic models for grid computing were investigated. The analysis covers the most popular models proposed since the inception of grid computing, provides discussion regarding strengths and weaknesses and indicates that no substantial work exists considering multiple economic models and switching between them for varying scenarios in a grid environment. The developed economic models are different from one another, depending on the way they are used for interaction among users and providers, for pricing and their ability to adapt to the different requirements. Among the crucial criteria for evaluating their strengths and weaknesses are computation, resource allocation and economic efficiency, handling of large number of users, decentralization, price stability, etc. A summary of the most popular models is presented in Table 1.

The *commodity market* and the *double action* are the most widely used models in the grid. In the commodity market model, resource owners specify their service price and charge users according to the amount of resources they consume. The pricing policy is based on various parameter services and priced in such a way to maintain market equilibrium, which is crucial for any market-oriented grid environment. Maintaining supply and demand by regulating price behavior ensures a higher probability of delivering the requested QoS, as well as an increased system performance. According to this model, if demand for a resource exceeds supply at a particular state, the price of that resource increases in a way such that the demand function shifts to the point closer to the available supply, a new equilibrium point. A number of approaches have been proposed for the determination of the equilibrium price, and they are usually based on:

- Flat fee;

- Usage Duration (Time);

- Subscription;

- Demand and Supply-based.

The resource value is defined as a function of many parameters:

Resource Value = Function (Resource strength, Cost of physical resources, Service overhead, Demand, Value perceived by the user, Preferences).

In the case of the *posted price* model, which is quite similar to the commodity market, brokers need not negotiate directly with service providers for price, but they rather use posted prices as they are generally cheaper compared to regular prices [44]. Although the posted-price offers may have usage conditions, they might be attractive for some users. For example, during holiday periods, when demand for resources is likely to be limited, service providers can post tempting offers or prices to attract users to increase resource utilization.

The *auction* model supports one-to-many negotiation between a service provider (seller) and many consumers (buyers) and reduces negotiation to a single value (i.e., price). The auctioneer sets the rules of auction that are acceptable for the consumers and the providers. Auctions use market forces to negotiate a clearing price for the service, and they can be conducted as open or closed. This depends on whether they allow back-and-forth offers and counter offers.

The *Double Auction (DA)* model has a decentralized nature and the ability to handle large number of users. It is the primary economic model for the trading of equities, commodities, and derivatives in stock markets. In the double auction model, buy orders (bids) and sell orders (asks) may be submitted anytime during the trading period. If at any time there are open bids and asks that match or are compatible in terms of price and requirements, such as quantity of goods or shares, a trade is executed immediately. In grid computing, users and providers are self-interested entities and appear with their individual optimization strategies. Hence, DA supports them by sorting their valuations and thus expediting the trading phase without any requirement of global information. The model has a high potential for grid computing.

In the *English auction* model, the auctioneer seeks to obtain the true market value of the source that has been set for auction. Users are free to increase their bids exceeding others for the resource that they are competing for. When no bidder is willing to increase their bids, the auction ends, and the auctioneer checks its reservation price with the last highest bid and determines the winner. This model is suitable for increasing revenue because it supports competition among users, selecting the user who bids the highest by using an iterative bidding policy. It also helps to identify the demand of a particular resource in the market. The main drawback of the model is that, due to its high communication demand, it may produce network congestion. Because the English auction is by nature an iterative model, too many messages are exchanged during the auction process.

An additional model that requires high communication demand is the *bargaining* model, which may not be a suitable choice in the case of many users. In the context of this model, users and providers can optimize their preferred interests by negotiating their preferences and reach a satisfactory SLA. Resource brokers bargain with service providers for lower access prices and higher usage duration. Both brokers and service providers have their own objective functions, and they negotiate with each other as long as their objectives are met. Negotiation stops as soon as they reach a mutually agreeable price or one side is not willing to negotiate any further. The objective functions are built upon preferences such as budget/job-execution-cost, deadline/job-execution-time, etc.

4.2.   Case Study: Resource Costs in a Public Computing Grid

Public-resource computing, also known as Global Computing, Volunteer Computing or Peer-to-peer computing (P2P), is a type of distributed computing in which computer owners donate their computing resources (such as processing power and storage) to one or more "projects" [49]. This computational model uses resources belonging to the general public, such as personal computers and game consoles, to perform scientific supercomputing. This paradigm enables previously infeasible research and encourages public awareness of current scientific research [50]. P2P systems provide the opportunity to expand PC grid computing to pool large amounts of distributed resources to enable Internet-scale applications using millions of compute engines [51]. Probably the most well-known collaborative application on these peer-to-peer networks is file sharing. Apart from file sharing, the distributed resources in P2P systems can also enable large-scale computing projects, seeking to aggregate the computing power in these networks to construct a large-scale parallel system. A list of the most well-known P2P systems can be found in [52].

Public resource computing depends on the availability of computing resources contributed by individuals. These resources can be increased by creating incentives to users, such as providing payment for the offered resources. However, there are costs associated with the provision of resources, and it is important that these costs are calculated to estimate the level of the payment to be offered, with a profit for the provider. These costs include, among others, opportunity costs, future value costs, penalties, utility costs, and fixed costs. A detailed analysis and calculation of these costs for the public grid model can be found in [51]. By defining a full accounting of the cost structure, the resource provider can determine whether it is profitable to participate in a public resource computing market. The main costs are as follows:

- fixed costs;

- utilization costs;

- time dependent costs;

- quality of service penalties.

Fixed costs are mainly identified as the capital costs to purchase the computing equipment. The expected revenues from public resource computing are usually small, so providers are unlikely to proceed with buying new infrastructure for the needs of the grid. So, equipment is typically purchased for another purpose while supplying computing resources to the grid. As a result, fixed costs can be usually ignored.

Utilization costs are variable costs associated with the actual use of the service. They are derived by adding together:

- *Power consumption* (up). It can be expressed as follows: $up = cp * p * T$, where cp is the energy cost per joule, T is the time that the resource is being utilized, and p is the wattage differential, i.e., the difference in power consumption between standby and normal modes. The last factor is added because the service is available when the computer is idle and likely in standby mode;

- *Network bandwidth* (un). Bandwidth provision is usually charged on a fixed cost basis regardless of its utilization, as in a typical home broadband connection. Corporate connections, on the other hand, may have a bandwidth cost. Therefore, network utilization cost can be expressed as follows: $un = (cbw * b + cn) * T$, where cbw is the bandwidth cost, b is the average bandwidth utilized by the client and cn the network cost per unit time;

- *Wear-and-tear* (uw). They correspond to the cost caused by the failure of the infrastructure as a result of usage. Although a number of sophisticated methods exist to determine this cost, a simple but reliable approach is to express it as a function of the mean time to failure ($MTTF$) metric. In this case, the uw function can be expressed as follows: $uw = (cr/MTTF) * T$, where cr is the cost of the source.

- *Resource utilization* (ur). They are derived as a result of the dedication of a limited resource, and they are inversely related to the availability of the resource. It is expressed as a function of the amortized fixed cost of the resource and the fraction of resources that are being used by the public computing grid. Simple models are linear, but more realistic models would make the cost inversely proportional or logarithmically related to the resource availability.

Time dependent costs are related to the costs that are the result of time scheduling procedures and the allocation of resources. In this context, there are a number of methodologies to be presented in the corresponding literature, a simple one being the heuristic according to which the more difficult a contract makes scheduling, the higher is the price.

Finally, *quality of service* costs are related to the availability and the reliability of the resources and the penalties to be accounted due to the lack of fulfilling the agreements. Penalties are set to give incentives to providers to become more reliable. Apart from the availability of the system, penalties may be set according to the availability of bandwidth, of CPU time, of memory, or any other resource.

Conclusion

This chapter discusses the resource usage rate and associated costs when processing scientific applications on the grid and also presents a user-centric approach and an economic basis for resource management and scheduling, together with the most widely used pricing methodologies in the grid ecosystem. The calculation of the resource costs in a public computing grid was considered as an example.

CPU usage rate depends on the application graph characteristics, such as the degree of parallelism, leading to resources that are partially idle and still consuming energy. Resource sharing among applications is a feasible solution to improve the systems usage rate and reduce costs. A review of the algorithm for resource sharing is presented here and is divided into two categories: a) time optimization and non-budget constrained scheduling and b) budget constrained scheduling. The former optimizes processing time without limiting the cost, and the latter optimizes time but is limited by a user defined budget.

Challenges to future grid resource managers are proposed, which consist mainly in applying Quality of Service scheduling, ensuring user deadlines and budgets by introducing flexibility to the resource manager, so that the amount of processors assigned to each job may change dynamically, and by introducing an economic model. The economic approach provides several additional advantages over conventional ones, including incentives for resource owners and resource users to obtain profit, and promotes the grid as a platform for mainstream computing.

Among the benefits of the grid economy is that it helps regulate the supply and demand for resources, offers uniform treatment of all resources, allows building a highly scalable system, as the decision-making process is distributed across all users and resource owners, and supports a simple and effective basis for offering differentiated services for different applications at different times.

Acknowledgments

This work is partially supported by Fundação para a Ciência e Tecnologia, PhD Grant FCT - DFRH - SFRH/BD/80061/2011, and by EU under the COST programme Action IC1305: Network for Sustainable Ultrascale Computing (NESUS).

References

[1] A. W. Mualem, D. G. Feitelson. Utilization, predictability, workloads, and user runtime estimates in scheduling the IBM SP2 with backfilling. *IEEE Transactions on Parallel and Distributed Systems*, Vol. 12, n. 6, pp. 529-543, 2001.

[2] James Broberg, Srikumar Venugopal, Rajkumar Buyya. Market-oriented Grids and Utility Computing: The State-of-the-art and Future Directions. *Journal of Grid Computing*, n. 6, pp.255-276, 2008.

[3] Gideon Juve, Ann Chervenak, Ewa Deelman, Shishir Bharathi, Gaurang Mehta, Karan Vahi. Characterizing and profiling scientific workflows. *Future Generation Computer Systems*, Vol. 29, pp. 682-692, 2013.

[4] G. B. Berriman, Ewa Deelman, John C. Good, Joseph C. Jacob, Daniel S. Katz, Carl Kesselman, Anastasia C. Laity, Thomas A. Prince, Gurmeet Singh, Mei-Hu Su. Montage: a grid-enabled engine for delivering custom science-grade mosaics on demand. *SPIE Conference 5487: Astronomical Telescopes*, 2004.

[5] R. F. da Silva, W. Chen, G. Juve, K. Vahi, E. Deelman. Community Resources for Enabling Research in Distributed Scientific Workflows. *10th IEEE International Conference on e-Science*, 2014.

[6] Xiao Zhang, Jian-Jun Lu, Xiao Qin, Xiao-Nan Zhao. A high-level energy consumption model for heterogeneous data centers. *Simulation Modelling Practice and Theory*, Vol.39, pp. 41-55, 2013.

[7] PBS Works. *PBS Professional 12.2*, User's Guide, September 2014. http://www.pbsworks.com.

[8] D.Jackson, Q.Snell, M.Clement. Core algorithms of the Maui scheduler. In D.G. Feitelson and L. Rudolph, editors, *Job Scheduling Strategies for Parallel Processing*, LNCS volume 2221, pages 87-102, 2001.

[9] *Adaptive Computing*. Moab workload manager administrator's guide, version 8.0.0, September 2014, http://docs.adaptivecomputing.com

[10] Y. Kwok, I. Ahmad. Static scheduling algorithms for allocating directed task graphs to multiprocessors. *ACM Computing Surveys*, 31(4), pp. 406-471, 1999.

[11] H. Topcuoglu, S. Hariri, M. Wu. Performance-effective and low-complexity task scheduling for heterogeneous computing. *IEEE Transactions on Parallel and Distributed Systems*, 13(3), pp. 260-274, 2002.

[12] Oliver Sinnen, Leonel Sousa, Frode Sandnes. Toward a Realistic Task Scheduling Model. *IEEE Transactions on Parallel and Distributed Systems*, Vol. 17, n. 3, pp.263–275, March 2006.

[13] Hamid Arabnejad, Jorge G. Barbosa. List Scheduling Algorithm for Heterogeneous Systems by an Optimistic Cost Table. *IEEE Transactions on Parallel and Distributed Systems*, Vol. 25, n. 3, pp. 682–694, March 2014.

[14] Hamid Arabnejad, Jorge G. Barbosa. A Budget Constrained Scheduling Algorithm for Workflow Applications. *Journal of Grid Computing*, DOI: 10.1007/s10723-014-9294-7, 2014.

[15] A. Dŏgan, F. Özgüner. Bi-objective scheduling algorithms for execution time reliability trade-off in heterogeneous computing systems. *Comput. J.* 48(3), pp. 300-314, 2005.

[16] Jack J. Dongarra, Emmanuel Jeannot, Erik Saule, Zhiao Shi. Bi-objective scheduling algorithms for optimizing makespan and reliability on heterogeneous systems. *Proceedings of the 9th ACM symposium on Parallel algorithms and architectures*, pp. 280–288, 2007.

[17] R. Prodan, M. Wieczorek. Bi-criteria scheduling of scientific grid workflows. *IEEE Trans. Autom. Sci. Eng.* 7(2), pp. 364-376, 2010.

[18] Hamid Arabnejad, Jorge Barbosa, Frédéric Suter. Fair Resource Sharing for Dynamic Scheduling of Workflows on Heterogeneous Systems. in High-Performance Computing on Complex Environments, by Emmanuel Jeannot and Julius Zilinskas, John Wiley & Sons, *Parallel and Distributed Computing Series* (51), pp. 147–167, June 2014.

[19] M.A. Iverson, F. Özgüner. Hierarchical, competitive scheduling of multiple dags in a dynamic heterogeneous environment. *Distributed System Engineering*, Vol. 1, n. 3, 1999.

[20] H. Zhao, R. Sakellariou. Scheduling multiple DAGs onto heterogeneous systems. In *International Parallel and Distributed Processing Symposium (IPDPS)*, pp. 1-14, IEEE, 2006.

[21] T. N'takpé, F. Suter. Concurrent scheduling of parallel task graphs on multi-clusters using constrained resource allocations. *International Symposium on Parallel and Distributed Processing (IPDPS)*, pp.1-8, 2009.

[22] L. Bittencourt, E. Madeira. Towards the scheduling of multiple workflows on computational grids. *Journal of Grid Computing*, vol. 8, pp. 419-441, 2010.

[23] H. Casanova, F. Desprez, F. Suter. On cluster resource allocation for multiple parallel task graphs. *Journal of Parallel and Distributed Computing*, vol. 70, pp. 1193-1203, 2010.

[24] A. Carbajal, A. Tchernykh, R. Yahyapour, J. García, T. Röblitz, and J. Alcaraz. Multiple workflow scheduling strategies with user run time estimates on a grid. *Journal of Grid Computing*, vol. 10, pp. 325-346, 2012.

[25] Z. Yu, W. Shi. A planner-guided scheduling strategy for multiple workflow applications. In *International Conference on Parallel Processing-Workshops* (ICPP-W'08), pp. 1-8, IEEE, 2008.

[26] C. Hsu, K. Huang, F. Wang. Online scheduling of workflow applications in grid environments, *Future Generation Computer Systems*. vol. 27, no. 6, pp. 860-870, 2011.

[27] H. Arabnejad, J. Barbosa. Fairness resource sharing for dynamic workflow scheduling on heterogeneous systems. In *International Symposium on Parallel and Distributed Processing with Applications (ISPA)*, pp. 633-639, *IEEE*, 2012.

[28] D. Karger, C. Stein, J.Wein. Scheduling algorithms. *CRC Handbook of Computer Science*, 1997.

[29] R. Ferreira da Silva, T. Glatard, F. Desprez. Workflow fairness control on online and non-clairvoyant distributed computing platforms. *19th International Conference Euro-Par* 2013, pp.1-12, 2013.

[30] W. Zheng, R. Sakellariou. Budget-deadline constrained workflow planning for admission control in market-oriented environments. In: *Economics of Grids, Clouds, Systems, and Services*, pp. 105-119, 2012.

[31] L. Bittencourt, E. Madeira. HCOC: a cost optimization algorithm for workflow scheduling in hybrid clouds. *Journal of Internet Services and Applications*, Vol. 2, n. 3, pp. 207–227, 2011.

[32] J. Yu, R. Buyya, C.K. Tham. Cost-based scheduling of scientific workflow applications on utility grids. In *First International Conference on e-Science and Grid Computing, IEEE*, pp. 147-154, 2005.

[33] W.-N. Chen, J. Zhang. An ant colony optimization approach to a grid workflow scheduling problem with various QoS requirements. *IEEE Trans. Syst. Man Cybern. Part C Appl. Rev.* 39(1), 29-43, 2009.

[34] J. Yu, R. Buyya. A budget constrained scheduling of workflow applications on utility grids using genetic algorithms. *IEEE Workshop on Workflows in Support of Large-Scale Science*, WORKS'06, pp. 1-10, 2006.

[35] J. Yu, R. Buyya. Scheduling scientific workflow applications with deadline and budget constraints using genetic algorithms. *Sci. Program.* 14(3), pp. 217-230, 2006.

[36] E.-K. Byun, Y.-S. Kee, J.-S. Kim, E. Deelman, S. Maeng. Bts: Resource capacity estimate for time-targeted science workflows. *J. Parallel Dist. Comput.* 71(6), pp. 848-862, 2011.

[37] R. Sakellariou, H. Zhao, E. Tsiakkouri, M. Dikaiakos. Scheduling workflows with budget constraints. *Integr. Res. Grid Computing*, pp. 189-202, 2007.

[38] Y. Jia, K. Ramamohanarao, R. Buyya. Deadline/budget based scheduling of workflows on utility grids. *Market-Oriented Grid Util. Comput.*, pp. 427-450, 2009.

[39] Wei Zheng, Rizos Sakellariou. Budget-deadline constrained workflow planning for admission control. *Journal of Grid Computing*, pp. 1-19, 2013.

[40] Hamid Arabnejad, Jorge G. Barbosa. Budget Constrained Scheduling Strategies for on-line Workflow Applications. In *14th International Conference on Computational Science and Its Applications (ICCSA)*, pp. 1–14, 2014.

[41] G. Stuer, K. Vanmechelen, and J. Broeckhove. A commodity market algorithm for pricing substitutable Grid resources. *Future Generation Computer Systems*, vol. 23, pp. 688-701, 2007.

[42] H. Izakian, A. Abraham, and B. T. Ladani. An auction method for resource allocation in computational grids. *Future Generation Computer Systems*, vol. 26, pp. 228–235, 2010.

[43] C. Kenyon and G. Cheliotis. Grid resource commercialization: Economic engineering and delivery scenarios. In *Grid Resource Management: State of the Art and Future Trends*, J. Nabrzyski, J. M. Schopf, and J. Weglarz, Eds., ed: Springer, pp. 465–478, 2004.

[44] R. Buyya. *Econommic-based distributed resource management and scheduling for grid computing*. Monash University, Melbourne, Australia, 2002.

[45] R. Buyya, D. Abramson, and S. Venugopal. The Grid Economy. *Proceedings of the IEEE*, vol. 93, pp. 698–714, 2005.

[46] C. S. Yeo and R. Buyya. Pricing for Utility-Driven Resource Management and Allocation in Clusters. *Int. Journal of High Performance Computing Applications*, vol. 21, pp. 405–418, 2007.

[47] R. Buyya, D. Abramson, J. Giddy, and H. Stockinger. Economic Models for Resource Management and Scheduling in Grid Computing. *Concurrency and Computation: Practice and Experience*, vol. 14, pp. 1507–1542, 2002.

[48] A. Haque, S. M. Alhashmi, and R. Parthiban. A survey of economic models in grid computing. *Future Generation Computer Systems*, vol. 27, pp. 1056–1069, 2011.

[49] Wikipedia. *Voluteer Computing.*
Available: http://en.wikipedia.org/wiki/Volunteer_computing.

[50] D. P. Anderson. BOINC: A System for Public-Resource Computing and Storage. *Proceedings of the 5th IEEE/ACM International Workshop on Grid Computing*, 2004.

[51] J. A. Chandy. An analysis of resource costs in a public computing grid. In *IEEE International Symposium on Parallel & Distributed Processing*, pp. 1–8, 2009.

[52] Wikipedia. *List of distributed computing projects.*
Available: http://en.wikipedia.org/wiki/List_of_distributed_computing_projects

In: Grid Computing: Techniques and Future Prospects   ISBN: 978-1-63117-704-0
Editors: J. G. Barbosa and I. Dutra, pp. 71-98   © 2015 Nova Science Publishers, Inc.

Chapter 3

On the Challenges in the Design of Efficient Job Scheduling Policies for Production HPC and Grid Environments

Dalibor Klusáček* and Šimon Tóth†
CESNET a.l.e., Prague, Czech Republic

Abstract

Resource management and job scheduling in large and heterogeneous systems like HPC clusters and Grids is still a very challenging task. During the past two decades many new approaches and scheduling algorithms have been proposed, yet only few are widely used in practice. Particularly, significant portion of the research has concentrated on heavily sanitized models of systems used in production. While this allows for a straightforward analysis of the proposed models and approaches, it severely limits the applicability of such solutions. In this chapter we describe the main problems a researcher should consider when developing or modifying a scheduling algorithm. Production systems generally represent a complex multi-criteria optimization problem combined with a set of operational constraints. We highlight several common problems that appear when simple or incomplete system models are used. Furthermore, even if accurate models are used, they do not guarantee that the proposed solutions will be truly useful, unless an appropriate evaluation is performed. For this purpose, we present several rules that must be followed in order to obtain realistic evaluation and/or simulation results. Throughout the chapter we provide several practical examples, in which we describe and demonstrate how an existing or newly developed solution should be analyzed, modeled and evaluated. We demonstrate, that the final solution is often achieved by using a set of various interacting scheduling policies, algorithms and carefully selected optimization criteria.

Keywords: Scheduling, Policy, Evaluation

AMS Subject Classification: 68M20

---

*E-mail address: klusacek@cesnet.cz
†E-mail address: simon@cesnet.cz

1. Introduction

Current HPC and Grid [16] systems are often distributed and decentralized computer environments composed of a large number of heterogeneous resources which are managed by different owners like companies, universities or another business or scientific organizations. Such resources may be of different type such as computational machines, data storage nodes, databases, scientific tools, etc; interconnected by (high speed) communication network. These systems tend to have *high dynamicity in time*, mainly due to the changing load of the system, available network bandwidth and also due to other dynamic events such as resource or network failures and recoveries [16, 27].

The main goal of a resource manager and underlying middleware is to manage this large and heterogeneous environment while allowing easy access to its resources for various users. It allows them to submit their jobs into the system, guaranteeing nontrivial Quality of Service (QoS), meanwhile hiding the complexity of the system itself by providing powerful but simple interfaces [16]. Moreover, not only users but also resource owners should be satisfied, i.e., the system should be safe and efficient, thus allowing proper utilization of its resources. Clearly, if both users' and resource owners' goals are to be met, multi-objective criteria have to be used. To meet these goals *automated and sophisticated scheduling techniques* should be applied.

1.1. Complexity of Job Scheduling

Unfortunately, job scheduling in such a highly dynamic, distributed, heterogeneous and decentralized environment is an extremely difficult task if good performance, nontrivial QoS, scalability, etc., are required. There are several reasons why efficient job scheduling is so demanding. First of all, it is well known that finding optimal schedules in large systems is, in general, NP-hard [44, 62]. For example, the Grid scheduling problem is a generalized reformulation of the *Multiprocessor Scheduling [SS8]*[1] problem which has been shown to be NP-hard [18]. In fact, since HPC and Grid environments are highly dynamic, it is often impossible to even *define the optimality of scheduling* [60], as it is defined in combinatorial optimization. In these systems, the scheduler runs as long as the system exists and thus the performance is measured not only for particular applications but also in the long run [60]. Moreover, it is easy to show that even significantly simplified subproblems are intractable [28]. To illustrate this fact, let us consider one machine with several CPUs which corresponds to several identical machines in parallel, denoted as P. A simplified subproblem involves one machine, sequential jobs, and the makespan as a single objective[2]. Let us assume that the problem is to be solved at the given time, thus the release dates of jobs can be omitted as well. Using the Graham's $\alpha|\beta|\gamma$ classification scheme of scheduling problems [21] — where α describes the machine environment, β provides (optional) details of the processing characteristics and the constraints, and γ specifies the optimality criterion — this problem is formulated as $P||C_{\max}$. Even this heavily simplified problem is known to be NP-hard [53], i.e., intractable for larger instances.

In contrast to that, the real issues faced when operating HPC or Grid systems are far

---

[1]The code in square brackets is a reference to the classification used in Garey and Johnson [18].
[2]The makespan is the completion time of the last job, often denoted as $C_{\max}$.

more complex, as we will describe closely in Sections 3-5. As a result, all mainstream schedulers applied in practice are using suboptimal scheduling techniques, typically a combination of several simple heuristics.

1.2. The Impact of Research on Existing Systems

For many years, researchers have been searching for a perfect job scheduling algorithm that would improve the performance of HPC and Grid-like systems. Still, there are few algorithms that are being used in practice [47] as can be seen in many production schedulers applied in nowadays general resource management systems. For example, the core of the system is generally based on the trivial first come first served (FCFS) approach and backfilling is typically the most advanced option available [1, 2, 41, 47]. Since backfilling was proposed in 1995 [37], it is obvious that there is some misunderstanding between the research community and system administrators concerning "what is really important".

The main reason is that classical research papers usually considered too simplified, thus unrealistic models. Therefore, their results are hardly achievable in production systems. Using our experience from the Czech National Grid Infrastructure *MetaCentrum* [38] we explain several additional challenges that appear when searching for a functional solution. For example, real life systems have to focus on maintaining fairness among users of the system [26, 59], rather than just trying to optimize simple criteria like the average slowdown or the makespan. In practice, it quickly turns out that those widely used "theoretical" models and optimization goals are mostly impractical in real life [17, 47].

1.3. Chapter Overview

In this chapter, we describe several important features that must be considered when developing a functional and realistic scheduling approach. First of all, we discuss the hierarchy of Grid and HPC scheduling and provide a detailed insight into a real, complex job scheduling system. In detail, we explain several important features that current resource managers offer to a system administrator in order to establish robust, efficient and fair computing infrastructure. Based on this description, we show the main parameters of a realistic system model, that are necessary in order to guarantee reasonably realistic outputs of this model, e.g., by means of simulation or analysis. Next section discusses the process of choosing proper optimization criteria. Finally, we show how results of the analysis or a simulation should be interpreted and presented in order to obtain realistic and useful outputs.

2. Hierarchy of Scheduling

By definition, HPC and especially Grid systems are distributed, decentralized, heterogeneous and highly dynamic computer environments consisting of various resources which are interconnected by a computer network [16], although some of these attributes are not always present in all systems. It is worth noticing, that job scheduling may also be distributed both physically and logically. For example, we may distinguish between centralized and decentralized scheduling. By *centralized scheduling* we usually understand scheduling approach based on a single Local Resource Management System (LRMS) such as PBS Pro [41], TORQUE [3] or Sun Grid Engine [19]. In this case, a set of computers or clusters (HPC system) or the whole Grid is managed by a single scheduler which has full control of all jobs and resources (see the *Centralized layer* in the bottom of Figure 1).

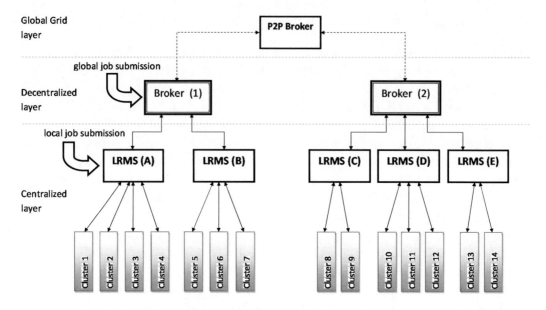

Figure 1. Hierarchy of Grid scheduling systems.

Decentralized scheduling usually applies some hierarchical model as depicted by Figure 1[3]. Here the scheduling process is broken down into a set of separate decisions on different levels, although some cooperation for effective solution is often required. Decentralized scheduling is often managed by one or more so called *Metaschedulers* or *Brokers* like GridWay [22] or Unicore [45]. These brokers often manage different underlying centralized LRMSs [54]. Moreover, several brokers may communicate together, establishing a *global Grid* consisting of several local Grids or resources [54]. In this case, one or more so called P2P Brokers can be applied to interconnect different Grids, allowing truly global Grid infrastructure. In such an environment it is often possible to submit jobs at different levels — local users prefer their local LRMS while brokers are used by the users from the outside [54].

Still, the problem of efficient scheduling cannot be handled satisfactory unless LRMSs are properly setup. Therefore, we will further discuss those centralized scheduling systems only, assuming that their schedulers have full control of all jobs and resources.

3. Main Components of a Resource Management System

The common mistake of many research papers is that they only focus on the scheduling policy, i.e., on the mechanism how jobs are selected for execution. However, typical resource management systems are far more complicated, containing several other components with

---

[3]Figure 1 is based on the scheme proposed in [54].

various functionalities and features that may easily represent a bottleneck that causes inefficient behavior of the whole system. Therefore, this section closely describes major parts of a typical resource management system, discussing their goals, interactions and possible problems that may appear if these parts are not configured properly.

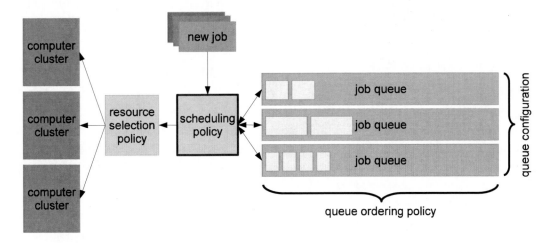

Figure 2. Main components of a common (local) resource management system.

A typical scheme of a resource management system is shown in Figure 2. The system consists of one or more *queues*, where waiting jobs are stored until they are chosen by a *scheduling policy* for execution. The system as a whole is often configured so that jobs are ordered within a queue(s) using a special *queue ordering policy*. Different *queue configuration* may be applied for queues, reflecting the needs of the system provider. Once a job is selected for execution, target machine(s) is chosen by a *resource selection policy*.

3.1. Queue Ordering Policy

Queue ordering policy determines the order of jobs in which they are then processed by a scheduling policy. Resource management systems usually provide a set of static ordering policies (ordering between two jobs does not change once established) as well as dynamic policies. Jobs can be either kept in the order of their arrival (static First Come First Served ordering), or can be ordered dynamically according to their length (Shortest Job First, Longest Job First), according to their resource requirements (Largest CPU/Memory Requirements First) or their (user configured) priority. Combinations of ordering policies are also possible [1, 24].

3.1.1. Fairshare

Fairshare is a dynamic priority ordering policy designed to provide user-to-user fairness. Job ordering is usually based on users previous resource consumption [24, 30]. Typically, the more resources are consumed by a particular user, the lower his/hers priority becomes. More precisely, if user A and a user B have identical priorities, they will receive the same amount of resources, when averaged over a reasonably long time period [24]. This is of course only true when both user A and user B actually request these resources. Fairshare self-balances itself around an equilibrium where all users have consumed the same amount of resources. Practical implementations of fairshare also *reflect aging* [24] by periodically decreasing all recorded consumption using the so called decay factor [1]. This is suitable for systems with faster job turnaround times (submission to completion) that puts a higher emphasis on more recent resource consumption.

3.1.2. Queue Selection Policy

Not only jobs, but also queues may be ordered. If multiple queues are present in the system, a separate policy is used to define the order in which queues will be selected by a scheduling policy. Typically, queues are selected in a fixed (priority-based) sequential order, or using a *Round-robin*-like algorithm [41]. Once the ordering is established, the scheduling policy either attempts to run one job from each queue or all jobs from the currently selected queue are checked before the next queue is processed. Also the combination of these approaches can be used [41]. Queues are typically selected according to their priorities which are set up by a system administrator.

3.2. Scheduling Policy

Resource management systems are rather conservative in their choices of scheduling policies and mostly rely on well established and robust approaches [47]. Due to the complex nature of the job scheduling problem, all mainstream resource managers are using some kind of heuristic-based policies, i.e., techniques to obtain high quality solutions in reasonable time. A heuristic does not guarantee that an optimal solution will be found, good solutions in (relatively) short time are preferred instead. However, in some situations we cannot reach a good solution or even decide how far or close the generated solution is from the optimal solution [43]. In practice, only few scheduling policies are used in mainstream systems. These range from trivial First Come First Served (FCFS), aggressive backfilling (no reservations), to EASY [37] or Conservative backfilling [24], each with its own shortcomings.

3.2.1. First Come First Served

All systems support a basic *First Come First Served (FCFS)* scheduling policy [1, 41, 48]. FCFS always schedules the first job in a queue, checking the availability of resources required by such a job. If all the resources required by the first job in a queue are available, it is immediately scheduled for execution, otherwise FCFS waits until all required resources become available. While the first job is waiting for execution none of those remaining jobs can be scheduled, even if required resources are available. The pseudo code of FCFS is shown in Algorithm 1.

Despite its simplicity, the FCFS approach presents several advantages. It does not require estimates of jobs processing times and it guarantees that the response time of the first job does not depend on the processing times of the remaining jobs. On the other hand, if parallel jobs are scheduled then this fairness-related property often implies a low utilization of

---

Algorithm 1 *First Come First Served*

1: *stopping condition* := **false**;
2: **while** *stopping condition* = **false** **and** *queue* is not empty **do**
3:     *j* := first job in *queue*;
4:     **if** *j* in *queue* can be executed **then**
5:         remove *j* from *queue* and execute it;
6:     **else**
7:         *stopping condition* := **true**;
8:     **end if**
9: **end while**

---

system resources, that cannot be used by some "less demanding" job(s) from a queue [51]. Approaches applied to solve this problem are described in the following Section 3.2.2.

3.2.2. Algorithms Using Backfilling

Algorithms using *backfilling* are an optimization of the FCFS algorithm that tries to maximize resource utilization [37]. Backfilling generally requires that each job specifies its estimated execution time, so that the scheduler can predict when jobs will be finished.

We start with EASY (Extensible Argonne Scheduler sYstem) backfilling [48] algorithm that is shown in Algorithm 2. It works as FCFS but when the first job in the queue cannot be scheduled because the specified amount of resources is not yet available (line 9), it calculates its earliest possible starting time using the processing time estimates of running jobs. Then, a resource reservation is made, starting at the pre-computed job start time (line 11). Next, it scans the queue of waiting jobs and schedules immediately every job not interfering with the reservation of the first job [37] (lines 4-8). Clearly, instead of strictly following the job order as mandated by the ordering policy it only guarantees the earliest possible start for the first job. The notions of "first job" and the order of jobs are mandated by the ordering policy as was described in Section 3.1. Backfilling increases resource utilization, since idle resources are *backfilled* with suitable jobs, while decreasing the average job wait time. The algorithm finishes when the whole queue has been tested (line 16).

EASY backfilling takes an aggressive approach that allows short jobs to skip ahead provided they do not delay the job at the head of the queue. The price for improved utilization of EASY backfilling is that execution guarantees cannot be made because it is hard to predict the size of delays of jobs in the queue. Since only the first job gets a reservation, the delays of other queued jobs may be, in general, unbounded [39][4]. EASY backfilling is supported by all major production systems including Moab [2], Maui [24], PBS Pro [41], LSF [42] or Condor [52].

While EASY backfilling makes a reservation for the first job only, Conservative backfilling [11, 36, 49] makes the reservation for every queued job which cannot be executed at a

---

[4]If a job is not the first in the queue, new jobs that arrive later may skip it in the queue. While such jobs do not delay the first job in the queue, they may delay all other jobs. Therefore, the system cannot predict when a queued job will eventually run [39].

Algorithm 2 *EASY backfilling*

 1: *stopping condition* := **false**; *reservation* := **null**; *job index* := 1;
 2: **while** *stopping condition* = **false** **and** *queue* is not empty **do**
 3:      *j* := job at position *job index* in the *queue*;
 4:      **if** job *j* can be executed not colliding with *reservation* **then**
 5:          remove *j* from *queue* and execute it;
 6:          **if** *job index* = 1 **then**
 7:              *reservation* = **null**;
 8:          **end if**
 9:      **else**
10:          **if** *job index* = 1 **and** *reservation* = **null then**
11:              *reservation* := make reservation for *j*;
12:          **end if**
13:          *job index* := *job index* + 1;
14:      **end if**
15:      **if** *job index* > size of *queue* **then**
16:          *stopping condition* := **true**; (the whole queue has been tested)
17:      **end if**
18: **end while**

---

given moment as shown in Algorithm 3. It means that backfilling is performed only when it does not delay any previous job in the queue. Here the scheduling decisions are made upon job submittal, thus we can predict when each job will run, giving users execution guarantees. Users can then plan ahead based on these guaranteed response times. Obviously, there is no danger of starvation as a reservation is made for every job that cannot be executed immediately. This places greater emphasis on predictability [11, 39].

Algorithm 3 shows the pseudo-code of Conservative backfilling. Unlike EASY backfilling, it makes a reservation for every job that cannot start at a given moment (see line 10), by calculating its earliest possible starting time using the processing time estimates of running jobs. The duration of a reservation period is based on a job's estimated processing time. These reservations are stored in a set (*reservations*). No job being scheduled for execution can collide with some reservation from this set (see line 4). When some job having a reservation is finally scheduled for execution its reservation is removed from the *reservations* set (line 7). The algorithm terminates when all jobs in the queue were either scheduled for execution or reservations for them were established (line 15).

3.2.3. Job Starvation

Job starvation is an undesirable condition where a particular job (or a user) is subject to excessive wait time due to the configuration of policies. The notion of excessive is of course subject to interpretation. For example, fairshare ordering priority will deliberately cause starvation of users with recent high resource consumption, which is however considered desirable. FCFS and Conservative backfilling algorithms provide anti-starvation mechanisms, guaranteeing that jobs are not excessively delayed. More aggressive forms of backfilling

Algorithm 3 *Conservative backfilling*

1: $reservations := \emptyset$; *stopping condition* := **false**; *job index* := 1;
2: **while** *stopping condition* = **false** **and** *queue* is not empty **do**
3:     $j :=$ job at position *job index* in the *queue*;
4:     **if** job j can be executed not colliding with existing *reservations* **then**
5:         remove j from *queue* and execute it;
6:         **if** $\exists reservation_j \in reservations$ for job j **then**
7:             $reservations := reservations \setminus reservation_j$;
8:         **end if**
9:     **else**
10:         $reservation_j :=$ make reservation for j;
11:         $reservations := reservations \bigcup reservation_j$
12:         *job index* := *job index* + 1;
13:     **end if**
14:     **if** *job index* > size of *queue* **then**
15:         *stopping condition* := **true**;
16:     **end if**
17: **end while**

like EASY or aggressive backfilling need to be combined with other mechanisms to prevent starvation, as they can delay the execution of certain jobs without any bounds [39].

3.3. Resource Selection Policy

When a job is chosen by the scheduling policy, it means that all resources it requires are available. If there are multiple choices (i.e., nodes or clusters) to execute that job a process called *resource selection policy* is used to select the "best resource" from the list of all currently suitable resources. Again, this process involves some heuristic that makes this decision. *First Fit (FF), Best Fit (BF), Min Load First (MLF)* or *Fastest Resource First (FRF)* are some of many policies which are used for this purpose in the production systems [2]. First Fit schedules jobs onto the first suitable resource, while Best Fit chooses the node that has the fewest available resources but still enough to successfully execute the job while respecting all job constraints. This helps to keep large nodes free for large jobs and lowers resource fragmentation. Min Load First does the exact opposite, i.e., the cluster with the highest number of idle CPUs is chosen [7, 2]. Fastest Resource First selects the fastest available resource. Again, a combination of policies is possible, and the final decision usually depends on the internal decisions of the responsible organization.

3.4. Queue Configuration

Previously presented policies provided by resource management systems are relatively simple. As such, a single policy cannot cover the usually complex requirements used in production systems. To deal with more complex requirements, resource management systems provide the concept of independently configurable queues. Then, it is the interaction between queue-specific policies and the global system policies that dictates the overall behavior of the system.

Queues can handle different policies, that are mostly represented by a set of various limits [1, 2, 41] that apply to jobs executed from that queue. These limits usually cover per-user, per-group and per-queue limitations concerning the maximum number of running jobs and/or amount of particular resource type (e.g., CPU cores). Also, the maximum execution time of jobs can be limited by imposing a global queue limit. Another possibility is to limit the queues to have access only to a subset of available resources, e.g., limiting a queue to a particular cluster of machines. Such policy establishes pools of resources, where several queues can compete for a limited set of resources, thus preventing a (potentially dangerous) saturation of the entire system.

While such configuration can increase resource fragmentation [24], it is necessary when dealing with different classes of users accessing the system. We need to be very careful when saturating the system with jobs from a single user, or even when saturating the system with a single class of jobs. For example, it would be very dangerous to saturate the system with long running jobs (i.e., jobs with expected runtime of several weeks). Such a situation would naturally lead to great deterioration in performance characteristics of the system (e.g., huge wait times for shorter jobs), as it would take several weeks before any other job would be executed.

3.5. Summary

Efficient setup of a local resource management system is very important. For example, queues and their limits are used to guide the access of users and their jobs to existing computational resources while fairshare is responsible for fair job ordering. The problem is *how to find an efficient setup* of a local resource manager.

As it turns out, there is no generally acceptable solution that would suit all systems. Still, there are some known best practices that one can build upon when searching for a good solution. For example, MetaCentrum uses several queues with different limits to balance the amount of resources available to different classes of jobs. The basic rule is that the number of available CPU cores is inversely proportional to the maximum execution time of jobs [32], limiting the problems related to long jobs while keeping low wait times for shorter jobs. Also, several modifications covering anti-starvation policy, fairshare and queue ordering have been made recently, significantly improving the overall performance of MetaCentrum [32]. An interesting fact is that the improvement was solely based on modifications that were not related to the actual scheduling policy.

Another example comes from the Zeus cluster in PL-Grid. Here all long jobs as well as jobs that require whole node(s) are planned ahead using reservations which enables a forward detection of potential problems [15].

In the Ohio Supercomputer Center several combined approaches are used together. For example, long serial jobs are only allowed if a user is able to reasonably explain why he or she needs to run such a long experiment [40]. Moreover, parallel jobs have in general smaller maximal runtime limits compared to sequential jobs. Also, per-user and per-group limits are used together with fairshare accounting [40].

A different, rather strict approach is used in the DAS-4 system in Netherlands. The default run time for jobs on DAS-4 is 15 minutes, which is also the maximum for jobs on DAS-4 during working hours. Only during the night and on the weekend, when DAS-4 is regularly idle, it is allowed to run longer jobs. In all other cases, a user will first have to negotiate advanced permission from the system administrators to make sure that he or she will not cause too much trouble for other users [57].

Obviously, there are several ways how to achieve good performance. Although we have shown some of them in the previous text and some further details can be found in, e.g., [32], a detailed study concerning suitable combinations of global policies and queue configurations is probably still missing.

4. Realistic Simulations Using Adequate System Model

When a researcher or a system administrator is trying to optimize an existing solution or develop a new one, the crucial starting point is to use a realistic system model. The model of the system shall follow all important parameters that are typical for the target system (see Section 3). Without doing so, the outcome of simulations will have limited or even no relevance, since they will probably provide misleading results [33, 47]. While Section 3 demonstrated the purpose and interactions of various parts of real resource management systems, this section discusses how such systems should be modeled in simulation. Especially, we mention some of those typical shortcomings that should be avoided in order to obtain a reasonable system model. These include resources, jobs, system dynamics and additional system-specific features like queue configuration or specific job requirements.

4.1. Detailed Resource and Job Models

Many problems are related to simplified resource and job models. Therefore, we now describe some of the most common problems related to these two areas, including real-life and experimental examples.

4.1.1. Resources

Concerning system resources, researchers usually use a simple model, where the system is composed of one or more computer clusters and each cluster is composed of several machines. Often, all machines within one cluster have the same parameters, e.g., the number of CPUs and the machine's CPU speed.

Together, a typical model of resources describes the number o clusters, machines and related number of CPUs and their speeds. However, there are several *additional parameters* that are very important and should be used in simulations, e.g., the number and type of GPUs, the size of machine's RAM, a local hard disk's capacity, parameters of network interconnections, etc. For starters, we would strongly suggest to consider at least RAM, as it is equally important as CPUs. It should be a rather easy task as many existing workload logs provide us with such data [12].

4.1.2.   Jobs

Job represents a user's application. Commonly, a job is modeled by its length (execution time), arrival time, and by the number of requested CPUs. A job may require one (sequential) or more CPUs (parallel). Such a specification is very common, however it is far from reality.

For example, an actual runtime is typically unknown to a scheduler until a job completes. Instead of that, only an *estimated runtime* is usually known in advance. In a real system, a runtime estimate or a queue time limit is the maximum time limit that a job can execute. In case that the actual job runtime is longer than the estimate, the job is killed since it exceeds its available runtime. This is essential to *ensure that reservations are respected* [55]. Therefore, users usually *overestimate* the job runtime to avoid premature termination of their jobs [39], making them very inaccurate [39, 55]. Therefore, if available, such an estimate should be always used by the scheduling algorithm instead of an actual execution time.

Furthermore, actual resource managers like Maui, Moab, PBS Pro, etc., are using more complicated job specifications. A job is specified by its per-node requests, instead of specifying aggregated resources. For example, instead of saying that a job requires 8 CPUs and 32 GB of RAM, a job requests two nodes each having 4 CPUs and 16 GB of RAM. Moreover, different per-node specifications are also allowed [1, 41]. Again, if available, these complex specifications should be used in simulations as they further increase their reliability.

Also, researchers often ignore other job requirements such as RAM or GPUs. However, these should be considered too. To illustrate the importance of considering RAM, we provide the following real-life example which is based on a real workload coming from the *Zewura* cluster, a part of MetaCentrum [38]. Zewura consists of 20 nodes, each having 80 CPUs and 512 GB of RAM. Figure 3 (left) shows the heterogeneity of CPU and RAM requirements of jobs that were executed on this cluster. Clearly, there are many jobs that use a lot of RAM while using only a fraction of CPUs. Similarly, Figure 3 (right) shows an example of CPUs and RAM usage on a selected node within the Zewura cluster. For nearly two weeks in July 2012, jobs were using at most 10% of CPUs while consuming all available RAM memory. Then, the remaining 90% of CPUs could not be used by other jobs due to the lack of available RAM. This example illustrates the importance of using complex job and cluster specification. If we would ignore the RAM and its usage in our experiments, we would obtain totally different results, i.e., very optimistic and completely wrong.

4.1.3.   Queue Configuration and Specific Job Requirements

So far we have defined typical parameters that are used to describe jobs and machines. Here the given job can be executed on any cluster that offers sufficient amount of CPUs (and RAM). However, this is a very basic constraint which is rarely sufficient in real life, where, e.g., a queue configuration as described in Section 3.4 is further applied. In heterogeneous environments, users often specify some subset of machines or clusters that can process their jobs. This subset is usually defined either by a resource owners' policy (a user is allowed to use such cluster), or by a user who requests some properties (library, software license, execution time limit, etc.) offered by some clusters or machines only. Also, the combination

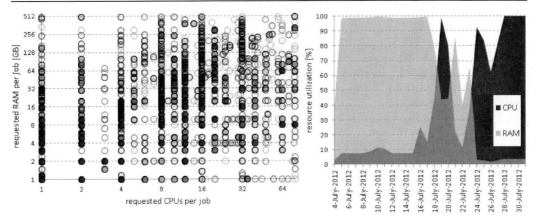

Figure 3. Heterogeneity of jobs CPU and RAM requirements (left) and an example of CPU and RAM utilization on one Zewura node (right).

of both owners' and users' restrictions is possible [27].

First of all, each cluster may have additional parameters that closely specify its properties. These parameters typically describe the architecture of the underlying machines (e.g. Opteron or Xeon), the available software licenses (e.g. Matlab or Gaussian), the operating system (e.g. Debian or SUSE), the list of queues allowed to use this cluster and their various limits, the network interface parameters (e.g. 10Gb/s or Infiniband), the available file systems (e.g. nfs or afs) or the cluster owner. Clearly, different clusters may support different properties.

Users may closely specify which cluster(s) is (are) suitable for their jobs by specifying required machine architecture, requested software licenses, operating system, network type, file system, etc. In other words, by setting these requirements, users can prevent a job from running on some of the cluster(s). In real life, there are several reasons to do so. Some users have strong security demands and do not allow their jobs (and data) to use "suspicious" clusters which are not managed by their own organization. Other users may need special software which is not available everywhere. Some clusters are dedicated for short jobs only and a user wanting more time is not allowed to use such cluster, and so on.

All these requests and constraints are often combined together and have to be included into the decision making process to satisfy all specific job requirements. If no suitable cluster is found, the job has to be canceled. Clearly, the specific job requirements cannot be used when the corresponding cluster parameters are not known. Without them, consideration of "job-to-machine" suitability is irrelevant. Therefore, it is very important to use complex workload traces that provide such data, e.g. from the Parallel Workloads Archive [12].

4.2. System Dynamics

It is important to notice that modeled systems are dynamic, which means that the state of the system is not static but changes dynamically in time. Hence, also the studied problem is dynamic since it changes over the time. We will closely discuss two major influences that affect the state of the system. Those are machine failures and restarts as well as user activity. As it turns out, both may have high impact on the performance of the system [27].

4.2.1. Machine Failures and Restarts

Actual systems consist of many machines that — naturally — are not immune against occasional failures or necessary maintenance and upgrade periods. Also, the size of the system is not fixed throughout the time as the number of connected machines may change. It is a common feature that machines are added or removed from the system as the time passes. *Machine failure* means that either one or more machines within a cluster are not available to execute jobs for some time period. Such failure may be caused by various reasons such as a power failure, a disk failure, a software upgrade, etc.

4.2.2. Influence of Users

In the same unpredictable fashion as failures influence the number of available machines, activities of users have impact on the number of jobs currently present in the system. An arrival time is determined by a user in most cases and can be influenced by both external and internal influences. An external influence is, e.g., current time. In geographically small systems, user activity is usually higher during the day causing higher load of the system compared with the off-peak night hours [10]. While such an influence is covered by existing workloads, additional system and scheduler-related (internal) influences are not usually covered by these workloads. For instance, if several scheduling algorithms are tested, then in the real world the submission pattern of a user may change if he or she knows that more resources are available at a particular moment [47]. Therefore, it is often useful to model users submission patterns separately, using original historic workload only as an input which is further (dynamically) modified.

4.3. Summary

To conclude this Section, let us now demonstrate how complex models including system dynamics, i.e., specific job requirements and machine failures, influence results of simulations. For this purpose we have used a complex MetaCentrum workload [27], that allows us to simulate both machine failures and specific job requirements. Figure 4 shows how simulation results concerning average job wait time evolve when more complex system models are applied. Clearly, the *simple model* does not show any dramatic difference among considered scheduling algorithms. However, as soon as more complex models involving either failures or specific job requirements or both (complex model) are applied, the differences among algorithms start to show up very clearly. Especially the tragic performance of plain FCFS algorithm is largely visible. This example demonstrates that — if available — complex simulation models should be used as they are more likely to show "interesting behavior".

5. Optimization Criteria and Corresponding Metrics

So far, we have described what the common features and constraints of resource managers and schedulers are and why it is important to incorporate them into the model. However, there is one very important aspect left — how to measure the quality of generated solutions? Most importantly, this question relates both to simulations as well to real, production

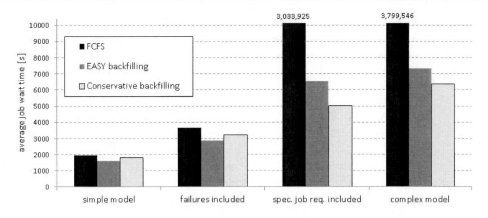

Figure 4. Example of various simulation results according to the complexity of applied simulation model.

systems. A common way is to use a set of optimization criteria, expressed in a form of objective functions (metrics) that are to be either minimized (e.g., the wait time) or maximized (e.g., the system utilization).

In the following text we present several common optimization criteria and discuss their suitability for realistic evaluation. As we demonstrate, the process of choosing proper metric and its interpretation is in fact a very challenging task. We start with criteria that are often applied to measure the performance of the system. Next, job related as well as user related criteria are presented.

5.1. System Aware Metrics

Probably the most popular system aware metric is the *machine usage/utilization* [14, 50, 60]. It expresses to what extent is the resource capacity utilized over the time and as such is a very common criterion used by resource owners who generally desire to maximize the utilization of their system. Since Grid and HPC systems often contain heterogeneous machines, these systems commonly employ a *weighted machine usage* criterion to represent the performance of machines [28], or another — even subjective — factor that reflects the relative importance of a particular machine [8]. For example, when a choice is to be made between two machines, it is better to highly utilize the fast machine rather than the slow machine since the fast machine computes more operations in the given time than the slow one. It is important to notice that such a scenario is not covered by the classic machine usage criterion where only the proportion of used and available CPUs is measured disregarding their relative performance.

There are several other system aware metrics that try to incorporate the overall efficiency of the system by focusing on its energy demands or its environmental impact. For example, *Power Usage Effectiveness (PUE)* is the metric used to determine the energy efficiency of a system. PUE is determined by dividing the amount of electric power entering a system by the power used to run the computer infrastructure within it [6].

Finally, the *makespan* ($C_{\max}$) which denotes the completion time of the last executed job in the system is widely used in the literature [61, 60]. Although it is a job aware metric, some authors use it to measure the general productivity of the system. As pointed out by Xhafa and Abraham in [60], small values of makespan mean that the whole workload is processed in short time, i.e., the scheduler is providing good and efficient planning of jobs to resources.

5.1.1. Problems with System Aware Metrics

Sadly, both makespan and machine usage are somehow problematic. As defined, makespan is suitable only for "off-line", static problems where all jobs are already known. If the system is running for months or even years, it makes little sense to optimize the makespan, since it cannot be even properly computed. The problem is that we do not know when the last job will arrive or complete. Of course, one can consider the otherwise dynamic problem as a static one, measuring "partial makespan" at each given time, considering only currently present jobs. Still, the usefulness of makespan is quite limited as it optimizes only the upper bound of the jobs completion times. Therefore, additional objectives should be applied [60].

Similar problems relate to machine usage. Typically, machine usage is measured in an aggregated fashion, expressing the average utilization of resources in a long time period. However, such an approach causes that the resulting values are very similar for all considered algorithms. This is not a surprising fact [17, 34] because common workloads used for algorithm evaluation usually represent several months of execution. At the same time, the average processing time of a job is much lower. In such case, the resulting makespan — which is used to calculate the maximal possible usage — is not controllable by the scheduler since it can never be smaller than the arrival time of the last job plus its processing time. Then, the utilization is rather a function of users activity than of scheduler's performance [17]. Moreover, as the infrastructure is becoming more and more heterogeneous, CPUs may not be the most restricting resource [20]. GPUs, RAM, etc., are also very important, therefore it is questionable whether CPU utilization is still a relevant measure.

To conclude, when the overall system performance is to be measured, it is important to choose a proper metric which is of course a highly individual — site-specific — problem. For example, the problems related to the "pure" machine usage criterion can be solved by considering (A) machine weights, (B) other users demands including, e.g., the RAM consumption and (C) adjusting the computation with respect to actual users demands. In case of (B), the good candidate is the so called *Processor Equivalent (PE)* metric [24], which allows to combine CPU and, e.g., RAM consumptions, translating job's multi-resource consumption requests into a scalar value. PE is based on the application of a *max* function that determines the most constraining resource for each job and translates it into the equivalent processor count. In case of (C), the problem related to users activity can be minimized by considering modified utilization metric proposed in [51]. Unlike the original machine utilization metric which uses the total number of CPUs in the system when computing the usage, the modified metric divide the amount of used CPUs by a value which is *the minimum* of the total number of CPUs in the system and number of CPUs requested by jobs present in the system at that time. Therefore, the modified metric is tolerant to situations when there are no or only a few jobs in the system.

5.2. Job Aware Metrics

Typical and widely used metrics are those that consider overall job performance. Among them, the most popular are the *average response time*, the *average wait time* or the *average slowdown*.

The average response time measures the mean time from job submission to its termination. The average wait time is the mean time that jobs spend waiting before their execution starts. The slowdown is the ratio of an actual response time of a job to a response time if executed without any waiting. While the response time only focuses on a time when a job terminates, the slowdown measures the responsiveness of the system with respect to a job length, i.e., jobs are completed within the time proportional to jobs demands [13]. The wait time supplies the slowdown and the response time. Short wait time prevents the users from feeling that the scheduler has "ignored" their jobs.

Although widely used, these job-related metrics are based on several assumptions that no longer hold in heterogeneous, multi-user, HPC and Grid-like environments, as we explain in the following text.

5.2.1. Problems with Job Priority

One of the main assumptions of standard job-related metrics is that a shorter job should receive higher priority in the system (see, e.g., the slowdown or the response time). Shorter jobs are easier to schedule and users with more complex (longer) requests are therefore to expect longer wait times.

This assumption is problematic on several levels. Firstly, as long as we are measuring the total job penalty or the average value (e.g., total/average slowdown/response time) this "shortest job first" priority advantage will remain absolute. This can very easily lead to huge starvation of (few) long jobs. Production systems usually employ a certain type of anti-starvation technique (see Section 3.2.3). Since this approach goes directly against the order suggested by the job-related metric, it naturally leads to skewed results [58]. HPC and Grid systems are indeed dynamic systems and the number of jobs submitted by a single user is, to a certain degree, proportional to the number of jobs successfully processed. Given the total job length dispersion (from several minutes to a month) [9, 39], users with extremely long jobs would hardly ever get their requests fulfilled.

Secondly, the correlation between the absolute job length and the job urgency is little to none. Again, due to the large dispersion of job lengths, the notion of a "short job" has very different meaning to different users. The increased benevolence towards wait times for long jobs is simply due to the increased absolute users runtime estimation error (10% imprecision on a month long job equates to 3 days) [58].

5.2.2. Problems with Resource Requirements

Similar issues occur when dealing with different job resource requirements. If one can split a large CPU demanding job into a set of smaller jobs, these will obtain a higher priority. This problem was previously addressed by normalizing the selected metric using the number of CPU cores a job is requesting [10, 25], as a weight.

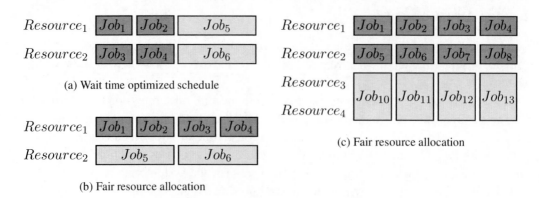

(a) Wait time optimized schedule

(b) Fair resource allocation

(c) Fair resource allocation

Figure 5. Examples of optimal schedules.

Unfortunately, nearly no metric is designed to reflect combined consumption of multiple resources [31] such as CPUs, RAM, GPUs, HDD, etc. When multiple resources are concerned, further measures need to be employed, like dominant resource [20] or processor equivalent [24] to properly reflect other than CPU-related job requirements.

5.2.3. Why Users Matter

We now demonstrate that job aware metrics are often impractical in real systems. Let us consider an example of a schedule optimized according to the average wait time (see Figure 5a). In this schedule we have two users (light-grey and dark-grey) and the optimization criterion favors the jobs of the dark-grey user due to their shorter length[5]. The total penalty for this schedule according to the average wait time would be $\frac{0+0+1+1+2+2}{6} = 1$. Unfortunately, the light-grey user will clearly not consider this schedule optimal. He or she is requesting the same amount of resources as the dark-grey user, but has to wait until all jobs of the dark-grey user are processed.

Let us consider a different schedule, this time using fair resource allocation among the dark-grey and the light-grey user (see Figure 5b). In this case both users receive one resource exclusively for their jobs and both users receive the complete results of their jobs at the same time. The total penalty for this schedule according to the average wait time would be $\frac{0+1+2+3+0+2}{6} = \frac{4}{3}$, which is more than in the previous example. Indeed, we would get similar results for both the response time and the slowdown.

An analogous unfair allocation occurs when we simulate a different situation where, instead of job runtimes, overall resource requirements are considered (see Figure 5c). Again the presented fair resource allocation among the dark-grey and the light-grey user is not considered optimal according to standard job aware metrics.

5.3. User Aware Metrics

User aware metrics aim at maximizing "benefits" regarding the users of the system. Very often, the metric applied for such a goal is related to fairness. In production environments, some type of fairness guaranteeing process/metric is usually provided (see Section 3.1.1).

---

[5] $Resource_1$ and $Resource_2$ represent resources, e.g., CPU cores.

These measures are highly dependent on the system itself and range from simple measures that try to maintain the order in which the requests entered the system [46] to much more complicated measures concerned with the combined consumption of various resources [20].

5.3.1.   Job-to-job Fairness

Fairness is often understood and represented as a *job-related* metric, meaning that every job should be treated in a fair fashion with respect to other jobs [46, 35, 49]. For example, a *fair start time* (*FST*) metric [46, 35] measures the influence of later arriving jobs on the execution start time of the current waiting jobs. *FST* is calculated for each job, by creating a schedule assuming no later jobs arrive. The resulting "unfairness" is the difference between *FST* and the actual start time. Similar metric is so called *fair slowdown* [49]. The fair slowdown is computed using *FST* and can be used to quantify the fairness of a scheduler by looking at the percentage of jobs that have a higher slowdown than is their fair slowdown [49]. Sadly, these job-to-job metrics do not guarantee fair behavior with respect to different users.

5.3.2.   User-to-user Fairness

Instead of job-to-job fairness, the resource management systems frequently prefer to guarantee fair performance to *different users*. One of the commonly employed techniques is *fairshare*, which we have closely described in Section 3.1.1. Fairshare-based fairness is supported in many production resource management systems such as in Moab, Maui [1], TORQUE [3], Quincy [23], PBS Pro [41] or in Hadoop Fair and Capacity Schedulers [5, 4].

While the methods applied in production fairshare algorithms are well documented [24], there is — surprisingly — no common agreement on how to actually measure, i.e., evaluate, analyze or even compare, the level of (un)fairness for such user-to-user approaches. Authors that need to employ such methods usually rely on measuring the variability (using, e.g., the standard deviation) of user-agnostic metrics [56, 29] such as slowdown or wait time.

For example, the so called *normalized user wait time* can be used [29], where a normalized user wait time is the total user wait time divided (normalized) by the total utilized CPU time of that user (a sum of products of the job runtime and the number of requested processors). Such a normalization is used in order to prioritize less active users over those who utilize the system resources very frequently [26], while considering their wait times as well. Next, the normalized user wait time is measured for each user of the system and, e.g., the arithmetic mean and the standard deviation are computed. In this case, the interpretation is as follows. The closer the resulting values of all users are to each other (lower deviation), the higher the fairness. Moreover, the lower the average value is, the more time users spent computing instead of waiting, which is advantageous.

5.4.   Summary

To conclude this section, we would like to stress that scheduling in HPC or Grid environments is typically a multi-objective optimization problem. Therefore, several criteria are to be followed simultaneously. For a researcher, it is very desirable if he or she can find out those critical criteria that are meaningful for the actual system that is analyzed or modeled.

It is not an easy task, as very often even the owners or the users of those systems do not have a clear idea of what they want. However, the closer a researcher's model follows the actual needs of system users and administrators, the higher is the chance that his or her research will be useful.

6.   Interpretation of Experimental Results

This section discusses how the results of experiments should be interpreted in order to provide realistic, detailed and non skewed outcomes. As we explained in the previous text, it is quite challenging to properly analyze or simulate a complex resource management system. There are several problems to be addressed, including the appropriate level of detail a simulation or an analysis should capture. Also, it is crucial and nontrivial to choose a proper set of optimization criteria. Once these problems are solved and the analysis or a simulation is completed, a researcher has to interpret the results. Sadly, even this process can be quite tricky, and — if underestimated by a researcher — can make the whole outcome worthless. Therefore, we now present some basic rules that should be followed in order to avoid this situation.

6.1.   Problems with Simple Statistical Measures

The most common problem when presenting the results of an experiment is the use of either too simple or inappropriate statistical measures [17]. Typically, researchers collect a per-job or per-user data and then compute, e.g., the arithmetic mean, which is then presented in their paper. Sadly, such results shall not be taken seriously unless closer analysis is performed. The problem with average values is that the distribution of the original data typically has a very long tail [17, 33]. Then, the resulting value is likely to be heavily influenced by those (few) extremes. Many further details and other examples covering these issues can be found in the following literature [17, 33, 47].

From this point of view, it is fair to look at the original data in greater detail. For example, it is fair to show a cumulative distribution function (CDF) of recorded values for each tested setup or scheduling algorithm. In order to demonstrate how misleading those simple statistical measures can be, let us demonstrate an example where the average job wait time is of interest[6]. We consider a scenario when a system administrator wants to select a scheduling algorithm for an existing system. For this purpose, he or she takes a historic workload[7] and uses it as an input for the simulator. Four different algorithms are tested, EASY and Conservative backfilling and their "fair" variants where jobs in a queue are dynamically reordered according to fairshare-based priorities. At first, the results of the experiment are presented using simple *average job wait time* as shown in Figure 6 (left). Second, the results are plotted as CDFs. Here, CDF is an $f(x)$-like function showing a fraction of jobs (y-axis) that have their job wait times less than or equal to x. The steeper the resulting curve, the sooner it reaches the maximum ($y = 1.0$) and the better is the performance of a given algorithm. As the resulting distributions have very long tails, the x-axis is not linear. The resulting CDFs are shown in Figure 6 (right).

---

[6]Of course, other measures, e.g., those presented in Section 5.2 can be used for this purpose.

[7]In this case the CTC SP2 workload log from the Parallel Workloads Archive [12].

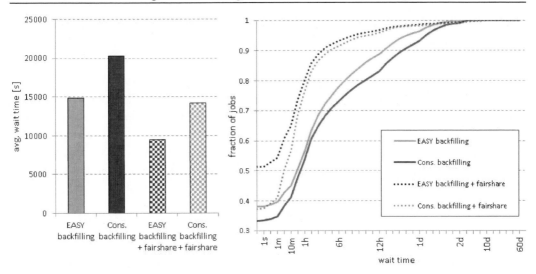

Figure 6. The benefits of using CDFs (right) instead of average values (left).

As we now show, the analysis based on average values (see Figure 6 (left)) is naive and leads to misleading conclusions. For example, it appears that there is a little difference between EASY backfilling without fairshare-based priorities and Conservative backfilling with fairshare-based priorities as their average wait times are very close (see the first and the last column in Figure 6 (left)). However, when we take a look at the corresponding CDFs in Figure 6 (right) we quickly realize, that for most of the jobs, EASY backfilling without fairshare-based priorities performs much worse, compared to Conservative backfilling with fairshare-based priorities. On the other hand, EASY backfilling has a shorter tail without those few huge extremes that are visible in case of Conservative backfilling with fairshare-based priorities. Clearly, simple statistical measures like the arithmetic mean are dangerous when the underlying distributions are far from being "normal".

6.2. Performance Heatmaps

In real systems, it is crucial to really understand "what is going on" before a new setup of the scheduling system is brought into operational status. In such a situation, even those cumulative distribution functions presented in the previous section may not be sufficient. Then, a highly detailed analysis tool can be very useful. A simple but powerful way to obtain such desired insight is to use the so called *performance heatmaps* [33, 58].

Let us once again consider the example from Section 6.1. So far, our analysis showed that for that particular workload, EASY backfilling with fairshare-based priorities is the best algorithm from those four considered when the wait time is used as a criterion. However, in real life we usually have to consider several criteria simultaneously, as discussed in Section 5. For example, we have to check that the solution is fair with respect to users. The problem is that neither the average value nor the CDF from Figure 6 allow us to verify that "fair" EASY backfilling is really a more fair solution than classical EASY backfilling. For such purpose we can use some simple metric measuring fairness (see Section 5.3), but the results may be misleading for similar reasons (the underlying distribution is not normal).

Instead, we will use heatmap as shown in Figure 7.

In this heatmap, we use the x-axis for time (1 unit represents two days) and the y-axis for users of the system. A color at the given coordinates then corresponds to the average wait time (minutes) of user's jobs that arrived during that point in time (see the legend on the right side of each heatmap). The heatmaps clearly show how the more fair variant decreases job wait times for most of the users. Clearly, many dark spots indicating huge wait times for particular users that are visible for classical EASY backfilling are eliminated as soon as fairshare-based priorities are applied. Still, two users (marked with ids 38 and 53 in the workload) have high average wait times in both configurations. A closer look at those two users quickly reveals that they are very active users with a lot of job submissions and high system utilization. Therefore, it is quite natural that they both have to wait longer compared to other users.

6.3. Summary

In this section we mentioned some problems that should be prevented when evaluating the results of an analysis or an experiment. The fact is that even a perfect experiment can be useless if its results are interpreted in a wrong way. The good news is that there is a lot of works that specifically address these issues [17, 33, 47, 58]. Although a good, deep analysis

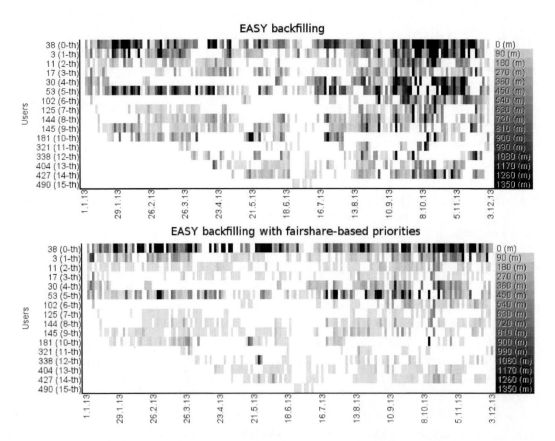

Figure 7. Heatmaps showing the average wait time wrt. users and time for classical EASY backfilling (top) and "fair" EASY backfilling with fairshare-based priorities (bottom).

is a challenging task, it is absolutely necessary when the tested scenario is a candidate for practical application in a production system.

Conclusion

We have shown that efficient job scheduling is a very complex problem when realistic scenarios are considered. In contrast to the popular belief that the whole problem can be solved by evaluating a scheduling algorithm using a simple system model, we have provided a detailed insight into the complexity of the problem, using several real-life based examples. We have stressed how several particular components of the system interact together and influence the resulting performance of the system. Using our experiences from a real system, we have mentioned several parts of the problem that must be carefully modeled and evaluated in order to obtain realistic and useful results. We hope that this chapter may help other researchers as well as practitioners to properly model, evaluate and/or develop functional scheduling solutions for real systems.

Acknowledgments

The gracious support and access to computing and storage facilities owned by parties and projects contributing to the National Grid Infrastructure MetaCentrum, provided under the programme "Projects of Large Infrastructure for Research, Development, and Innovations" (LM2010005), are greatly appreciated.

References

[1] Adaptive Computing Enterprises, Inc. *Maui Scheduler Administrator's Guide, version 3.2*, January 2014. http://docs.adaptivecomputing.com.

[2] Adaptive Computing Enterprises, Inc. *Moab workload manager administrator's guide, version 7.2.6*, January 2014. http://docs.adaptivecomputing.com.

[3] Adaptive Computing Enterprises, Inc. *TORQUE Admininstrator Guide, version 4.2.6*, January 2014. http://docs.adaptivecomputing.com.

[4] Apache.org. *Hadoop Capacity Scheduler*, January 2014. http://hadoop.apache.org/docs/r1.2.1/capacity_scheduler.html.

[5] Apache.org. *Hadoop Fair Scheduler*, January 2014. http://hadoop.apache.org/docs/r1.2.1/fair_scheduler.html.

[6] C. Belady, A. Rawson, J. Pfleuger, and T. Cader. Green grid data center power efficiency metrics: PUE and DCIE. Technical Report 6, The Green Grid, 2008.

[7] A. Bucur and D. Epema. Local versus global schedulers with processor co-allocation in multicluster systems. In D. G. Feitelson, L. Rudolph, and U. Schwiegelshohn, editors, *Job Scheduling Strategies for Parallel Processing*, volume 2537 of *LNCS*, pages 184–204. Springer Verlag, 2002.

[8] D. G. Carmichael. *Project Planning, and Control.* Taylor & Francis, 2006.

[9] W. Cirne and F. Berman. A comprehensive model of the supercomputer workload. In *2001 IEEE International Workshop on Workload Characterization (WWC 2001)*, pages 140–148. IEEE Computer Society, 2001.

[10] C. Ernemann, V. Hamscher, and R. Yahyapour. Benefits of global Grid computing for job scheduling. In *GRID '04: Proceedings of the 5th IEEE/ACM International Workshop on Grid Computing*, pages 374–379. IEEE, 2004.

[11] D. G. Feitelson. Experimental analysis of the root causes of performance evaluation results: A backfilling case study. *IEEE Transactions on Parallel and Distributed Systems*, 16(2):175–182, 2005.

[12] D. G. Feitelson. Parallel workloads archive, July 2014. http://www.cs.huji.ac.il/labs/parallel/workload/.

[13] D. G. Feitelson, L. Rudolph, U. Schwiegelshohn, K. C. Sevcik, and P. Wong. Theory and practice in parallel job scheduling. In D. G. Feitelson and L. Rudolph, editors, *Job Scheduling Strategies for Parallel Processing*, volume 1291 of *LNCS*, pages 1–34. Springer Verlag, 1997.

[14] D. G. Feitelson and A. M. Weil. Utilization and predictability in scheduling the IBM SP2 with backfilling. In *12th International Parallel Processing Symposium*, pages 542–546. IEEE, 1998.

[15] L. Flis, P. Lason, M. Magrys, A. Ozieblo, and M. Twardy. Effective utilization of mixed computing resources on zeus cluster. In *Cracow Grid Workshop*, pages 105–106. ACC Cyfronet AGH, 2012.

[16] I. Foster and C. Kesselman. *The Grid 2: Blueprint for a New Computing Infrastructure, second edition.* Morgan Kaufmann, 2004.

[17] E. Frachtenberg and D. G. Feitelson. Pitfalls in parallel job scheduling evaluation. In D. G. Feitelson, E. Frachtenberg, L. Rudolph, and U. Schwiegelshohn, editors, *Job Scheduling Strategies for Parallel Processing*, volume 3834 of *LNCS*, pages 257–282. Springer Verlag, 2005.

[18] M. R. Garey and D. S. Johnson. *Computers and Intractability; A Guide to the Theory of NP-Completeness.* W. H. Freeman & Co., New York, NY, USA, 1990.

[19] W. Gentzsch. Sun Grid Engine: towards creating a compute power Grid. In *Proceedings of the First IEEE/ACM International Symposium on Cluster Computing and the Grid*, pages 35–36, 2001.

[20] A. Ghodsi, M. Zaharia, B. Hindman, A. Konwinski, S. Shenker, and I. Stoica. Dominant resource fairness: fair allocation of multiple resource types. In *8th USENIX Symposium on Networked Systems Design and Implementation*, 2011.

[21] R. L. Graham, E. L. Lawler, J. K. Lenstra, and A. R. Kan. Optimization and approximation in deterministic sequencing and scheduling: A survey. *Annals of Discrete Mathematics*, 5:287–326, 1979.

[22] E. Huedo, R. Montero, and I. Llorente. The GridWay framework for adaptive scheduling and execution on Grids. *Scalable Computing: Practice and Experience*, 6(3):1–8, 2005.

[23] M. Isard, V. Prabhakaran, J. Currey, U. Wieder, K. Talwar, and A. Goldberg. Quincy: Fair scheduling for distributed computing clusters. In *ACM SIGOPS 22nd Symposium on Operating Systems Principles*, pages 261–276, 2009.

[24] D. Jackson, Q. Snell, and M. Clement. Core algorithms of the Maui scheduler. In D. G. Feitelson and L. Rudolph, editors, *Job Scheduling Strategies for Parallel Processing*, volume 2221 of *LNCS*, pages 87–102. Springer, 2001.

[25] H. D. Karatza. Performance of gang scheduling strategies in a parallel system. *Simulation Modelling Practice and Theory*, 17(2):430 – 441, 2009.

[26] S. D. Kleban and S. H. Clearwater. Fair share on high performance computing systems: What does fair really mean? In *Third IEEE International Symposium on Cluster Computing and the Grid*, pages 146 – 153. IEEE Computer Society, 2003.

[27] D. Klusáček and H. Rudová. The importance of complete data sets for job scheduling simulations. In E. Frachtenberg and U. Schwiegelshohn, editors, *Job Scheduling Strategies for Parallel Processing*, volume 6253 of *LNCS*, pages 132–153. Springer Verlag, 2010.

[28] D. Klusáček and H. Rudová. Efficient Grid scheduling through the incremental schedule-based approach. *Computational Intelligence*, 27(1):4–22, 2011.

[29] D. Klusáček and H. Rudová. Performance and fairness for users in parallel job scheduling. In W. Cirne, editor, *Job Scheduling Strategies for Parallel Processing*, volume 7698 of *LNCS*, pages 235–252. Springer, 2012.

[30] D. Klusáček and H. Rudová. Multi-resource aware fairsharing for heterogeneous systems. In *Job Scheduling Strategies for Parallel Processing*, LNCS. Springer, 2015. To appear.

[31] D. Klusáček, H. Rudová, and M. Jaroš. Multi resource fairness: Problems and challenges. In N. Desai and W. Cirne, editors, *Job Scheduling Strategies for Parallel Processing*, volume 8429 of *LNCS*, pages 81–95. Springer, 2014.

[32] D. Klusáček and Š. Tóth. On interactions among scheduling policies: Finding efficient queue setup using high-resolution simulations. In F. Silva, I. Dutra, and V. S. Costa, editors, *Euro-Par 2014*, volume 8632 of *LNCS*, pages 138–149. Springer, 2014.

[33] D. Krakov and D. G. Feitelson. Comparing performance heatmaps. In N. Desai and W. Cirne, editors, *Job Scheduling Strategies for Parallel Processing*, volume 8429 of *LNCS*, pages 42–61. Springer, 2014.

[34] C. B. Lee. *On the User-Scheduler Relationship in High-Performance Computing*. PhD thesis, University of California, San Diego, 2009.

[35] V. J. Leung, G. Sabin, and P. Sadayappan. Parallel job scheduling policies to improve fairness: a case study. Technical Report SAND2008-1310, Sandia National Laboratories, 2008.

[36] B. Li and D. Zhao. Performance impact of advance reservations from the Grid on backfill algorithms. In *Sixth International Conference on Grid and Cooperative Computing (GCC 2007)*, pages 456–461, 2007.

[37] D. A. Lifka. The ANL/IBM SP Scheduling System. In D. G. Feitelson and L. Rudolph, editors, *Job Scheduling Strategies for Parallel Processing*, volume 949 of *LNCS*, pages 295–303. Springer-Verlag, 1995.

[38] MetaCentrum, July 2014. http://www.metacentrum.cz/.

[39] A. W. Mu'alem and D. G. Feitelson. Utilization, predictability, workloads, and user runtime estimates in scheduling the IBM SP2 with backfilling. *IEEE Transactions on Parallel and Distributed Systems*, 12(6):529–543, 2001.

[40] Ohio Supercomputer Center. *Batch Processing at OSC*, February 2014. https://www.osc.edu/supercomputing/batch-processing-at-osc.

[41] PBS Works. *PBS Professional 12.1, Administrator's Guide*, January 2014. http://www.pbsworks.com.

[42] Platform Computing Corporation, Canada. *Administering Platform LSF*, 6.2 edition, 2006.

[43] C. R. Reeves. Moder heuristic techniques. In V. J. Rayward-Smith, I. H. Osman, C. R. Reeves, and G. D. Smith, editors, *Modern Heuristic Search Methods*, chapter 1, pages 1–25. Wiley, 1996.

[44] G. Ritchie and J. Levine. A hybrid ant algorithm for scheduling independent jobs in heterogeneous computing environments. In *PlanSIG2004: Proceedings of the 23rd annual workshop of the UK Planning and Scheduling Special Interest Group*, 2004.

[45] M. Romberg. UNICORE: Beyond web-based job-submission. In *Proceedings of the 42nd Cray User Group Conference*, pages 22–26, 2000.

[46] G. Sabin, G. Kochhar, and P. Sadayappan. Job fairness in non-preemptive job scheduling. In *International Conference on Parallel Processing (ICPP'04)*, pages 186–194. IEEE Computer Society, 2004.

[47] U. Schwiegelshohn. How to design a job scheduling algorithm. In *Job Scheduling Strategies for Parallel Processing*, LNCS. Springer, 2015. To appear.

[48] J. Skovira, W. Chan, H. Zhou, and D. Lifka. The EASY – LoadLeveler API project. In D. G. Feitelson and L. Rudolph, editors, *Job Scheduling Strategies for Parallel Processing*, volume 1162 of *LNCS*, pages 41–47. Springer, 1996.

[49] S. Srinivasan, R. Kettimuthu, V. Subramani, and P. Sadayappan. Selective reservation strategies for backfill job scheduling. In D. G. Feitelson, L. Rudolph, and U. Schwiegelshohn, editors, *Job Scheduling Strategies for Parallel Processing*, volume 2537 of *LNCS*, pages 55–71. Springer Verlag, 2002.

[50] D. Talby and D. G. Feitelson. Supporting priorities and improving utilization of the IBM SP scheduler using slack-based backfilling. In *IPPS '99/SPDP '99: Proceedings of the 13th International Symposium on Parallel Processing and the 10th Symposium on Parallel and Distributed Processing*, pages 513–517. IEEE Computer Society, 1999.

[51] A. D. Techiouba, G. Capannini, R. Baraglia, D. Puppin, and M. Pasquali. Backfilling strategies for scheduling streams of jobs on computational farms. In *Making Grids Work*, pages 103–115. Springer, USA, 2008.

[52] D. Thain, T. Tannenbaum, and M. Livny. Condor and the Grid. In F. Berman, G. Fox, and T. Hey, editors, *Grid Computing: Making the Global Infrastructure a Reality*. Wiley, 2002.

[53] V. T'kindt and J.-C. Billaut. *Multicriteria Scheduling, Theory, Models and Algorithms*. Springer, second edition, 2006.

[54] N. Tonellotto, P. Wieder, and R. Yahyapour. A proposal for a generic Grid scheduling architecture. In S. Gorlatch and M. Danelutto, editors, *Proceedings of the Integrated Research in Grid Computing Workshop*, pages 337–346. University di Pisa, 2005.

[55] D. Tsafrir, Y. Etsion, and D. G. Feitelson. Modeling user runtime estimates. In D. G. Feitelson, E. Frachtenberg, L. Rudolph, and U. Schwiegelshohn, editors, *Job Scheduling Strategies for Parallel Processing*, volume 3834 of *LNCS*, pages 1–35. Springer, 2005.

[56] S. Vasupongayya and S.-H. Chiang. On job fairness in non-preemptive parallel job scheduling. In S. Q. Zheng, editor, *International Conference on Parallel and Distributed Computing Systems (PDCS 2005)*, pages 100–105. IASTED/ACTA Press, 2005.

[57] Vrije Universiteit Amsterdam. *DAS-4 Job Execution*, June 2014. http://www.cs.vu.nl/das4/jobs.shtml.

[58] Šimon Tóth and D. Klusáček. User-aware metrics for measuring quality of parallel job schedules. In *Job Scheduling Strategies for Parallel Processing*, 2014.

[59] A. Wierman and M. Harchol-Balter. Classifying scheduling policies with respect to unfairness in an M/GI/1. In *2003 ACM SIGMETRICS International Conference on Measurement and Modeling of Computer Systems*, pages 238–249. ACM, 2003.

[60] F. Xhafa and A. Abraham. Computational models and heuristic methods for Grid scheduling problems. *Future Generation Computer Systems*, 26(4):608–621, 2010.

[61] F. Xhafa, J. Carretero, E. Alba, and B. Dorronsoro. Design and evaluation of Tabu search method for job scheduling in distributed environments. In *International Symposium on Parallel and Distributed Processing (IPDPS 2008)*, pages 1–8. IEEE, 2008.

[62] J. XU, A. Y. Lam, and V. O. Li. Chemical reaction optimization for the Grid scheduling problem. In *2010 IEEE International Conference on Communications*, pages 1–5. IEEE, 2010.

In: Grid Computing: Techniques and Future Prospects ISBN: 978-1-63117-704-0
Editors: J. G. Barbosa and I. Dutra, pp. 99-128 © 2015 Nova Science Publishers, Inc.

Chapter 4

SCALABILITY ANALYSIS OF BoT APPLICATIONS ON LARGE DISTRIBUTED COMPUTING SYSTEMS

Fabricio A. B. Silva[1,*] *and Hermes Senger*[2,†]
[1]Oswaldo Cruz Foundation - FIOCRUZ
Scientific Computing Department, Rio de Janeiro - RJ, Brazil
[2]Federal University of São Carlos - UFSCar
Computer Science Department, São Carlos - SP, Brazil

PACS: 05.45-a, 52.35.Mw, 96.50.Fm

Keywords: Multiprocessor systems, scalability analysis, bag-of tasks

1. Introduction

In this chapter, we study the scalability of Bag-of-tasks (BoT) applications executing on master-slave and hierarchical platforms. We also consider several contention scenarios involving input and output data transfers. BoT applications are composed of sequential and independent tasks which present no communication or dependencies (as observed in embarrassingly parallel applications). The input for each task is composed of one or more files, and one file can be input for more than one task. Each task generates a set composed of one or more output files. Examples of BoT applications include Monte Carlo simulations, massive searches (such as for breaking cryptographic keys), image manipulation applications and data mining applications. They are frequent in areas such as bioinformatics, astronomy, high-energy physics, and others. Note that BoT applications are often referred in the literature as Parameter-Sweep applications [1] [a]. For instance, a significant fraction of jobs in the workloads observed in real distributed systems is submitted in the form of BoT applications in LHC Computing Grid (LCG), NorduGrid, TeraGrid, and Open Science Grid [35].

---

*E-mail address: fabs@fiocruz.br

†E-mail address: hermes@dc.ufscar.br.

Hermes Senger would like to thank CNPQ (Process:305879/2012-0) and FAPESP for their support.

[a]In this chapter we use the terms "Bag-of-Tasks" and "Parameter-Sweep" interchangeably.

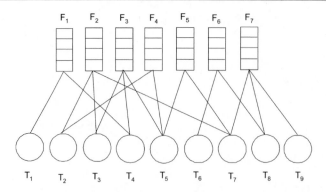

Figure 1. A BoT application composed of 9 tasks and 7 input files.

For the sake of illustration, a BoT application can be represented as a bipartite graph in which one set of nodes represent input files, the other set represents tasks, and links represent dependencies among tasks and files [3] (e.g. see Figure 1). In this chapter we consider that both the size of the input files and the dependencies among input files and tasks are known in advance.

Because of task independence and the absence of communication among tasks, BoT are ideal applications to execute on loosely coupled platforms such as computational clusters and grids, and master-slave and hierarchical topologies have been widely employed to execute BoT applications in such distributed platforms [11, 12]. In master-slave platforms, there is one master node which is responsible for scheduling computations among a set of working nodes, dubbed slave nodes. Usually, the master node is also responsible for transmitting input files to the nodes where tasks will be executed, as well as for collecting the resulting data [11, 12]. Whenever it is possible, the whole scheme can overlap computation and communication, i.e., both the master and slave nodes can perform computation at the same time that input files are transmitted to slave nodes and output files are sent back to the master.

The master-slave paradigm has well known limitations. Either the communications between the master and slave nodes or the contention due to the access to a centralized file repository may become performance bottlenecks and severely limit the scalability. In this chapter we pay special attention to the impact of contention in the completion phase on scalability.

Hierarchical platforms are multiple-node machines where the nodes are organized as a multiple level tree (e.g., as illustrated in Figure 2). In hierarchical platforms, a root node (supervisor) is responsible for scheduling computation tasks among the several master nodes and collecting the results. The masters are non-leaf nodes which receive workloads from upper level nodes (e.g., from the root node) and schedule computations among the lower level nodes in the hierarchy. The leaf nodes in the hierarchy are defined as slaves and they only perform computations. We also consider that all input files are initially stored in the root node of the hierarchical platform, which serves as the repository of all input and output files. Each input file required by a task has to be transferred from the root node to the processing node on which the task is scheduled, but only if the file does not exist in that node.

Non-root nodes have a local disk where temporary files can be stored. Examples of real implementations of hierarchical platforms include high performance computing platforms such as clusters, multi-clusters and grids.

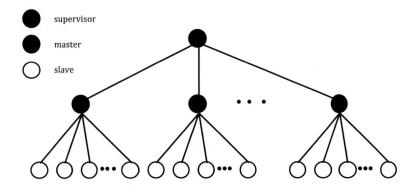

Figure 2. Example of a hierarchical platform.

Contention in the completion phase may happen when individual tasks send the results of its computation back to the master or supervisor node. Depending on the characteristics of the platform, the impact of this type of contention on scalability may be significant. Contention may be caused, for instance, by disk write serialization of large output files in a Master node or concurrent access to a common input port. Contention in the completion phase increases the total makespan of a job and reduces parallel execution efficiency. In this chapter, we assess the impact of contention in the completion phase on scalability for several different scenarios.

In a previous paper, we studied the performance and scalability of real data mining applications executing as BoT application on a cluster of PCs [4]. Further, we demonstrated that the execution of BoT applications whose tasks share files can be remarkably more scalable on hierarchical platforms than in a pure master-slave platform [5]. In [6], we proved the scalability lower bound on the isoefficiency function for BoT applications executing on master-slave platforms. For the sake of simplicity, we prove such lower bounds while assuming that the underlying communication paradigm is the one-port model. In this model, at any given time there are at most two communications involving a given server, one sent and the other received. As pointed out by [2], the one port model is nicely suited to LAN network connections. In the same paper, we also showed how scalability of real applications can be improved by means of task grouping, by proposing the *Dynamic Clustering* Algorithm. In [36] we demonstrate the scalability limits for a set of multi-level hierarchical platforms that extend the pure master-slave paradigm. In a subsequent paper, we have stated the lower bounds on the isoefficiency function for a master-slave platforms under several communication paradigms other than the one-port communication model, e.g., when data transfer is carried out over TCP links [38]. In this chapter, we review, summarize and discuss several results presented in the papers mentioned in this paragraph.

The remainder of this chapter is organized as follows: section 2 presents the related work. In section 3 some useful definitions are stated, among them the definitions of scalability and isoefficiency function. In section 4 we define the concept of *Input File Affinity* and state several lower bounds on the isoefficiency function for master-slave platforms. Section 5 includes several theorems related to scalability lower bounds for hierarchical platforms. In this section the problem of contention in the completion phase on hierarchical platforms is also discussed. Section 6 presents several simulation results, while section 7 presents an overall discussion about the theoretical and experimental results of this chapter and section 8 contains our final remarks.

2. Related Work

The class of BoT applications composed of independent tasks with file sharing has been studied in several papers in the literature such as in [1, 3, 6, 10–18]. Because of their relevance, specialized tools which aim to facilitate the execution of large BoT applications on computational grids and clusters have been proposed, such as the AppLeS Parameter Sweep Template (APST) [11] and MyGrid [12].

Because of its simplicity, the master-slave framework is widely employed to execute BoT applications composed of independent tasks on computational clusters and grids [3, 10]. In this framework, slave processors execute application tasks under the centralized supervision of a master processor. For this reason, the framework has two fundamental limitations: both the communication between master and slaves, and access to file repositories may become bottlenecks to the overall scheduling scheme, causing scalability problems.

Casanova et al. [1] proposed scheduling heuristics which consider file sharing, so that the files required by every scheduled task which have been previously transmitted to the processors do not need to be retransmitted. This improvement allowed for a reduction of the bottleneck in the master processor. Additional examples of scheduling heuristics which aim at reducing the master's bottleneck by means of improving scheduling efficiency and reducing communication can be found in [3].

In [20], Chaintreau presents a scalability analysis applied to distributed systems. The author describes a model where the graph describing task dependencies is organized as Euclidean lattice. The main assumption of this work is that the precedence relation between these tasks is invariant by translation, so that the evolution of the system follows Uniform Recurrence Equations. The author proves that, under these special circumstances and by definition of a criterion called "sharpness", the system is scalable.

In [39], Yero and Henriques present a scalability analysis of masterslave heterogeneous clusters. Despite some similarities with this work, all models considered in that paper are different from the ones considered in this chapter. Indeed, the authors initially disregard the effects of communication contention in the execution model. When the authors explicitly consider contention, they conclude that the system is not scalable when contention is proportional to the number of processors. In this chapter we demonstrate that the execution of BoT applications on master-slave and hierarchical platforms may be scalable, even when contention is proportional to the number of processors, in several scenarios.

In a previous paper we have studied the scalability of BoT applications executing on master-slave platforms [6]. In that paper we proposed a scheduling algorithm which is oblivious to task execution times dubbed Dynamic Clustering (DC). We have shown that the scalability performance of the DC algorithm is similar to the scalability obtainable by non-oblivious algorithms in several circumstances. In the same paper, we assessed the scalability of BoT applications executing on master-slave platforms that adopt the one-port communication model, and proved that the lower bound on the isoefficiency function is $\Omega(P^2)$. In [36] we have demonstrated the scalability limits for a set of multi-level hierarchical platforms that extend the pure master-slave platforms, for several communication paradigms. We also presented a brief analysis of the scalability of heterogeneous hierarchical platforms. In this paper we proved that hierarchical platforms can be more scalable than master-slave platforms. An example of a recent work that has confirmed this conclusion specifically for cloud platforms is [39]. In another paper [38] we further elaborate on the scalability study of BoT applications on master-slave platforms whose communication follows the multiplexed and broadcast models. We also evaluate the impact of output file contention on the scalability of the pair master slave platform/BoT application under the one-port model.

3. Background and Preliminary

Scalability may be defined as "the system ability to increase speedup as the number of processors increase" [21]. Another definition that is not based in the concept of speedup is the following: "An algorithm-machine combination is scalable if the achieved average speed of the algorithm on the given machine can remain constant with the increasing number of processors, provided that the problem size can be increased with the system size" [22]. This later definition is important because it relates the scalability to the combination of a machine and an algorithm, instead of being a property of either the machine or the algorithm.

Kumar and Rao proposed the concept of isoefficiency function [23] to characterize the scalability of an algorithm on a given architecture. The basic idea is to fix the efficiency to a certain value and to measure by how much the work must be increased to keep the efficiency unchanged as the machine scales up. The amount of work W is defined as the sum of the amount of computation of all tasks composing the application. The isoefficiency function $f(P)$ relates machine size (P) to the amount of work needed to maintain the efficiency, which can be defined as follows.

One limiting factor for the scalability of parallel systems is the overhead. Let T_P be the time spent for a parallel execution to solve the problem on a parallel computer with p processors. Then, the total time collectively spent by all the processing elements is pT_P time units. T_S time units are spent with useful work, and the remainder is overhead. Thus, the total overhead of a parallel system can be expressed by an *overhead function* as follows

$$T_0 = pT_P - T_S \tag{1}$$

where pT_P is the total time spent by p processors to solve the problem, and T_S is the runtime of the fastest known sequential algorithm to solve the problem on a sequential computer. Let the *problem size W* be equal to T_S, then we can define parallel runtime as

$$T_P = \frac{W + T_0(W,p)}{p}, \tag{2}$$

where $T_0(W, p)$ is the system overhead for a workload W executing with p processors.

Scalability may be defined as "the system ability to increase speedup as the number of processors increase" [23]. This notion of scalability can be measured by speedup as:

$$S = \frac{W}{T_P}$$
$$= \frac{pW}{W + T_0(W,p)}. \tag{3}$$

Then, efficiency can be denoted as

$$E = \frac{S}{p}$$
$$= \frac{W}{W + T_0(W,p)} \tag{4}$$
$$= \frac{1}{1 + \frac{T_0(W,p)}{W}}$$

For scalable parallel systems, efficiency can be maintained at some desired level (between 0 and 1) if the ratio $T_0(W,p)/W$ can be maintained at some fixed value as the number p of processors is increased. If W needs to grow only linearly with p, then the system is highly scalable. Thus, for some desired level E of efficiency,

$$E = \frac{1}{1 + \frac{T_0(W,p)}{W}},$$
$$\frac{T_0(W,p)}{W} = \frac{1 - E}{E}, \tag{5}$$
$$W = \frac{E}{1 - E} T_0(W,p).$$

With this idea on mind, Kumar and Rao proposed the isoefficiency concept [48]. The basic idea is to fix the efficiency and measure how much work must be increased to keep the efficiency unchanged as the machine scales up. The expression for the *isoefficiency function* can be defined as

$$f(p) = KT_0(W,p), \tag{6}$$

where $K = \frac{E}{(1-E)}$ is a constant value dependent on the desired efficiency level. Thus, the isoefficiency function f(P) relates machine size p to the amount of work needed to maintain the efficiency. It shows the growth rate of W necessary to maintain the desired efficiency value as p increases. Notice that $f(p)$ does not exist for an unscalable system, since efficiency cannot be maintained at any fixed value as p increases, no matter how fast the problem size W is increased. A small value of $f(p)$ means that a small increment in the amount of work is enough to maintain high efficiency as p increases. On the other hand, a large value of $f(p)$ means that even with large increases on the workload W cannot maintain efficiency as the number of processors increase.

4. Bounds on Scalability of BoT Applications Running on Master-Slave Platforms

We begin this section by describing the models considered in the theoretical scalability analysis presented. We also introduce in this section the *Input File Affinity* Measure.

4.1. Platform Model

We assume a set of $P = \{p_1, \ldots, p_p\}$ processors. One processor is the master and the other processors are slaves. Communication among master and slaves is carried out through a shared link, and the master can only send files through the network to a single slave at a given time. We assume that the communication link is full-duplex, i.e., the master can receive an output file from a slave at the same time it sends an input file to another slave. Note that this communication model corresponds to the one port model: at any given time there are at most two communications involving a given server, one sent and the other received. The main reason for choosing the one port model is its simplicity, that allows us to abstract from a myriad of complex and unnecessary details, while capturing the essential behavior of a master slave platform. Furthermore, as pointed out by Yang et al. [2], the one port model is nicely suited to LAN network connections. Further, in section 6 we present some experimental results that demonstrate that the scalability bounds for more realistic communication model. [b] We also assume that computation on a slave node begins as soon as the input files are completely received. This assumption is coherent to BoT master-slave platforms that are currently available [35].

4.2. Application Model

Typically, a BoT application is composed of independent tasks $\{T\}_{i=t_1..t_t}$. From the standpoint of workload scheduling, we assume that tasks constitute the basic workload unit, i.e., tasks cannot be subdivided, and each task t_i has an associated computational cost denoted by $comp(t_i)$. In practice, $comp(t_i)$ could be a measure of the total number of instructions, or the floating point operations to be executed. We also assume that $comp(t_i)$ may vary for each task t_i, and it is not known in advance. Clearly, in this scenario $comp(t_i)$ is fixed for any given task t_i, since the amount of computation associated to t_i does not change. In other words, we cannot arbitrarily change $comp(t_i)$ it is the case for divisible loads application model [2].

Each task depends on one or more input files for execution. The communication cost of each task, denoted by $comm(t_i)$, is the total amount of input data that must be transmitted to the node before task t_i can be executed. Clearly, since the same file can be input for more than one task, transmission cost for a group of tasks can be amortized when two or more tasks that share files can be grouped together and scheduled to execute in the same processor. For instance, if a task t_j will execute after t_i in the same processor p_k (assume that p_k has a local storage) and these two tasks share one or more files, then $comm(T_j)$ can be amortized because $comm(\{t_i, t_j\}) < comm(t_i) + comm(t_j)$. Thus, the communication cost

---

[b]For the interested reader, more details about the impact of communication models on the scalability of BoT applications on master slave platforms can be found in [38]

of a group of tasks $comm(\{t_i,..,t_j\})$ (and the cost of an entire application) may be affected by scheduling decisions.

4.3. Execution Model

Typically, each BoT application task goes through three phases during its execution:

- An initialization phase (t_{init}), where the necessary files are sent to the slave node and the task is started. Note that this phase includes the overhead incurred by a master to initiate a data transfer to a slave. There is a queue of waiting tasks in the master node.

- A computation phase (t_{comp}), where the task processes the parameter file at the slave node and produces an output file. Any additional overhead related to the reception of input files by a slave node and writing input files to a local file system is also included in this phase.

- A completion phase (t_{end}), where the output file is sent back to the master and the task is completed. This phase may require some processing at upper level nodes, mainly related to writing output files received from lower level nodes to a disk. Since this writing may be deferred until the disk is available [25], under specific conditions it is possible to assume that this processing time is negligible. Therefore, we consider initially that the initialization phase of one slave can occur concurrently with the completion phase of another slave node.

Regarding the duration of the completion phase for a given task, two possibilities are considered: in the first one, time to transfer the output files from one node to the upper level node depends on the number of nodes in the same level, i.e., the number of lower level nodes directly connected to the upper level node. This situation may happen when there is contention related to the transfer of output files from the lower-level nodes to the master.

The second possibility is when there is no contention, i.e., the duration of the completion phase is constant, independently of the number of lower level processors. In this case, typically, there is an underlying distributed file system on which output files are written, such as in [37]. Indeed, for the best case in [37], aggregate write rates are increase linearly the number of clients grows.

We assume, in the following sections, that the communication link is full-duplex, i.e., the master can receive an output file from a slave at the same time it sends an input file to another slave. We also assume that computation on a slave node begins as soon as the input files are completely received.

4.4. The Input File Affinity Measure

In this section we introduce the input file affinity (I_{aff}) measure. In order to do so, first we describe a simplified execution model that clarifies several issues related with the execution of BoT applications on dedicated, homogeneous masterslave platforms. It should be stressed that several assumptions presented in the model described in this section have been simplified for clarification purposes, aiming to introduce the concept of input file affinity in a more concise form. However, it should be noted that the concept of input file affinity is seamlessly applicable to the more general model described in the introduction of the paper.

As detailed in the previous subsection, each task goes through three phases during execution of a parameter-sweep application:

- An initialization phase, with duration equal to t_{init}.

- A completion phase, with duration equal to t_{end}.

- A computation phase on a particular processor, with duration equal to t_{comp}.

Given these three phases, the total execution time of a task is equal to

$$t_{total} = t_{init} + t_{comp} + t_{end} \qquad (7)$$

For the sake of simplicity and without loss of generality, we consider in this section that there is no contention related to the transmission of output files from slave nodes to the master. Indeed, it is possible to merge the computation phase with the completion phase without affecting the results of this section. Therefore, we merge both phases as t'_{comp} in the equations that follow.

A slave node is idle when it is not involved with the execution of any of the three phases of a task. For the equations below, the task model is composed of T homogeneous tasks. All tasks and files have the same size, and each task depends upon a single non-shared file. Note that the problem of scheduling a BoT application where each task depends upon a single nonshared file, all tasks and files have the same size and the masterslave platform is homogeneous, has polynomial complexity [3], with the optimal scheduling algorithm being the simple greedy round-robin algorithm. These simplified assumptions are considered in the analysis that follows, since they provide absolute lower bounds on the isoefficiency function [38].

We define the *effective number of processors* (P_{eff}) as the maximum number of slave processors needed to run an application with no idle periods on any slave processor. Taking into account the task and platform models described in this section, a processor may have idle periods if:

$$t'_{comp} < (P-1)t_{init} \qquad (8)$$

P_{eff} is then given by the following equation:

$$P_{eff} = \lfloor \frac{t'_{comp}}{t_{init}} + 1 \rfloor \qquad (9)$$

The total number of tasks to be executed on a processor is at most

$$M = \lceil \frac{T}{P} \rceil \qquad (10)$$

For a platform with P_{eff} processors, the upper bound for the total execution time (makespan) will be

$$\lceil t_{makespan} \rceil = M(t_{init} + t'_{comp}) + (P-1)t_{init} \qquad (11)$$

The second term in the right side of Eq. 11 shows the time needed to start the first $(P-1)$ tasks in $P-1$ processors. Note that Eq. 11 corresponds to the maximum makespan of all P individual processors. If we have a platform where the number of processors is larger than P_{eff}, the overall makespan is dominated by communication times between the master and the slaves. We then have

$$\lceil t_{makespan} \rceil = MPt_{init} + t'_{comp} \tag{12}$$

It is worth noting that Eq. 11 is valid when slaves are constantly busy, either performing computation or communication. Eq. 12 is applicable when slaves have idle periods, i.e., are not performing either computation or communication. Remember that, as we have idle periods when $P > P_{eff}$ using a round-robin scheduling algorithm, Eq. 8 holds. Eq. 8 occurs mainly in two cases:

- For very large platforms (P large).

- For applications with a small $\frac{t_{comp}}{t_{init}}$ ratio, such as fine-grain applications.

In order to measure the degree of affinity of a set of tasks concerning their input files, we introduce the concept of input file affinity. Given a set G of tasks, composed of K tasks, $G = \{T_1, T_2, ..., T_K\}$, and the set F of the Y input files needed by the tasks belonging to group G, $F = \{f_1, f_2, f_3, ..., f_Y\}$, we define I_{aff} as follows:

$$I_{aff}(G) = \frac{\sum_{i=1}^{Y}(N_i - 1)|f_i|}{\sum_{i=1}^{Y} N_i |f_i|} \tag{13}$$

where $|f_i|$ is the size in bytes of file f_i and $N_i (1 \leq N_i \leq K)$ is the number of tasks in group G which have file f_i as an input file. The term $(N_i - 1)$ in the numerator of the above equation can be explained as follows: if N_i tasks share an input file f_i, that file may be sent only once (instead of N_i times) when the group of tasks is executed on a slave node. The potential reduction of the number of bytes transferred from a master node to a slave node considering only input file f_i is then $(N_i - 1)|f_i|$. Therefore, the input file affinity indicates the overall reduction of the amount of data that needs to be transferred to a slave node, when all tasks of a group are sent to that node. Note that $0 \leq I_{aff} < 1$. For the special case where all tasks share the same input file $I_{aff} = \frac{K-1}{K}$, where K is the number of tasks of a group, and $f_i = F$ for all i, F fixed (see Eq. 13). Note that, in this particular case, $I_{aff} \to 1$ as $K \to \infty$. An input file affinity of zero indicates that there is no sharing of files among tasks of a group.

4.5.   A Lower Bound for the Isoefficiency Function of BoT Applications

The purpose of our study is to assess scalability limits of BoT computations in the best possible case. Such limits can be expressed by the lower bounds on the isoefficiency function under specific circumstances. We assume a BoT application composed of T tasks executing on P homogeneous and dedicated processors that communicate through a homogeneous interconnection network (e.g., similar to computers in a cluster). Then, we propose the definition of Scalable Bag-of-Tasks Applications (SBA).

Definition 1. Scalable Bag-of-Tasks Applications (SBA): *A SBA is composed by T homogeneous tasks that are evenly distributed among P homogeneous processors for execution. Thus, we consider that computational cost cost*(t_i) *is the same for every task* t_i *(1 ≤ i ≤ T). We assume round-robin scheduling, that is optimal and minimizes execution time in such scenario. Since T is significantly larger than P (i.e., T ≫ P), we can assume (without loss of generality) that T is multiple of P, thus each processor executes the same amount of work* $T/P \cdot cost(t_i)$. *In other words, we assume perfect load balancing among the processors.*

Furthermore, we assume that communication costs for the whole application is also minimum. This can be achieved when all tasks share the same input file (or the same set of input files). In this scenario, the set of input files is transmitted only once for a given processor p_i *before the processor can execute any task. However, when the input files are transmitted for* p_i *to execute its first task, all the remaining tasks assigned to the same processor can be executed with no retransmission of the input files. This definition is important since we focus on the highest possible scalability in ideal conditions.*

Given this definition, we can find a lower bound on the isoefficiency function for BoT applications as follows.

Theorem 1. *The lower bound on the isoefficiency for a BoT application running on a homogeneous master-slave platform with P processors is* $\Omega(P^2)$. [c]

Proof. Consider a SBA program running on an homogeneous master-slave platform with P processors. Under such circumstances, the number of tasks T must grow at least $\Theta(P)$, otherwise processors will eventually become idle as P increases. Then, the amount of work assigned to each processor can be executed in time $\Theta(T \cdot comp(t_i)/P)$, which reduces to $\Theta(1)$ because $T = \Theta(p)$ and $comp(t_i)$ is constant. However, parallel execution time must also take into account the time to transmit input files to every processor $P \cdot comm(t_i)$. In the other hand, serial execution time can be estimated as the execution time for the best sequential algorithm to execute T tasks, which is $\Theta(T \cdot comp(t_i)) = \Theta(P)$. Thus, substituting these costs in Equation 1 we can find an expression for the overhead function as

$$T_0 = P.T_P - T_S \qquad (14)$$

$$= P\left(\Theta\left(P \cdot comm(t_i) + \frac{T \cdot cost(t_i)}{P}\right)\right) - \Theta(P) \qquad \text{[c]}$$

$$= P\left(\Theta(P) + \frac{\Theta(P)}{P}\right) - \Theta(P)$$

$$= \Theta(P^2) + \Theta(P) - \Theta(P)$$

$$= \Theta(P^2).$$

And the isoefficiency function for SBA programs under such conditions can be defined as $f(P) = KT_0(W,p)$ (according to equation 6), where $K = \frac{E}{(1-E)}$ is a constant value dependent on the desired efficiency level. Hence, we conclude that the isoefficiency function for any BoT application running on a master-slave platform is $\Omega(P^2)$.

□

---

[c]Formally, Ω, and Θ may be defined as follows: $\Omega(g(n)) = \{f(n) :$ for any positive constant $c > 0$, there exists a constant $n_0 > 0$ such that $cg(n) \geq f(n)$ for all $n \geq n_0\}$. $\Theta(g(n)) = \{f(n) :$ for any positive constants $c_1, c_2 > 0$, and $n_0 > 0$ such that $0 \leq c_1 g(n) \leq f(n) \leq c_2 g(n)$ for all $n \geq n_0\}$.

Theorem 1 defines the lower bound on scalability achievable by BoT applications running on masterslave platforms. However, it does reveal one necessary condition so that BoT applications can be effectively scalable. The next theorem shows that the lower bound on the isoefficiency function is only achievable for applications having maximum input file affinity.

Theorem 2. *The lower bound for the isoefficiency function for a homogeneous BoT application running on a homogeneous, dedicated masterslave platform is $\Omega(P^2)$ for BoT applications having maximum Input File Affinity*

Proof. In this case all T tasks share common input files, and the set of T tasks can be grouped into K groups of tasks, where "larger" means that at least one of the K tasks includes at least two of the original T tasks. It takes a time t_{init} to send the files necessary to one of the K tasks to one node. Consider also that the new average task cost is z, $z = \frac{W}{K}$. Clearly $K = \Theta(P)$ since the number of "larger" tasks has to be of the same order of magnitude of the number of processors. Note that z is also given by $\Theta(P)$, in order to maintain the efficiency at a predefined level α when the number of processors of the platform increase. Since the input file affinity of the application is $\frac{T-1}{T}$, we have to send $\Theta(P)$ sets of input files to processors in $\Theta(z)$ time. Since the transfer of each set of input files takes t_{init} time, z has to grow at a rate higher than $\Theta(t_{init}P)$. Considering that $W = Kz$ we get the isoefficiency function to be $W = \Theta(P^2)$.

$\square$

4.6.   Contention in the Completion Phase

This subsection considers contention in the completion phase, i.e., in this section we do not consider the duration of the completion phase as constant, independently of the number of processors. The objective of this section is to assess the impact of completion phase contention (due to transmission of output files back to the master node) in the scalability of BoT applications running on master-slave platforms.

Contention may be caused, for instance, by disk write serialization of large output files in a Master node or concurrent access to a common input port. Contention in the completion phase increases the total makespan of a job and reduces parallel execution efficiency. Therefore, contention in the completion phase may have a significant impact on the isoefficiency function and may change the lower bounds stated in the previous subsection. For the results presented in this subsection we assume without loss of generality two possible scenarios regarding the contention in the transmission of the output files: *(i)* in this scenario we assume each individual task produces an output file of small, fixed size (this is true for several real BoT applications, e.g. in [17], whose individual task receives input files of arbitrary size, and produces an output file whose size typically ranges from a few dozen to some hundred bytes). In this scenario, all the output files produced in one node can be grouped and sent to the master node as a single aggregated output file immediately after the processor completes the execution of its local tasks; and *(ii)*, a scenario composed of BoT applications whose individual tasks produce output files of arbitrary size, whose completion phase is subject to severe contention conditions. For the theorems below we refer to these two scenarios as fixed size output files and large output files, respectively.

Theorem 3. *If the one-port model and output files of fixed size are assumed, the lower bound on the isoefficiency function for a BoT application running on a master-slave platform with P processors is* $\Omega(P^2)$.

Proof. Assume an application composed of k subtasks, and that it takes at most τ time units to transfer the necessary files between two nodes (output and input files). It is possible to decompose τ as $\tau_i + \tau_s$, where τ_i is the time needed to transfer input files and τ_s is the time needed to transfer output files. Also, consider that the average task size is $z, z = W/k$. Clearly $k = \Omega(P)$ since the number of tasks has to be at least of the order of magnitude of the number of processors. This is necessarily true; otherwise the efficiency will decrease as the number of processors increase. Since it takes τ time units to transfer files, z has to grow at a rate higher than $\Theta(\tau_i P + \tau_s P)$, where $\tau_i P$ is the time needed to transfer the input files from the master to the P slaves; and $\tau_s P$ is the time it takes for the P slaves to transfer the P aggregated output files to the master (one aggregated file at a time). Now, since $W = kz$, substituting lower bounds for k and z, we get the isoefficiency function to be $W = \Omega(P^2)$.

$\square$

For the next theorem we assume that each task produces an output file of arbitrary size. When tasks finish their computation phase the output files produced are transmitted to the master one at a time.

Theorem 4. *For the scenario in which one-port model and output files of arbitrary size are assumed, the lower bound on the isoefficiency function for a BoT application running on a master-slave platform with P processors is* $\Omega(P^2)$.

Proof. Assume an application composed of k subtasks, and that it takes at most τ time units to transfer the necessary files between two nodes (output and input files). It is possible to decompose τ as $\tau_i + \tau_s$, where τ_i is the time needed to transfer input files and τ_s is the time needed to transfer output files for each task. Also, consider that the average task size is $z, z = W/k$. Since it takes τ time units to transfer files, z has to grow at a rate higher than $\Theta(\tau_i P + \tau_s P)$, where $\Theta(\tau_i)$ is the time needed to transfer the input files from the master to the P slaves (it is worth noting that input files are sent only once for each node); and $\Theta(\tau_s P)$ is the time it takes to transfer k output files from the slaves to the master node (it is worth noting that there is at least one output file per completed task). Now, since $W = kz$, substituting lower bounds for k and z, we get the isoefficiency function to be $W = \Omega(k(P+k))$. Clearly, $k = \Omega(P)$ since the number of tasks has to be at least of the order of magnitude of the number of processors. This is necessarily true; otherwise the efficiency will decrease as the number of processors increase. Then we can write $W = \Omega(k^2)$. In this case, there are two possibilities for the asymptotical behavior of k:

- In the best possible case, k grows equal than P (i.e., $k = \Theta(P)$): in this case, since $W = kz$, substituting lower bounds for k and z, we get the isoefficiency function to be $W = \Omega(k.(P+k)) = \Omega(P^2)$;

- Another (much more realistic) possibility is that the growing of k is at least one order of magnitude higher than P (i.e., $k = \omega(P)$) (see note on small omega notation [d]). For

---

[d]Formally, small omega can be defined as $\omega(g(n)) = \{f(n) :$ for any positive constant $c > 0$, there exists a constant $n_0 > 0$ such that $0 \le cg(n) \le f(n)$ for all $n \ge n_0\}$ [33].

instance, consider without loss of generality, that $k = (P \log P)$. In this case, since $W = kz$, substituting lower bounds for k and z, we get the isoefficiency function to be $W = \Omega(P^2 (\log P)^2)$ (see footnote [e]). In order to simplify our analysis, the asymptotic behavior for the isoefficiency function in this case is significantly higher than in the previous case.

$\square$

5. Bounds on Scalability of BoT Applications Running on Hierarchical Platforms

In this section we present bounds on the isoefficiency function for hierarchical platforms. Two main topologies are considered in the theorems that follow: 2-level hierarchical platforms (as shown in Figure 2 and n-ary trees. 2-level hierarchical platforms represent multi-cluster platforms. In this case we consider an upper level front end (a supervisor node) which has access to a number of clusters, each one with its own front end. This particular topology is quite common today, and it is representative, for instance, of several multi-clusters and multi-cluster grid infrastructures. Such large distributed systems are typically implemented by several clusters composed of multiple-processor nodes interconnected by high performance hardware, such as InfiniBand, Myrinet, Crossbar, and SP Switch (www.top500.org). Inter-cluster communication can be implemented either by specialized interconnection hardware or WAN networks [34,36].

N-ary trees were included because they define the lowest achievable bound for several configurations, as it is proved in the following sections. It is worth noting that those topologies may be deployed either physically or logically. For instance, a multi-cluster platform is an example of topology defined by the interconnection of its nodes. On the other hand, it is possible to deploy a n-ary tree of resource managers on Warehouse-Scale Computers [41], which is composed of a large number of nodes in just one site.

5.1. Scalability of BoT Applications Running on Hierarchical Platforms

For the following theorems we assume the one-port communication model, and that there is no contention in the completion phase, when output files are transferred back to the upper level node.

The first theorem is stated below. It defines the lower bound on the isoefficiency function achievable for a class of 2-level hierarchical topologies. The objective when stating Theorems 1 and 2 is to highlight the relation between hierarchical topologies and scalability. Depending on how processors are organized, some hierarchical topologies provide better scalability than other different hierarchical topologies. In Theorem 5, a specific 2-level topology (similar to the platform illustrated in Figure 2) is considered, as stated below:

Theorem 5. *If there is no contention in the completion phase, the lower bound on the isoefficiency function for a BoT application running on a 2-level hierarchical platform with*

---

[e]In [32], authors show that a possible ordering of complexity functions is: $\log n, \sqrt{n}, n \log n, n^2, n^3, \cdots, 2^n$.

P processors, when either the number of master nodes or the maximum number of slave nodes per master is limited, is $\Omega(P^2)$.

Proof. Assume an application composed of k subtasks, and that takes at most τ time units to transfer the necessary files between two nodes (output and input files). It is possible to decompose τ as $\tau_i + \tau_s$, where τ_i is the time needed to transfer input files and τ_s is the time needed to transfer output files. Also, consider that the average task size is z, $z = W/k$. Clearly $k = \Omega(P)$ since the number of tasks has to be at least of the order of magnitude of the number of processors. This is necessarily true; otherwise the efficiency will decrease as the number of processors increases. Two different possibilities for the behavior of z are discussed below:

- If the number of masters is limited by a constant $M(P > M)$, the scalability is bounded by the maximum number of slaves per master, which is equal to $\lceil P/M \rceil$. Since it takes τ_i time units to transfer input files and τ_s time units to transfer output files, z has to grow at a rate higher than $\Theta(\tau_i M + \tau_i P/M)$, where $\tau_i M$ is the time needed to transfer the input files from the supervisor to the M masters, and $\tau_i P/M$ is the time it takes to transfer input files from M masters to the P slaves. Since no contention is considered and output files can be sent to the user machine after the application has been completed, τ_s is not considered here. Now, since $W = kz$, substituting lower bounds for k and z, we get the isoefficiency function to be $W = \Omega(P^2)$.

- If the maximum number of slaves per master is limited by a constant $S(P > S)$, scalability is bounded by the number of masters, which is equal to $\lceil P/S \rceil$. Since it takes τ_i time units to transfer input files and τ_s time units to transfer output files, z has to grow at a rate higher than $\Theta(\tau_i P/S + \tau_i S)$, where $\tau_i P/S$ the time to transfer input files from the root node to the $\lceil P/S \rceil$ masters, and $\tau_i S$ is the time it takes to transfer the input files from any of the $\lceil P/S \rceil$ masters to the S slaves (it is worth noting that in the best case input files are sent only once for each processor). Now, since $W = kz$, substituting lower bounds for k and z, we get the isoefficiency function to be $W = \Omega(P^2)$.

$\square$

Theorem 6. *The lower bound on the isoefficiency function for BoT running on a hierarchical platform organized as a balanced n-ary tree is* $\Omega(P \log P)$.

Proof. Assume an application composed of k subtasks, and that it takes a time τ to transfer the necessary files between two nodes (upper and lower levels). Consider also that the average task size is z, $z = W/k$. Clearly $k = \Omega(P)$ since the number of tasks has to be at least of the order of magnitude of the number of processors. Note that z is given by $\Omega(\log P)$. This is due to the fact that, in a hierarchical system organized as a n-ary tree, at least n messages should be sent from a upper level node to lower level processors in $\Theta(z)$ time. It is also worth noting that, in this particular case, the number of transfers from an upper level node to a lower level one is always bounded by n, which is not the case for theorem 5. Since the transfer of input files takes τ_i time units, and the number of levels of the tree is limited by $\lceil \log P \rceil$, z has to grow at a rate higher than $W = \Omega(n\tau_i \log P)$. Now, since $W = kz$, substituting lower bounds for k and z, we get the isoefficiency function to be $W = \Omega(P \log P)$.

□

Theorem 7. *For the one-port model, the lower bound on the isoefficiency function achievable by BoT applications running on hierarchical platforms is $\Omega(P \log P)$.*

Proof. Consider a master (i.e., a non-leaf) node in the hierarchy, and its children (i.e., the nodes in the lower level that are directly connected to the master). Under the one-port model, the time needed to transfer input files from any master to its children will always be a function of the number of children processors below the master. This happens because, under the one-port model, any master can only send one message (i.e. a file) to one child node at a given time-step. Considering that the average task size is z, $z = W/k$, and $k = \Omega(P)$, to have a lower bound of the isoefficiency function of $\Omega(P)$ the communication time between any node and its children should be a constant, independently of the number of processors. As stated before, this is not possible under the one-port model.

□

5.2. Hierarchical Platforms - Contention in the Completion Phase

This section considers contention in the completion phase, i.e., in this section we do not consider the duration of the completion phase as constant, independently of the number of processors in a given level. The objective of this section is to assess the impact of completion phase contention (due to transmission of output files back to the root of the hierarchy) in the scalability of BoT applications running on hierarchical platforms. The relevance of output file contention is attested either by the support provided by several execution management systems (such as in [12,32]), and by studies on the impact of transmission of output files in performance (such as in [10,19,31]).

The analysis of this section focus on the one-port communication model. Contention may be caused, for instance, by disk write serialization of large output files in a Master node or concurrent access to a common input port. Contention in the completion phase increases the total makespan of a job and reduces parallel execution efficiency. We consider in this subsection the same scenarios described in subsection 4.6.

For the next theorem, we assume output files with a small, fixed size. This scenario is representative for applications (such as in [17]), whose tasks produce small output files (typically of dozens to a few hundred bytes) containing results and summarized data. In this case, lower level processors can group the output files produced by its local tasks and send them altogether to the upper level nodes when all its local tasks have been executed. According to the one-port model, each master can receive output files from one slave processor at a time, as well as the supervisor can receive output files from one master at a time. Thus, in this scenario the completion phase is subject to contention.

Theorem 8. *If the one-port model and output files of fixed size are assumed, the lower bound on the isoefficiency function for a BoT application running on a 2-level hierarchical platform with P processors, when either the number of master nodes or maximum number of slave nodes per master is limited, is $\Omega(P^2)$.*

Proof. Assume an application composed of k subtasks, and that takes at most τ time units to transfer the necessary files between two nodes (output and input files). It is possible to decompose τ as $\tau_i + \tau_s$, where τ_i is the time needed to transfer input files and τ_s is the time needed to transfer output files. Also, consider that the average task size is z, $z = W/k$. Clearly $k = \Omega(P)$ since the number of tasks has to be at least of the order of magnitude of the number of processors. This is necessarily true; otherwise the efficiency will decrease as the number of processors increases. Two different possibilities for the behavior of z are discussed below:

- If the number of masters is limited by a constant $M(P > M)$, the scalability is bounded by the maximum number of slaves per master, which is equal to $\lceil P/M \rceil$. Since it takes τ_i time units to transfer input files and τ_s time units to transfer output files, z has to grow at a rate higher than $\Theta(\tau_i M + \frac{\tau_i P}{M} + \frac{\tau_s P}{M} + \tau_s P)$, where $\tau_i M$ is the time needed to transfer the input files from the supervisor to the M masters; $\frac{\tau_i P}{M}$ is the time it takes to transfer input files from M masters to the P slaves; $\frac{\tau_s P}{M}$ is the time it takes to transfer back P aggregated output files to the M masters; and $\tau_s P$ is the time needed to the M masters to transfer P aggregated output files to the supervisor. Now, since $W = kz$, substituting lower bounds for k and z, we get the isoefficiency function to be $W = \Omega(P^2)$.

- If the maximum number of slaves per master is limited by a constant $S(P > S)$, scalability is bounded by the number of masters, which is equal to $\lceil \frac{P}{S} \rceil$. Since it takes τ_i time units to transfer input files and τ_s time units to transfer output files, z has to grow at a rate higher than $\Theta(\tau_i \frac{P}{S} + \tau_i S + \tau_s S + \tau_s P)$, where $\tau_i \frac{P}{S}$ the time to transfer input files from the supervisor to the $\lceil \frac{P}{S} \rceil$ masters; $\tau_i S$ is the time it takes to transfer the input files from any of the $\lceil P/S \rceil$ masters to the slaves; $\tau_s S$ is the time it takes for the $\lceil \frac{P}{S} \rceil$ masters to receive the aggregated files from lower level nodes; and $\tau_s P$ is the time needed to the M masters to transfer P aggregated output files to the supervisor. Now, since $W = kz$, substituting lower bounds for k and z, we get the isoefficiency function to be $W = \Omega(P^2)$.

$\square$

For the next theorems we assume that each task produces an output file of arbitrary size. When tasks finish their computation phase the output files produced are transmitted to the upper level one at a time. According to the one-port model, each master can receive output files from slave nodes one at a time, as well as the supervisor can receive output files from one master at a time. Thus, in this scenario the completion phase is subject to contention.

Theorem 9. *For the scenario in which one-port model and output files of arbitrary size are assumed, the lower bound on the isoefficiency function for a BoT application running on a 2-level hierarchical platform with P processors, when either the number of master nodes or maximum number of slave nodes per master is limited, is $\Omega(P^3)$.*

Proof. Assume an application composed of k subtasks, and that takes at most a τ time units to transfer the necessary files betweenn two nodes (output and input files). It is possible to decompose τ as $\tau_i + \tau_s$, where τ_i is the time needed to transfer input files and τ_s is the time needed to transfer output files. Also, consider that the average task size is z, $z = W/k$. Clearly $k = \Omega(P)$ since the number of tasks has to be at least of the order of magnitude of the number of processors. This is necessarily true; otherwise the efficiency will decrease as the number of processors increases. Two different possibilities for the behavior of z are discussed below:

- If the number of masters is limited by a constant $M (P > M)$, the scalability is bounded by the maximum number of slaves per master, which is equal to $\lceil P/M \rceil$. Since it takes τ_i time units to transfer input files and τ_s time units to transfer output files, z has to grow at a rate higher than $\Theta(\tau_i M + \frac{\tau_i P}{M} + \frac{\tau_s k}{M} + \tau_s k)$, where $\tau_i M$ is the time needed to transfer the input files from the supervisor to the M masters; $\frac{\tau_i P}{M}$ is the time it takes to transfer input files from M masters to the P slaves; $\frac{\tau_s k}{M}$ is the time it takes to transfer back k output files from P slaves to M masters; and $\tau_s k$ is the time needed to the M masters to transfer k output files to the supervisor. Now, since $W = kz$, substituting lower bounds for k and z, we get the isoefficiency function to be $W = \Omega(P^2 k)$. In the best possible case, we have $k = \Theta(P)$ and $W = \Omega(P^3)$

- If the maximum number of slaves per master is limited by a constant $S (P > S)$, scalability is bounded by the number of masters, which is equal to $\lceil \frac{P}{S} \rceil$. Since it takes τ_i time units to transfer input files and τ_s time units to transfer output files, z has to grow at a rate higher than $\Theta(\tau_i \frac{P}{S} + \tau_i S + \frac{\tau_s k}{P/S} + \tau_s k)$, where $\tau_i \frac{P}{S}$ the time to transfer input files from the supervisor to the $\lceil \frac{P}{S} \rceil$ masters; $\tau_i S$ is the time it takes to transfer the input files from any of the $\lceil P/S \rceil$ masters to the slaves (S slaves per master); $\frac{\tau_s k}{P/S}$ is the time it takes to transfer back k output files from P slaves to $\lceil \frac{P}{S} \rceil$ masters; and $\tau_s k$ is the time needed to transfer k output files to the supervisor. Now, since $W = kz$, substituting lower bounds for k and z, we get the isoefficiency function to be $W = \Omega(P^2 k)$. In the best possible case, we have $k = \Theta(P)$ and $W = \Omega(P^3)$

$\square$

Theorem 10. *The lower bound on the isoefficiency function for BoT applications running on a hierarchical platform organized as a balanced n-ary tree is $\Omega(P^2 \log P)$, when there is contention in the completion phase for the one-port communication model.*

Proof. As in the previous theorem, when contention is taken into account, $\tau = \Omega(k)$, where k is the number of tasks of the application. Again, the average task size is z, $z = W/k$. Clearly $k = \Omega(P)$ since the number of tasks has to be at least of the order of magnitude of the number of processors. Note that z is given by $\Omega(\log P)$. This is due to the fact that, in a hierarchical system organized as a n-ary tree, at least n messages should be sent from an upper level node to lower level processors in $\Theta(z)$ time. Since the transfer of files (input and output) takes τ time units, and the number of levels of the tree is limited by $\lceil \log P \rceil$, z has to grow at a rate higher than $\Omega(n\tau \log P)$. Now, since $W = kz$, substituting lower bounds for k and z, we get the isoefficiency function to be $W = \Omega(P^2 \log P)$.

$\square$

5.3.   Heterogeneous Platforms

The theorems of the previous subsections considered only homogeneous platforms, i.e., all processors having the same computing power. In this section we briefly analyze the impact of processor heterogeneity in the previously stated lower bounds. The main question associated with this section is to determine whenever heterogeneity may impose lower bounds different from those stated in the previous section. In order to investigate this question one should consider the heterogeneity-aware variations of current scalability metrics described in the literature (e.g. see [42, 43] for isoefficiency and [44] for isospeed).

For the analysis of this section, given a P processors heterogeneous platform, we propose an equivalent homogeneous platform based on the concept of Homogeneous-Equivalent Computing Rate (HECR) as defined in [45]. In the following analysis, it is assumed that there is no contention in the completion phase.

Definition 2. *Given a heterogeneous platform with P processors, an equivalent homogeneous platform is defined as a P processors homogeneous platform where the processing power corresponds to the Homogeneous-Equivalent Computing Rate (HECR) as defined in [45]. The interconnection network of both platforms are the same.*

Essentially, the equivalent homogeneous platform is capable of completing the same amount of work of its heterogeneous counterpart in L time units under the FIFO work-sharing protocol [45, 46]. That is, both the heterogeneous platform and its HECR counterpart should have the same X-measure, as defined in [45]. It is worth noting that the X-measure "tracks" how much work is completed in L time units. If we defined the amount of work a particular platform with P processors complete in L time units as $W(L,P)$, then $W(L,P_1) \geq W(L,P_2)$ if and only if $X(P_1) \geq X(P_2)$. Note also that in the definition of the *Cluster Exploitation Problem*, that guides the derivation of the X-measure, all tasks of the application have the same complexity (i.e. can be considered homogeneous) and requires the distribution of a single package of work for each computing node in a single message Therefore, we can consider that the amount of data transferred between upper level and lower level nodes is constant, independently of the number of tasks mapped on a processor. Scalability is then maximized due to the applications high I_{aff}, which is directly related to a low communication-to-computation ratio (ccr).

The theorem below proves that, for a given dedicated heterogeneous platform and a maximum IFA BoT application executed with efficiency level α, it is always possible to achieve an efficiency equal or higher than α in an equivalent homogeneous platform for the corresponding BoT application. Therefore, the bounds defined in the previous sections are valid for both homogeneous and heterogeneous dedicated platforms.

Theorem 11. *Considering a maximum IFA application executed on a dedicated heterogeneous platform with efficiency level α, there is an equivalent homogeneous platform where the same application can be executed with efficiency equal or above α.*

Proof. As defined in [42, 43], the efficiency of a parallel (either homogeneous or heterogeneous) system can be defined as the ratio between the best response time achievable for solving a specific problem in that system and the real response time achieved during algorithm execution. The best response time will be obtained when the workload is evenly distributed among all nodes and the overhead time is minimized. For this best case we have:

$$EF = \frac{W}{T_R \sum_i \frac{W_i}{T_i}} \tag{15}$$

where EF is the efficiency (α), W is the total amount of work, T_R is the total response time, W_i is the amount of work done by processor i and T_i is the time required for processor I to complete W_i. Note that the ratio $\frac{W_i}{T_i}$ corresponds to the processing power of processor Pi.

On the other hand, an application where all tasks share the same input file (Maximum I_{aff}) minimizes the execution overhead since the input file needs to be sent only once to each node, if not already locally stored. Therefore, for an application with maximum IFA we can consider that:

$$EF_{HETER} = \frac{W_{HETER}}{T_R \sum_i \frac{W_i}{T_i}} \tag{16}$$

Since the application execution is perfectly load-balanced, we have:

$$T_i = T_R \tag{17}$$

$$\sum_i W_i = W_{HETER} \tag{18}$$

For the corresponding HECR platform we have:

$$EF_{HECR} = \frac{W_{HECR}}{T_R \sum_i \frac{W_i}{T_R}} \tag{19}$$

where $\sum_i W_i = W_{HECR}$. Since the X-measure of the HECR platforms may be larger than or equal to the X-measure of the heterogeneous platform [45], we can consider that both platforms execute the same amount of work in a time T_R. Therefore:

$$W_{HECR} = W_{HETER} \tag{20}$$

We can conclude that $EF_{HECR} = EF_{HETER}$. $\square$

6. Experimental Results

In this section, we confirm the results presented in sections 4 and 5 twofold. First, we present simulation experiments that validate previous analytical results. Second, we further discuss the results presented in the previous sections, clarifying choices and assumptions and how they impact the results. We also comment on the impact of the results of this chapter on platform topology definition and application design.

Regarding the choice of presenting simulation results instead of actual platform experimentation, it is worth noting that the motivation for the current study comes from background acquired in previous experimental studies [5,17,18]. However, experimental studies are likely subject to the influence of specific characteristics of the platform/application and several conditions that may not be controlled, in particular for a large number of processors as required for a scalability analysis.

For the present study, we consider that each task has an associated computational cost, which cannot be changed. Also, each task has an associated communication cost that is due to input and output file transfer. It is considered that the communication cost of each task cannot be changed. Such assumptions are consistent with other solid studies on scheduling BoT applications (e.g., in [3, 10, 19]).

Various studies on scheduling BoT applications (e.g., in [3]) adopt a measure to express the ratio between the communication and computation costs, dubbed the communication-to-computation ratio (ccr). It is worth noting that the present study focuses on BoT applications in which both the execution times and communication times are influential factors for the application makespan. We do not consider only the case where the ccr is close to zero (i.e., we do not consider the case of negligible communication times, for instance). Under this perspective, the ccr is likely to affect the isoefficiency function of a bag-of-tasks application. However, it affects the isoefficiency function only by some constant value. The ccr does not change the asymptotic behavior of the isoefficiency function for BoT applications running on hierarchical or master-slave platforms. This aspect is illustrated in the simulation results of this section.

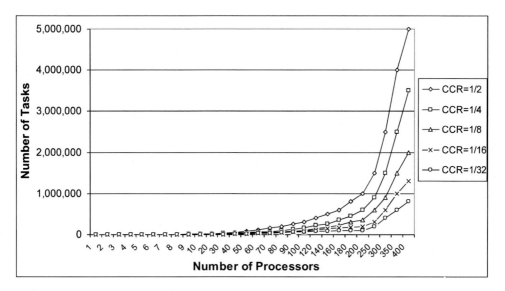

Figure 3. Isoefficiency function (i.e., the number of tasks needed to maintain the efficiency at 0.99) for the execution considering the input file affinity.

For the simulation experiments presented in this section, we assume that both the processors and communication links are homogeneous and dedicated. We assume that both the amount of time units to transmit the input and output files and the time units to execute an application task are related according to the communication-to-computation ratio (ccr). This is important for the evaluation of applications with different characteristics (i.e., different levels of ccr). Our simulator implements a round robin strategy to map tasks to processors because the round-robin strategy is optimal for running homogeneous BoT applications on homogeneous and dedicated masterslave platforms [3]. Such assumptions are important, since our experiments aim at validating the lower bounds presented in previous

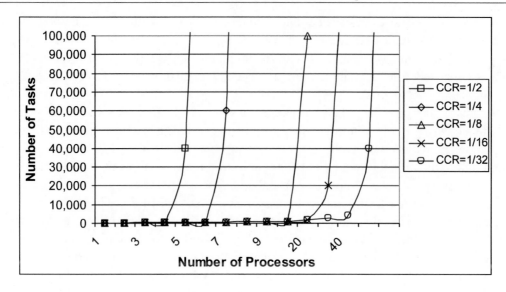

Figure 4. Isoefficiency function (i.e., the number of tasks needed to maintain the efficiency at 0.99) for the execution without considering the input file affinity.

sections.

6.1. Master-slave Platforms - Experimental Evaluation of Scalability Bounds

In this section, we present experimental results to compare the scalability of two scheduling algorithms, with and without taking into account the input file affinity. Our objective in this section is to confirm the analytical results presented in section 4. The experiments whose results are presented in this section were generated using the SimGrid package [47]. First we present results of the execution when the input file affinity is explicitly taken into consideration. The platform simulated was composed of up to 400 homogeneous and dedicated processors, and the application was composed of a variable number of tasks sharing one single input file. Each task takes 8 time units to complete (t_{comp}), and the amount of time needed to send the input files (t_{init}) varies in order to obtain different values of the communication-to-computation ratio (ccr), which can be computed as $ccr = \frac{t_{init}}{t_{comp}}$. In the following experiments we simulated the following ccr: 1/2, 1/4, 1/8, 1/16 and 1/32. It is worth noting that these ratios indicate the granularity of the tasks that compose the BoT application. The efficiency is kept around 0.99 for all ratios. Figure 3 shows the corresponding isoefficiency functions. By analyzing the curves shown in Figure 3 it becomes clear that the execution of applications with high input file affinity is scalable independently of the granularity of the tasks, if the input file affinity is explicitly considered. It is also clear that the curves shown are coherent with theorems presented in section 4. We also executed the same application when the input file affinity is not taken into consideration. In this case a round robin strategy was used to map tasks to processors. As stated in section 4, the round-robin strategy is optimal for running homogeneous BoT applications on masterslave platforms that are homogeneous and dedicated [3]. For those executions the input files are sent to slave nodes before each task execution. Figure 4 shows the corresponding isoefficiency functions, for efficiencies around 0.99. It can be seen that the execution of a BoT application without considering the input file affinity is not scalable. It is worth noting that each execution can keep the efficiency to platforms up to P_{eff} processors. For a number of processors larger than P_{eff} it is simply not possible to maintain the efficiency, independently of the granularity of the tasks. This result is also coherent to Theorem 2 and the observations of Section 4.

6.2.   The Scalability for a Master-Slave Architecture - TCP links

The experiments described in this section were carried out on a machine with two Intel Xeon E5420 2.50 GHz quad core processors with a 6MB cache and memory of 16 GB. For instance, the simulation of a master-slave platform with 1,000 nodes consumed 68,821 seconds (more than 19 hours) in the above mentioned machine. For this particular experiment instance, it was necessary to simulate about 1,345,510 tasks in order to keep the efficiency above 0.9. Experiments simulate the allocation and utilization of resources such as communication links, the master, and slave nodes for the execution of tasks and the transmission of files on the master-slave platform according to the communication models. In our experiments, the efficiency level was set as 0.9 in order to compute values of the isoefficiency function, i.e., our experiments searched for the minimum number of tasks that is necessary to maintain the computational efficiency above this threshold, which can be acceptable for real master-slave implementations such as grids and clusters. For instance, setting efficiency as 0.99 could rise the computational cost to run our simulation experiments without the corresponding benefits in accuracy (as the efficiency level dos not change the asymptotic behavior of the isoefficiency function).

The next experiment assesses the scalability of BoT applications running on master-slave platforms implemented with TCP links. Our objective is to verify experimentally if bounds found for the one-port model are valid also for other communication models. Such experiments explore Simgrid capability of simulating both local TCP links, and multi-hop routes over wide area TCP links. Results from this experiment are depicted in Figure 5.

As illustrated in Figure 5, the lower bound on the isoefficiency function $F(P)$ is $O(P^2)$ for master-slave platforms with TCP links. These results show that $O(P^2)$ is lower bound on the isoefficiency function for master-slave platforms deployed over the Internet. A log-log scale graphics is provided to illustrate the asymptotic behavior of the isoefficiency function, and curves for P, $P \log P$, and P^2 are also provided for reference.

6.3.   Hierarchical Platforms

For the first experiment presented in this subsection, we considered a 2-level hierarchical architecture with a fixed number of masters (M = 10) and a binary tree, and no contention in the transmission of output files. Figure 6 illustrates the results for our experiments on the isoefficiency function for these two architectures under the one-port communication model. Experiments simulate three ccr levels to evaluate communication-bound applications (ccr = 0.1), CPU-bound applications (ccr = 10.0), and balanced applications (ccr = 1.0). As illustrated in Figure 6, under the one-port model the lower bound on the isoefficiency function $F(P)$ present the same growth rate as $\Omega(P^2)$ for 2-level hierarchical platforms, and the lower bound for a n-ary hierarchical platform present the same growth rate as $\Omega(P \log P)$.

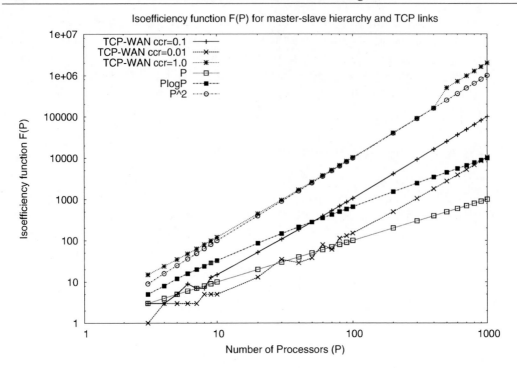

Figure 5. The isoefficiency function for the pair BoT applications/master-slave platforms with communication infrastructure based on multi-hop TCP links implemented on the top of WAN networks, with no output file contention. The log-log scale highlights the growth rate of each curve. Parallel lines means that they have similar growth rates. For instance, the isoefficiency bounds for 2-level tree present growth rate taht is equivalent to P^2 line, while the isoefficiency curves for binary tree present growth rate similar to $P \log P$.

These results confirm theoretical results presented in section 5, regardless of the ccr of the application. A loglog scale graphics was provided to illustrate the asymptotic behavior of the isoefficiency function, and curves for P, $P \log P$, and P^2 are also provided for reference.

Considering contention in the completion phase, Results presented in Fig. 7 confirm that the lower bound on the isoefficiency function $F(P)$ for 2-level hierarchical platforms under the one-port model is $\Omega(P^2)$, when tasks with output files of fixed size are considered. Likewise, results of this experiment confirm that the lower bound on the isoefficiency function $F(P)$ for 2-level hierarchical platforms under the oneport model is $\Omega(P^3)$, when tasks with output files of arbitrary size are considered. In fact, it is possible to observe from this experiment that, for a given number of processors P, the ccr affects the actual value of $F(P)$. This behavior is expected, since it will be necessary more tasks to maintain the computational efficiency at a given threshold for applications with larger values of ccr. However, it is worth noting that the asymptotic behavior of $F(P)$ is not affected by the ccr. In other words, results stated in subsection 5.2 hold, regardless of the ccr.

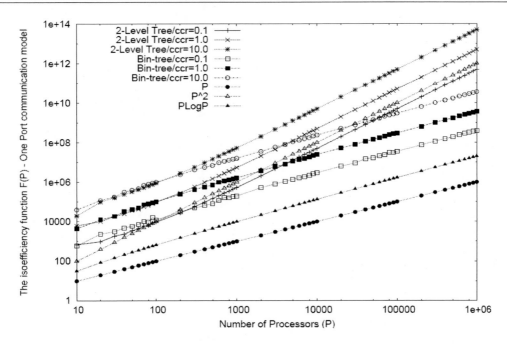

Figure 6. The isoefficiency function for the 2-level hierarchy and binary tree topologies under the one-port communication model, with three levels of communication-to-computation ratio (ccr).

7. Discussion

When output file contention should be taken into consideration, is worth noting that the relative scalability performance of different topologies does not change from the case with no completion phase contention. For instance, for the one-port communication model, the balanced n-ary tree will always have a lower bound on the isoefficiency function when compared to 2-level platforms for the cases with no contention, fixed size output file contention and arbitrary size output file contention. However, some adjustments in BoT application design may be necessary in order to guarantee application execution scalability. For arbitrary size output file contention the application designer should keep the number of tasks in the same order of magnitude of the number of nodes to ensure application execution scalability.

It was also formally demonstrated in this chapter that homogeneous BoT applications with maximum I_{aff} can achieve the lower bounds on the isoefficiency function in homogeneous and dedicated platforms. In order to approximate this lower bound it may be necessary to combine a number of techniques and mechanisms for BoT application scheduling and execution that have already been proposed in the literature. Therefore, so that an application can achieve maximum scalability on homogeneous and dedicated platforms, the workload should be evenly distributed among tasks, and input files should be shared among tasks as much as possible. Another useful technique is to group tasks that share common files in order to reduce the communication-to-computation ratio, as discussed in [6]. What becomes clear from the results presented in this chapter is that, regarding scalability, the combination of these strategies is better than simply deploying a single one.

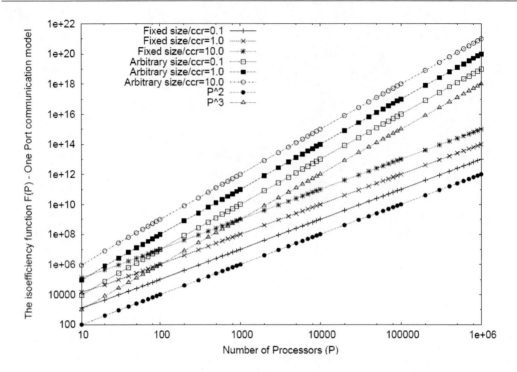

Figure 7. The isoefficiency function for the 2-level hierarchy under the oneport communication model, with two scenarios of contention in the output file transmission (output files of fixed size and output files of arbitrary size) and three levels of communication-to-computation ratio.

Conclusion

This chapter presents an analysis of the scalability of BoT applications running on master-slave and hierarchical platforms for the one-port communication model, with and without contention in the completion phase. In general, scalability depends on both the communication model and on the characteristics of the application with respect to input and output files.

Completion phase contention may also have a direct impact on BoT application execution when output files have arbitrary size. In this particular case, it is important that the total number of tasks be of the same order of magnitude of the number of processors. Otherwise BoT application execution may not be scalable at all.

The previous results were derived for homogeneous platforms. Platform heterogeneity does not have a direct effect on the isoefficiency function lower bound assessment. However, for an average case analysis, heterogeneity may impact scalability execution. A thorough investigation of this issue will be the subject of future work.

References

[1] H. Casanova, A. Legrand, D. Zagorodnov, F. Berman, Heuristics for Scheduling Parameter-Sweep Applications in Grid Environments. In *9th Heterogeneous Computing workshop (HCW'2000)*, pp. 349-363. IEEE Press, New York (2000).

[2] Y. Yang, K. Raadt and H. Casanova, Multiround Algorithms for Scheduling Divisible Loads. *IEEE Trans. on Parallel and Distributed Systems*, 16(11):1092-1102, (2005).

[3] A. Giersch, Y. Robert and F. Vivien, Scheduling task sharing files on heterogeneous master-slave platforms. *J. Systems Architecture*, 52(2):88–104, (2006).

[4] H. Senger, E.R. Hruschka, F.A.B. Silva, L.M. Sato, C.P. Bianchini and B.F. Jerosch, Exploiting Idle Cycles to Execute Data Mining Applications on Clusters of PCs. *J. Systems and Software*, 80(5):778–790, (2007).

[5] H. Senger, F.A.B. Silva, W.M. Nascimento, Hierarchical Scheduling of Independent Tasks with Shared Files. In *6th IEEE International Symposium on Cluster Computing and the Grid Workshops*, pp. 51-56. IEEE CS Press, New York, 2006.

[6] F.A.B. Silva and H. Senger, Improving Scalability of Bag-of-Tasks Applications Running on Master-Slave Platforms. *Parallel Computing*, 35(2):57–71, (2009).

[7] K. Li, Parallel Processing of Divisible Loads on Partitionable Static Interconnection Networks. *Cluster Computing*, 6(1): 47–55, (2003).

[8] V. Bharadwaj, D. Ghose and V. Mani, Multi-Installment Load Distribution in Tree Networks With Delays.*IEEE Trans. on Aerospace and Electronic Sys.*, 31(2):555–567, (1995).

[9] Y.-C. Cheng and T. Robertazzi, Distributed Computation for a Tree-Network With Communication Delay. *IEEE Trans. on Aerospace and Electronic Syst.*, 26(3):511–516, (1990).

[10] O. Beaumont, L. Carter, J. Ferrante, A. Legrand, L. Marchal and Y. Robert, Scheduling multiple bags of tasks on heterogeneous master-worker platforms: centralized versus distributed solutions. *Research Report No 2005-45, Ecole Normale Superieure de Lyon*, 2005. Available at: http://www.ens-lyon.fr/LIP/Pub/Rapports/RR/RR2005/RR2005-45.pdf.

[11] F. Berman, R. Wolski, H. Casanova, W. Cirne, H. Dail, M. Faerman, S. Figueira, J. Hayes, G. Obertelli, J. Schopf, G. Shao, S. Smallen, N. Spring, A. Su and D. Zagorodnov, Adaptive Computing on the Grid Using AppLeS. *IEEE Transactions in Parallel and Distributed Systems*, 14(4):369–382, (2003).

[12] W. Cirne, D. Paranhos, L. Costa, E. Santos-Neto, F. Brasileiro, J. Sauve, F.A.B. Silva, C.O. Barros and C. Silveira, Running Bag-of-Tasks Applications on Computational Grids: The MyGrid Approach. In *International Conference on Parallel Processing (ICPP'03)*, pp.407-416. IEEE Press, New York, 2003.

[13] T. Hagerup, Allocating Independent Tasks to Parallel Processors: An Experimental Study. *J. Parallel and Distributed Computing*, 47(2):185–197, (1997).

[14] K. Kaya and C. Aykanat, Iterative-Improvement-Based Heuristics for Adaptive Scheduling of Tasks Sharing Files on Heterogeneous Master-Slave Environments. *IEEE Transactions on Parallel and Distributed Systems*, 17(8):883–896,(2006).

[15] M. Maheswaran, S. Ali, H.J. Siegel, D. Hensgen and R.F. Freund, Dynamic Matching and Scheduling of a Class of Independent Tasks onto Heterogeneous Computing Systems. In: *Heterogeneous Computing Workshop (HCW'99)*, pp. 30-44. IEEE CS Press, New York, 1999.

[16] E. Santos-Neto, W. Cirne, F. Brasileiro and A. Lima, Exploiting Replication and Data Reuse to Efficiently Schedule Data-intensive Applications on Grids. In: *Workshop on Job Scheduling Strategies for Parallel Processing (JSSPP'04)*. LNCS, vol. 3277, pp. 210-232, Springer, Heidelberg, 2004.

[17] F.A.B. Silva, S. Carvalho, H. Senger, E.R. Hruschka and C.R.G. Farias, Running Data Mining Applications on the Grid: a Bag-of-Tasks Approach. In: *Intl. Conf. Computational Science and its Applications (ICCSA 2004)*. LNCS, vol. 3044, pp.168-177. Springer, Heidelberg, 2004.

[18] F.A.B. Silva, S. Carvalho and E.R. Hruschka, A Scheduling Algorithm for Running Data Mining Applications on the Grid. In *Euro-Par*. LNCS, vol. 3419, pp. 254-262. Springer, Heidelberg, 2004.

[19] Y.C. Lee and A.Y. Zomaya, Practical Scheduling of Bag-of-Tasks Applications on Grids with Dynamic Resilience. *IEEE Trans. on Computers*, 56(6):815–825, (2007).

[20] A. Chaintreau, Sharpness: A tight condition for Throughput Scalability. In *15th International Colloquium on Structural Information and Communication Complexity (SIROCCO)*, June 2008.

[21] A. Grama, A. Gupta and V. Kumar, Isoefficiency: Measuring the Scalability of Parallel Algorithms and Architectures. *IEEE Parallel and Dist. Tech.*, 1(3):12–21, (1993).

[22] X. Sun and D.T. Rover, Scalability of Parallel Algorithm-Machine Combinations. *IEEE Transactions on Parallel and Distributed Systems*, 5(6):599-613, (1994).

[23] V. Kumar, V.N. Rao, Parallel Depth-First Search on Multiprocessors Part II: Analysis. *International Journal of Parallel Programming*, 16(6):501–519, (1987).

[24] H. Casanova, A. Legrand and M. Quinson, SimGrid: a Generic Framework for Large-Scale Distributed Experiments. In *10th IEEE International Conference on Computer Modeling and Simulation*, 126–131, IEEE Press, New York, 2008.

[25] R. Schmidt and F. Pedone, Consistent Main-Memory Database Federations under Deferred Disk Writes. In *24th IEEE Symposium on Reliable Distributed Systems*, IEEE Press, New York, 2005.

[26] J. Liu, A.R. Mamidala and D.K. Panda. Fast and Scalable MPI-Level Broadcast using InfiniBand's Hardware Multicast Support. In *Proc. of IEEE International Parallel and Distributed Processing Symposium*, 2004.

[27] A.R. Mamidala, L. Chai, H-W Jin and D.K. Panda, Efficient SMP-Aware MPI-Level Broadcast over InfiniBand's Hardware Multicast. In *Proc. of IEEE International Parallel and Distributed Processing Symposium*, 2006.

[28] T. Hoefler, C.Siebert and W. Rehm, A practically constant-time MPI Broadcast Algorithm for large-scale InfiniBand Clusters with Multicast, In *Proc. IEEE International Parallel and Distributed Processing Symposium*, pp. 285, 2007.

[29] J. L. Traff and A. Ripkea, Optimal broadcast for fully connected processor-node networks. *Journal of Parallel and Distributed Computing*, 68(7):887–901,(2008).

[30] D. Thain, T. Tannenbaum and M. Livny, Distributed computing in practice: the Condor experience. *Concurrency and Computation: Practice and Experience*, 17(2-4):323–356, John Wiley & Sons, Ltd. http://dx.doi.org/10.1002/cpe.938

[31] O.Beaumont, L.Carter, J. Ferrante, A.Legrand, L.Marchal and Y.Robert, Centralized versus Distributed Schedulers for Bag-of-Tasks Applications, *IEEE Transactions on Parallel and Distributed Systems*, 19(5):698–709, (2008).

[32] M.T. Goodrich, R. Tamassia, *Algorithm Design: Foundations, Analysis, and Internet Examples*. (John Wiley & Sons, 2002).

[33] T.H. Cormen, C.E. Leiserson, R.L. Rivest and C. Stein, *Introduction to Algorithms 2nd ed.*. (The MIT Press, 2001).

[34] A. Iosup, O. Sonmez, S. Anoep and D. Epema. The Performance of Bags-of-Tasks in Large-Scale Distributed Systems. In *High Performance Distributed Computing, (HPDC'08)*, Boston, USA, pp. 97-108, 2008.

[35] A. Iosup, H. Li, M. Jan, S. Anoep, C. Dumitrescu, L. Wolters, D.H.J. Epema, The Grid Workloads Archive, *Future Generation Computer Systems*, 24(7):672–686, (2008).

[36] F.A.B. da Silva, H.Senger, Scalability limits of Bag-of-Tasks applications running on hierarchical platforms, *Journal of Parallel and Distributed Computing*, 71(6): 788-801, 2011. Available online, DOI: 10.1016/j.jpdc.2011.01.002, 2011.

[37] S.Ghemawat,H.Gobioff,S.Leung,The google file system. In: *Proceedings of the 2003 ACM Symposium on Operating Systems Principles*, 2003.

[38] H.Senger, F.A.B. da Silva. Bounds on the scalability of bag-of-tasks applications running on master-slave platforms, *Parallel Processing Letters*, 22(2), 2012.

[39] E. Yero, M. Henriques, Speedup and scalabiltity analysis of masterslave applications on large heterogeneous clusters, *Journal of Parallel and Distributed Computing* 67: 11551167, 2007

[40] K.A. Nagaty. Cloud Tree: A Hierarchical Organization as a Platform for Cloud Computing. *International Journal of Computer & Electrical Engineering* 6.1, 2014.

[41] L.A. Barroso, U. Hlzle, The Datacenter as a Computer: An Introduction to the Design of Warehouse-Scale Machines, in: *Synthesis Lectures on Computer Architecture*, Morgan and Claypool Publishers, 2009.

[42] J.L. Bosque, L.P. Perez, Theoretical scalability analysis for heterogeneous clusters, in: *Proceedings of the 2004 IEEE International Symposium on Cluster Computing and the Grid*, 2004.

[43] L.P. Perez, J.L. Bosque, An efficiency and scalalabiltiy model for heterogeneous clusters, in: *Proceedings of the 2001 IEEE International Symposium on Cluster Computing*, 2001.

[44] Y. Chen, X.-H. Sun, M. Wu, Algorithm-system scalability of heterogeneous computing, *Journal of Parallel and Distributed Computing* 68 (11) (2008) 14031412.

[45] A.L. Rosenberg, R.C. Chiang, Toward understanding heterogeneity in computing, in: *Proceedings of the 2010 IEEE International Parallel and Distributed Processing Symposium*, 2010.

[46] M. Adler, Y. Gong, A.L. Rosenberg, On exploiting node-heterogeneous clusters optimally, *Theory of Computing Systems* 42 (2008) 465487.

[47] Versatile, Scalable, and Accurate Simulation of Distributed Applications and Platforms H. Casanova, A. Giersch, A. Legrand, M. Quinson, F. Suter *Journal of Parallel and Distributed Computing* 74(110) 2899-2917, (2014).

[48] V. Kumar, V. Nageshwara Rao. Parallel depth first search. Part II. analysis. *International Journal of Parallel Programming*, 16(6):501–519, (1987).

In: Grid Computing: Techniques and Future Prospects
Editors: J. G. Barbosa and I. Dutra, pp. 129-155
ISBN: 978-1-63117-704-0
© 2015 Nova Science Publishers, Inc.

Chapter 5

PARALLEL GRID APPLICATIONS

E. Atanassov, T. Gurov and A. Karaivanova*

Institute of Information and Communication Technologies,
Bulgarian Academy of Sciences, Sofia, Bulgaria

Abstract

In this chapter we discuss the development of parallel applications using the Grid environment. Two alternative strategies are widely used: (i) executing large number of batch jobs in a coordinated way, and, (ii) executing parallel jobs (using MPI and/or OpenMP). The chapter starts with a short description of the parallel computing and MPI standard, then goes on to present and discuss various parallelization strategies in Grid environment, including integration of MPI in the Grid middleware. A special attention has been given to tools which speed-up the job execution, such as a service developed by us called JTS (Job Track Service), as well as some techniques for the map-reduce processing model. Finally, the Grid application SALUTE (Stochastic Algorithms for Ultrafast Electron Transport) is presented as a case study, in order to illustrate some practical aspects of the above topics, covering the Grid implementation schemes with and without MPI, graphical interface, use of reservation services, visualization and scalability results.

Since in practice a large part of the computational resources, interconnected in Grids, is used for various types of Monte Carlo simulations, many of the tools and services that we describe are geared towards such problems. In order to support the execution of such computations, researchers use frameworks, libraries and services for launching, monitoring and output gathering. In our scientific research we have great experience with using Monte Carlo Methods in various applied areas. Our experience with the successfully used tools and techniques is also presented in this chapter.

Keywords: grid computing, parallel computing, Message Passing Interface (MPI), grid services, Monte Carlo Grid applications

---

* Corresponding Author Todor Gurov: Address: IICT-BAS, Acad. G. Bonchev St., bl. 25A, Sofia 1113, Bulgaria. Email: gurov@parallel.bas.bg.

1. Parallel Computing and MPI

1.1. Parallel Computing

The parallel computing philosophy is based on the idea of using many processing units in parallel in order to accomplish a computing task faster. Many techniques have been developed in order to achieve efficient parallel execution. The "divide and conquer" paradigm is used when the initial task can be divided into independent smaller tasks. When these tasks are similar, it is more common to speak of the "map-reduce" paradigm [28], where the aggregation of results of the tasks also can be done in parallel. Many of the techniques for parallel computing require tighter coordination of the computations, e.g., "domain decomposition" involves regular exchange of information around the interfaces.

The separate computational processes are usually executed on separate processors. In general, parallel codes run on shared memory multiprocessors, distributed memory multi-computers, clusters of workstations or heterogeneous systems that combine some of the above. The parallelization approach differs depending on the type of the target hardware architecture. Parallelism on shared memory systems (ranging from workstations to large supercomputers) is usuallybased on using compiler directives, following standards such as OpenMP [52]. On the other hand, MPI (Message Passing Interface) [35] is a standard that specifies operations for information exchange that can be used with distributed memory as well as with shared memory model. With recent innovations and multi-core machines becoming the norm, today's HPC (High Performance Computing) systems can optimally employ both of the above programming approaches, thus making hybrid parallel programming (MPI+OpenMP) perhaps the most efficient approach for solving large scale problems.

1.2. MPI Standard

This section is devoted to the usage of MPI in a GRID environment, which is supported by the operating system and middleware. First of all it has to be noted that MPI is not a programming language, but rather a specification (standard) of the parallel programming interface which each MPI implementation has to fulfill.

The implementations of the interface come as libraries of functions that can be invoked from user codes. Although the standard specifies Fortran/C bindings, many popular implementations support the use of C++. Because of the usefulness of the MPI paradigm, bindings are also available for other popular programming languages, like Python, R, Java, although they do not have the same level of support.

There are a number of open-source MPI implementations such as MPICH, LAM, OpenMPI etc., with varying degree of support for the standard versions. Commercial vendors like Intel, IBM, PGI, etc. also provide MPI implementations.

In general terms the idea of MPI is to offer a standard way of developing highly scalable parallel applications, using the message passing paradigm. Throughout the years the MPI standard has evolved offering relatively low-level access to advanced communications hardware. Two types of operations are available in MPI, collective and point-to-point. Although collective communications can be implemented with series of point-to-point communications, MPI implementations strive to achieve better performance using hardware features where such are available. They also allow for more concise and easy to read programs. As a first step towards understanding MPI, one can consider developing parallel applications using only the following functions:

- MPI_Init and MPI_Finalize for starting and finishing the parallel program;
- MPI_Send and MPI_Recv for sending and receiving messages.

Later-on one can add collective operations where it is suitable. One important issue for achieving acceptable parallel performance is to overlap communications and computations, which is usually done using non-blocking operations.

The most important hardware characteristics that determine the efficiency of parallel execution are bandwidth and latency. Consequently the parallel applications can be divided in two classes, bandwidth- and latency-sensitive.

1.3. Message Structures and MPI Data Types

An MPI message consists of useful data (payload) as well as envelope, which contains information about the source of the message, the destination, tag and communicator.

The tag is a way of marking different messages so that the target process can wait for messages with a specific tag. The communicator denotes a group of processes that participate jointly in collective operations. Communication between processes can be "blocking" or "non-blocking". Semantically the call to a blocking operation returns only after the operation is completed in the sense that the send buffer can be safely reused or the receive buffer is filled with valid data. The non-blocking calls may return before the communication is finished and the status of the operation should be checked with additional calls. While the use of non-blocking point-to-point operations is widespread, non-blocking versions of the collective operations became available in the newest versions of the MPI standard.

It should be noted that MPI standard is portable across different computer architectures and even at runtime it is possible to use machines with substantially different processor architectures, e.g., of different endianness. In such case MPI guarantees that data is correctly converted on-the-fly. The MPI data types are created to support such kind of portability. The correspondence between MPI data types and the C data types is shown below:

- MPI_INT - signed int.;
- MPI_UNSIGNED - unsigned int.;
- MPI_FLOAT - float;
- MPI_DOUBLE - double;
- MPI_CHAR - char.

There is a possibility for users to create their own types, combining the basic types, which is useful in order to aggregate several MPI operations into one. MPI operations are performed over arrays of basic or user-defined types. In order to maximize bandwidth utilization, one should strive to use larger messages.

2. Parallelization Strategies in Grid Environment

2.1. 'Conversion' of a Serial into a Parallel Algorithm

In most practical cases the application developers have an already developed sequential algorithm as a starting point and prefer to use the same algorithm for the parallel execution. The conversion of a serial into a parallel algorithm goes through several stages - planning, analysis and re-synthesis.

An important point during the planning stage is to decide on the acceptable trade-offs and the target systems for the parallel execution. Since the Grid is usually heterogeneous, it can be expected that the application will use only certain parts of the available Grid resources. Conceptually one can distinguish between parallel execution on one machine (frequently called "worker node"), one cluster or several clusters. The case of "one machine" is the simplest since the difference between executing on the developer's machine and the Grid worker node will come mainly from the hardware, plus the overhead of launching a Grid job. The precise hardware configuration of the target system can be obtained from the Grid information system. For example, on the EGI grid infrastructure [41] the information system has detailed information about CPU and RAM available through ldap queries.

The case of using a single cluster is perhaps the most common one and will be considered in detail. The case of combining multiple clusters is also important for large scale computing tasks, but it involves solving significant challenges. We shall consider the two main characteristics of the parallel system in this case: bandwidth and latency. The bandwidth in this case will be limited by the bandwidth of the WAN connection being used. It should be noted that a cluster with 1Gbps or 10Gbps Ethernet connection between the nodes may achieve acceptable parallel performance, especially when non-blocking switches are used, because the total amount aggregate bandwidth of the system is much more than the bandwidth of a single link. However, when two clusters are interconnected over WAN this connection becomes effectively a bottleneck and thus the algorithms should be aware of the network topology for maximum efficiency.

In terms of latency the situation is similar. Inside a cluster one can deploy advanced interconnects like Infiniband which offer latencies in the order of 1 microsecond, while using WAN connections. One has to take into account that messages may pass through several routers and switches in their way, plus the fact that messages cannot travel faster than the speed of light.

Users should also consider the possibility of saturation of the network link, which can lead to queuing of packages and even package loss, which is highly undesirable. Since it is natural to have different hardware configurations at the different Grid sites/clusters, the balanced distribution of the computational loads among them will be a non-trivial problem.

Based on these considerations, we can expect that most applications will be targeting either single worker node or single cluster on the Grid, reserving the case of multiple clusters for applications with much higher computational requirements.

Now we concentrate on the process of developing a Grid application that uses parallel execution. Initially we explain a simple way towards parallelising an algorithm.

Although some algorithms require advanced techniques to achieve efficient parallel version, there are many practical cases where this approach will be sufficient: Finding parts of the serial algorithm which can be executed in parallel, i.e., at the same time. This requires a thorough understanding of the initial algorithm functioning and rewriting the algorithm by using:

- Functional decomposition:Division of the problem in smaller chunks which can be executed (processed) in parallel;
- Data decomposition:Division of the data used by the algorithm in smaller chunks;

Frequently it is easier to perform data decomposition than functional decomposition; In any case one should be aware of any interdependency between the resulting tasks. The stages during the development of the programme (future application) are:

- Choice of programming paradigm;
- Choice of the hardware/ middleware environment;
- Communication harmonisation:Communication means and modes, communication frequency, synchronisation, communication overhead adaptation etc;
- External execution control;
- Debugging, optimisation;
- Application wrapping based on the developed programme, required libraries, starting scripts, etc.

2.2. Exploiting Parallelism on the Grid

There are various approaches for using parallel computing on the Grid environment. Apart from MPI one can use other inter-process communication libraries or one can use multithreading. With regards to multithreading one can use OS-agnostic or OS-specific libraries or rely on the OpenMP standard, which has rich features and it is supported by compilers and tools. Multithreading may be preferable on SMP systems [55], but is limited to a single machine. Apart from MPI there are other standards, tools and libraries that support inter-process communication between multiple machines. The Advanced Message Queuing Protocol [39] is an evolving standard with support from multiple vendors. Libraries like ZeroMQ [63] may also be used. Some technologies attempt to hide the fact that one is using multiple machines, providing single system image or unifying the memory of the distributed system.

Overall we discern several possibilities for running parallel applications on the Grid:

- Single-job, single-site parallel application;
- Single-job, multi-site parallel application;
- Single-job, parameter study application;
- Workflow application with single-site parallelism;
- Workflow application with multi-site parallelism;
- Parameter study at workflow level.

Parameter study application means an application which has to compute results over a set of input parameters. A workflow application is an application that has several stages that have dependencies between them.

2.2.1. Single-Job, Single-Site Parallel Application

Parallel Grid applications result either from parallelization of existing sequential code or creating from scratch a new parallel application. Because of the difficulty in debugging applications that run on the Grid one can use a local cluster for developing the application. If the access to local cluster is not available, a workstation can also be used, if the amount of memory is not a problem.

Obviously one has more freedom when creating a new parallel application, but in any case using the MPI standard is a good choice. Many developers find OpenMP to be easier to use, but this will limit the size of problems that can be solved mostly due to the amount of available RAM.

At this stage it is important to understand the memory requirements of the application - as a whole and per process so that these requirements can be fulfilled during Grid execution.

It is also necessary to perform some initial benchmarking in order to understand the optimal number of processes and worker nodes that should be requested.

Since usually Grid jobs are processed as batch jobs, i.e., they do not stream information back to the user, during development and testing one can use messaging technology, for example via AMQP [39] or ZeroMQ [63], in order to be able to observe in near real-time the progress of the job and collect some monitoring information.

2.2.2. Single-Job, Multi-Site Parallel Application

An MPI application can be executed on several Grid sites in a parallel way. There are different ways how to launch such an application. From the point of view of program logic, the parallel application is an ordinary MPI application. However, care should be taken to avoid cross-site communications as much as possible. Thus applications that run on multiple sites should be aware of the network topology and should be less latency sensitive. There are different combinations of middleware that can achieve the launch of such application. When the previous versions of the Globus Toolkit [43] were used as grid middleware, it was possible to launch using the MPICH-G2 software [51]. A more general way to launch such a cross-site job is to start an mpd daemon process (from the *MPICH2* or *Intel MPI* implementation) on one node with external connectivity and to make all nodes in the multi-site configuration to connect to it, joining the MPI ring. We should note that there were efforts to develop or use other protocols instead of TCP for MPI communication between different clusters. For example some implementations of MPI make it possible to use the SCTP protocol, which is message-oriented (like UDP) but also reliable and with congestion control (like TCP). We should note that use of protocols like SCTP may require administrator's assistance (for example, the standard deployment of Linux OS on the European Grid Infrastructure [41] did not enable SCTP protocol). For TCP-based MPI communication to work, one also has to take care of the firewall restrictions. Since usually incoming communication is possible in the port range 20000-25000, one should make sure that ports are opened only in this port range. Obviously, it will be hard to interconnect clusters that have worker nodes behind a NAT.

2.2.3. Single-Job, Parameter Study Application

One of the most promising ways of exploiting the large number of Grid resources is the use of parameter studies on the Grid. A parameter study is performed when the same code is executed with many different sets of parameters. Since the computations are independent, all these runs can be done simultaneously, exploiting different Grid resources. The code to be executed in the parameter study can be sequential or parallel on its own. In the latter case the grid broker should select only resources where the required number of processors is available (SMPs, clusters or supercomputers). There are many frameworks that help in launching, monitoring and gathering of the results of such applications. Examples are the DIANE framework [45], the GANGA framework [46], portals like P-GRADE which has become WS-PGRADE [60] etc.

2.2.4. Workflow Application with Single-Site Parallelism

Workflow applications can be considered as a combination of interdependent operations, which are represented by graphs, where the nodes of the graphs are jobs or Grid services and the directed arcs represent the job execution dependencies and/or the necessary file transfers among the component jobs. Workflow applications are used widely on the Grid since the different components (jobs) can be executed on different Grid sites.

Workflow applications enable the exploitation of parallelism at two levels:

- Inside a workflow node.

If a node of the workflow is a multi-threaded and/or MPI job, this job is assigned to a Grid site where the necessary number of processors is available. It is executed, using several available nodes/processors on the Grid site. In this way it uses intra-node (e.g., inside an SMP worker node) and/or intra-site (e.g., inside a cluster) parallelism.

- Among several workflow nodes.

If there is a parallel branch inside the workflow, then the nodes of the parallel branches can be executed in parallel at different Grid sites. This is often called inter-site (multi-cluster) parallelism. If the parallel branches contain multi-threaded and/or MPI jobs, then both intra-node/intra-site and inter-site parallelism can be exploited at the same time.

2.2.5. Workflow Application with Multi-Site Parallelism

If communication between sites is possible on a particular Grid, then multi-site parallelism of MPI nodes of the workflow is available, as described in 2.2.2. However, there are additional options when the workflow engine can orchestrate the simultaneous execution of several MPI applications that communicate through other protocols, for example using AMQP or ZeroMQ. Embarrassingly parallel applications can run with less modification in such a setting, while more complex applications need an extra layer at the top. An example of such application is optimization using genetic algorithms, which is described in [15]. The additional complexity of implementing this type of parallelism means that it should be used only if the size of the problems justifies the efforts.

2.2.6. Parameter Study at Workflow Level

As already mentioned, the parameter study approach is a very important class of Grid applications and hence it should be supported not only at the job level but also at the workflow level.

The simplest approach of supporting parameter studies at the workflow level is based on the "black box" execution semantics. It means that we consider a workflow as a black box that should be executed with many different parameter sets.

2.3. Use of Grid Services to Speed-up Job Execution

One of the problems that we have not discussed before is the scheduling of parallel jobs. If a parallel job is created out of a combination of single-CPU job, e.g., by having the single-CPU jobs launch a process that joins the MPI ring, we may have to wait until sufficient number of processes have joined. If a parallel job is started as one job in the batch queue, we have to consider that it may have to wait until sufficient number of free resources are found. This waiting time may effectively destroy the advantage of an MPI job versus a single processor job. That is why services are developed that allow for smoother execution of parallel jobs in Grid environment. For example, the Job Track Service (JTS) [6] is a new Grid service for administration of user reservations, which manages requests for reservations from users automatically, in order to ensure that a parallel job will have resources ready when it is submitted.The service tries to ensure adequate priorities and faster start of the users"jobs. The users of the Grid are authenticated with their voms proxy [59] certificates and request in advance Grid resources and manage these reservations. The service provides Quality of Service in the Grid infrastructure, which is otherwise unavailable, since Grid usage is mostly opportunistic. The service was tested on the regional Grid infrastructure in South Eastern Europe, used by several Grid applications with high resource requirements.

The service is based on the messaging paradigm and uses standard protocols like AMQP (Advanced Message Queuing Protocol) [39] and XMPP (eXtensible Messaging and Presence Protocol) [62] for real-time communication, while its security model is based on GSI authentication with voms proxies [59]. It enables resource owners to provide the most popular types of Quality of Service (QoS) of execution to some of their users, using a standardized model.

In the next subsections we describe in detail the architecture of this service and its main features and advantages. Examples from real-life use of the service by parallel applications are provided.

2.3.1. Motivation for Development of JTS

The idea to develop the *Job Track Service* (JTS) comes from experience in operating or using Grid clusters from the Grid infrastructures, offered by the Enabling Grids for E-SciencE

(EGEE) and SEE-GRID infrastructures [54]. Currently, these two grid infrastructures form the European Grid Infrastructure (EGI) [41, 44]. In these types of Grid infrastructures the jobs are sent to Grid clusters (also called Grid sites) through a Computing Element (CE), which is a standard Grid service that contrls the access to a batch queuing system, which in turn controls the access to the Worker Nodes (WN). In large percentage of the clusters the batch system is torque [58] and the jobs are scheduled at the site level using the maui scheduler [48]. Both torqueand mauiare open source products, developed by Cluster Resources, Inc. At the highest level in these Grid infrastructures, the scheduling is performed by a so-called Workload Management System (WMS), which distributes the jobs towards Computing Elements following the resource requirements, imposed by the user. The predominant types of jobs that run on these clusters are sequential jobs, especially those sent from Virtual Organizations (VOs) related to the LHC experiment at CERN [47]. Some virtual organizations, related to bioinformatics or Earth Science, submit also MPI jobs.

In this situation it is usually the case that the series of sequential jobs take over the clusters and prevent MPI jobs from running, especially when the required number of processors of the MPI job is high with respect to the total number of CPUs in the cluster. Considering the fact that some of the CERN-related jobs can take a few days to complete, it is understandable that parallel jobs may be locked out. It is hard for system administrators to take measures against such situations, since they risk the under-utilization of the equipment. In this way the high waiting time becomes the main source of MPI job failures and results in user dissatisfaction with the service. These issues are studied in more detail in [29]. The performance of the regional Grid infrastructure has been studied also in [23]. Different methodologies are used in [22].

An interesting comparison that underlines the point about losing the benefit of parallel execution in case of high waiting times can be seen in [34]. Our test cases were problem instances from environmental modeling and prediction, where a typical job involves at least 8 CPUs with an optimal number of allocated CPUs either 16 or 32.

These works motivated the search for an interface that could allow a user to request certain number of CPUs for a period of time or to dynamically adjust the Quality of Service (QoS) for his or her jobs, depending on the membership and roles in the VOs. The availability of dedicated resources greatly enhances the user experience, particularly during development or testing of Grid applications. This is especially important if an application is being developed directly on the Grid, when researchers do not have local resources of the same size.

For example, in order to verify a certain model one may need to execute several hundred jobs, each one using approximately 8 hours on 8 CPU cores. This can be done on a powerful Grid cluster of medium size in a few days, while it will take a month on a small local cluster.

The principles of the Grid architecture are outlined in [12, 14] while in [1, 30, 38] we can see other approaches at ensuring QoS in Grid context.

The main advantage of using this service is that the mauiconfiguration is updated dynamically, based on the limitations specified by administrators, thus relieving them of the need to make frequent manual adjustments. Taking into account our experience and application requirementswe developed a Grid service which allows the users to perform advanced reservations and manage Quality of Service for their jobsin our particular Grid environment, thus relieving site administrators from the task of monitoringand adjusting the maui configuration in order to achieve good overall result. In the next sections we describe in detail the architecture of the service and its features and advantages.

2.3.2. Architecture of the JTS

The service is based on exchange of messages, based on the developing standard in messaging middleware called Advanced Message Queuing Protocol (AMQP). More information about this protocol can be obtained from [39]. This protocol is still under active development. We should note that version 1.0 is substantially different from the 0.8 version, upon which we based our work. We choose the RabitMQ [53] implementation because of its interoperability and robustness. It is written in the Erlang programming language [40] which has certain features that enable load balancing and fault tolerance.

There are well known examples of Erlang applications that achieve exceptionally high availability and we believe basing the Grid services onsuch foundation can be beneficial in the long run. In [10] one can see how services written in Erlang may be enhanced with Grid authentication/authorization. The RabbitMQ messaging broker has a module which can interoperate with instant messaging clients using the XMPP protocol. This protocol is used by the Jabber services and also by GoogleTalk/Gmail applications.

In our previous work [5] we have used the RabbitMQbroker to organize reliable execution of job workflows and to communicate progress reports back to the user. Our experience was positive and we concluded that interfacing with the broker is a relatively straightforward process.

In this way we put at the core of our architecture a RabbitMQ broker (collocated with JTS server on Figure 1). The Computing Elements connect with the Broker and register their corresponding queues. The clients connect with the broker on behalf of the user and interact with the Computing Elements via messages. The messages are always signed and encrypted using the corresponding keys and both parties authenticate following the usual scheme in the gLite middleware [42].

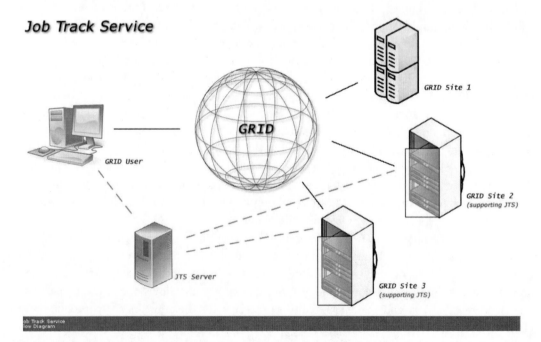

Figure 1. JTS working scheme.

There is a certain freedom in the development of clients for the service and we will see later more information about our implementations. When developing the service that is to be deployed on the Computing Elements, we tested to make sure it does not interfere with the components that are already working there.

In our experience the main sources of failures of the Computing Elements deployed in the regional South Eastern Grid infrastructure is the high CPU load and/or batch system instability. Taking into account that there are two supported client software stacks for access to the RabbitMQ broker - one in Java andone in C#, we decided to investigate the use of the C# bindings via the Mono open source framework [50]. We also considered the possible ways to store information about requests that are being handled. Since they are persistent across possible restarts of the Computing Element, we added a lightweight database back-end to the service, based on SQLite [57]. The requests to the service are divided in two categories. The requests of the first category require certain number of working nodes for a given period of time.The requests of the second category change the default QoS for the user for a defined period of time into one of several possibilities.

Three grid-wide QoS types are defined: high, low and bonus. The precise meaning of these QoS are not yet established, thus administrators are free to map these names into local names, which they implement as they see appropriate.

It is expected that jobs with high priority will have faster start-up, while jobs with low priority will have slower start-up and users may tolerate larger delays. The bonus jobs are those where the users can tolerate job failures. Such jobs allow the administrators to give priority to other jobs by preempting the execution of the bonus jobs. In return for that the users expect better overall throughput.

The requests are processed by the server following the local policy. We use an xml file for storing policy information. Three levels of granularity are defined - user, VO and total. For each user or virtual organization the site administrator describes the kinds of QoS that are allowed for them, as well as the number of Worker Nodes that they can pre-allocate. It is also possible to set a limit on the total number of Worker Nodes that can be allocated.

If a request is granted following the policy a reply is sent to the user and corresponding entries are inserted in the database.

If the request is about reserving worker nodes, a connection with the maui scheduler is performed and corresponding command is issued.

In order to achieve that, we follow the maui socket protocol, described in [48]. The JTS component does not have to run with root privileges, but only to use the appropriate key for authentication. In the other case, when the user specifies a QoS, the server first maps the grid-wide QoS (currently high, low, bonus) into a locally defined QoS name, following the local policy. A record in the database is inserted, setting the default QoS for this user. The actual change happens when the jobs from the user arrive. All user jobs pass through the so-called torque submit filter. This filter is usually a perl script specified in the torque configuration file. In our case we added a connection with the database to check if there is a record for that user. If there is such record and it is valid for this point in time, the QoS for the job is changed and then the job proceeds to submission. Reports about success/failures of the QoS requests are sent back to the core JTS server via AMQP messages.

Our experience with this architecture of the server at the Computing Element is positive and we believe that such modifications to Grid services are necessary when there is substantial number of MPI jobs.

The clients for the service need to use AMQP and to be able to perform a rather minimal set of tasks, like submission of requests and reception of acceptance/rejection messages. We found out that the C# bindings provided by RabbitMQ can be used to write a GUI client, that supports all the features that we require and hasa nice look due to use of wxWidgets library [61]. A screenshot of the client can be seen in Figure 2.

In this way we obtain an executable file that can be used in Linux as well as Windows, since *wxWidgets* and *Mono* have versions for both platforms and thus the executable works without modification. A command line client which may be more usable in some situations (for instance for writing scripts) has been implemented in Python. In this way we have implemented a Grid service providing useful functionality and providing appropriate interfaces for use by users and applications, while remaining extendable in the sense that more clients and new types of requests can be added.

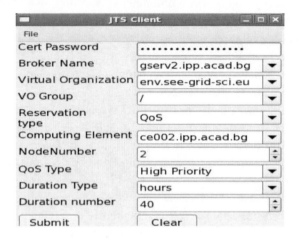

Figure 2. JTS client user interface.

2.3.3. Initial Experiences

The service has been tested initially on several Bulgarian Grid sites, which are part of the European and regional production Grid infrastructures [41, 54] serving more than 15 different virtual organizations. These sites are typical medium size Grid clusters, as follows:

- BG01-IPP - heterogeneous site with 576 CPUs;
- BG03-NGCC - homogeneous site with 200 CPUs;
- BG04-ACAD - homogeneous site with 80 CPUs.

All of these clusters have Worker Nodes with Intel Xeon or AMD CPUs and have deployed gLite middleware [42].

The current set of features is a result of taking into account user's experience with the beta versions. It is notable that the running of this service did not interfere with the availability and reliability of the Computing Elements.

For example, the BG01-IPP grid site is frequently rated in the top ten reliable sites and it achieved 99% reliability and availability [49]. The service has been enabled for use by members of the *env.see-grid-sci.eu* Virtual Organization and it greatly improved their perception of the Grid.

For this Virtual Organization the parallel multi-CPU jobs are the norm, with medium number of nodes used equal to 8. Using the JTS service users from this VO take over several worker nodes in a Grid site and use them until they complete a given simulation. It has also been used to fill-up the gaps that happen because of allowing certain jobs from another virtual organization (*meteo.see-grid-sci.eu*) to run at a given time period for 2 hours each day. For the site administrators the benefit was mostly in the improved utilization of the site and reduced administrative burden of dealing with users' requests and complaints.

Overall we believe that our goals to achieve certain functionality without adding heavyweight deployment requirements have been successfully attained.

2.3.4. Further Considerations

We believe that such services that improve the observed behaviour of the Grid infrastructure when launching parallel jobs can be of benefit to users, while having little impact on overall operations of the clusters. Depending on user demand, they can be enhanced with more collaborative features, enabling users to share reservations.

3. SALUTE: MPI Grid Application

We have chosen to present an application that uses Monte Carlo methods as this type of applications are very popular in grid environment.

Monte Carlo (MC) methods are based on the simulation of stochastic processes, whose expected values, are equal to quantities of interest. MC methods are constructed naturally when a physical process is being modeled, for example when considering evolution of dynamical systems. There are wide classes of problems where MC methods are the only known computational methods of solution. MC methods form the computational foundation for many fields of science and engineering including transport theory, quantum physics, computational chemistry, finance, etc.

Here we describe a Grid application, which solves a computationally intensive problem arising from semiconductor physics. The underlying stochastic algorithms are of Monte Carlo type. The application is called SALUTE (Stochastic Algorithms for Ultrafast Electron Transport) for simplicity.

When using MC method, a set of computational random numbers has to be generated and used to statistically estimate a quantity of interest. The probabilistic convergence rate is known to be approximately $O(N^{-1/2})$, where N is the number of computed random samples (random walks). A serious drawback of MC methods is that achieving higher accuracy is increasingly harder due to the slow rate of convergence. Many methods and techniques have been developed with the aim to accelerate the convergence rate of the MC methods. Variance reduction methods, like antithetic varieties, stratification and importance sampling [20], reduce the variance, which is a quantity that measures the probabilistic uncertainty. Another way to improve the convergence is to use quasi-random sequences instead of pseudo random. While pseudo random numbers are constructed to imitate the behavior of the truly random numbers, quasi-random sequences are deterministic and constructed to be as uniform as possible at the cost of correlation. The quality of the distribution of quasi-random numbers is measured with quantities that are defined in different ways. The most popular such measure is the discrepancy, which is why we are speaking of low-discrepancy sequences.

Parallelism is an alternative way to achieve the results of a MC computation faster. If n processors execute an independent copies of a MC computation, the accumulated result will have a variance n times smaller than that of a single copy. Due to the nature of MC methods, it is appropriate to have as many executions as possible to reduce the overall statistical error. On the other hand, for a distributed MC application: once a distributed task starts it can usually be executed independently with almost no inter-process communications. Due to this natural parallelism it may happen that an MC algorithm is preferable than a deterministic algorithm with faster convergence by worse parallelism. The subsequent growth of computing power, especially that of the parallel computers and distributed systems, allowed for distributed MC applications to carry out more and more ambitious calculations [24, 27]. Actually, many MC applications and software packages in science and engineering, for example, CHARMM [11] for macromolecular dynamics simulation implemented using MPI, PMC [36, 37] for nuclear physics simulation on Livermore Message Passing System, and MESYST for simulation of 3D tracer dispersion in atmosphere, have already taken advantage of the power of parallel systems to achieve a more accurate description of the problem or better performance of the computations.

In order to implement correctly the principle of parallel execution of MC computations, it is necessary to use independent random number streams in each subtask. The main techniques used in parallel random number generators to distribute sequentially generated random number sequences among different processors include sequence splitting and leapfrog. One problem with the sequence splitting and leapfrog techniques is that one must either assume that the number of nodes is fixed or at least bounded which will prevent the use of dynamically scaling distributed MC computations. Another way to generate parallel random number sequences is to produce independent sequences by parameterizing the pseudo random generators in an appropriate way [26]. The SPRNG (Scalable Parallel Random Number Generators) library [56] is designed to use parameterized pseudo random generators to provide independent random streams. Some generators in SPRNG can generate up to $2^{31}-1$ independent random number streams with sufficiently long periods and good quality[56]. These generators meet the requirements of most grid-based MC applications.

The intrinsically parallel aspect of MC applications makes them an ideal fit for the grid-computing paradigm. In general, grid-based MC applications can divide the MC task into a number of subtasks and utilize the grid''s scheduling services to dispatch these independent subtasks to different nodes [25]. We should point out that the same Grid environment may offer different ways to access the computational resources, for example, directly choosing the target clusters or leaving the choice to the grid scheduler services. The grid connectivity services provide communications options when two grid nodes need to communicate. The execution of a subtask takes advantage of the storage services of the grid to store intermediate results or to store each subtask''s final or partial result. When the subtasks are completed, a collection service may be used to gather the results and generate the final result of the entire computation.

The inherent characteristics of MC applications motivate the use of grid computing to effectively perform large-scale MC computations. Furthermore, within this MC grid-computing paradigm, we can use the statistical nature of MC computations and the cryptographic aspects of random numbers to reduce wall clock time and to enforce the trustworthiness of the computation.

We should point out that MC algorithms that are based on independent trajectories are resilient to failures, which is a desirable property in the Grid environment, since various types of failures may happen.

3.1. Description of the Application SALUTE

Many problems of interest in transport theory and related areas can be cast as a Fredholm integral equation of the second kind. It is instructive to rewrite such an equation as:

$$f = K f + \varphi,$$

where K is an integral operator, and f, φ are functions in a Banach space of integrable functions.

We present the integral equation in a form that shows the explicit appearance of application of the kernel, K, as a linear operator. Monte Carlo methods are merely probabilistic ways of applying linear operators. With suitable K's the formal solution of the equation is presented as a Neumann series. With MC methods the conventional integral equations problems are to calculate linear functional of the solution of the form:

$$J(f) = \int_D h(x) f(x) dx = (h, f),$$

with $h(x)$ a given function. In order to develop a Monte Carlo method for this problem one has to define a suitable random variable, whose mathematical expectation is equal to the solution, to determine appropriate initial and transition probability densities (usually, using the kernel of the integral operator with some transformations) for the chosen random process, to apply one or more variance reduction techniques to reduce the statistical error, and, finally, to ensure the accumulation in the appropriate statistical estimator.

The development and application of the MC methods for simulation of quantum transport processes in semiconductors and semiconductor devices has been initiated with works like [13, 19]. The stochastic approach relies on the numerical MC theory applied to the integral form of the generalized electron-phonon Wigner equation. The evolution at such a time scale cannot be described in terms of the Boltzmann transport and therefore a quantum description is needed [31]. The importance of active investigations in this field is underlined by the fact that nowadays nanotechnology uses devices and structures where the carrier transport occurs at nanometer and femtosecond scales.

A Wigner equation for the nanometer and femtosecond transport regime has been derived from a three equations set model based on the generalized Wigner function [32]. The full version of the equation poses serious numerical challenges. A simplified version of the equation (in the homogeneous case: the Levinson or Barker-Ferry equation, [16, 17]) is analyzed using SALUTE. The physical model describes a femtosecond relaxation process of optically excited electrons which interact with phonons in single-band semiconductor. The interaction with phonons is switched on after a laser pulse creates an initial electron distribution (results are shown in Figure 3).

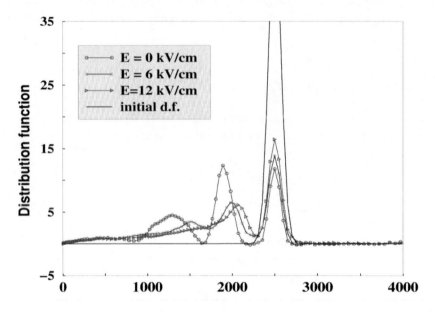

Figure 3. Intracollisional field effect in GaAs. MC solutions $|k|f(0,k_z,t)$ versus $|k|^2 10^{14}$ m^{-2}, at positive direction on the z-axis and different values of the electric field E. The evolution time t is 300 fs and the number of the random walks per point is N=24 millions.

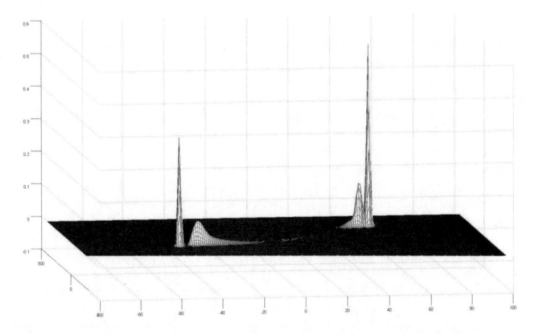

Figure 4. Evolution of optically generated distribution of electrons in a quantum wire. The Wigner function solution at 180 fs presented in the plane z × k_z. The electric field is 15 kW/cm along to the nanowire. The number of the random walks per point is N=10 millions.

Another version of the Wigner equation considers inhomogeneous case when the electron-phonon interaction described on the quantum-kinetic level depends on the energy and space coordinates [18, 33]. The problem is relevant, e.g., for description of the ultrafast dynamics of optically generated carriers. Particularly we consider a quantum wire, where the carriers are confined in the plane normal to the wire by infinite potentials. Here we assume a Gaussian initial condition both in energy and space coordinates and allow for an electric field to be applied along the wire. The MC methods can be used successfully for solving this limit case of the equation. The obtained simulation results over Grid characterize the space and energy dependence of the evolution time (Figure 4).

The SALUTE application integrates a set of Monte Carlo algorithms for simulation of ultra-fast carrier transport in semiconductors considered in above mentioned versions of the Wigner equation. A detailed description of the algorithms can be found in [7, 17, 18]. Since development of grid-specific features of an application requires certain programming effort, it is important to be able to re-use parts of the code-base for different tasks.

In all cases we explore the regime of early time evolution of the initially excited electrons. Experimentally, such processes can be investigated by using ultra-fast spectroscopy, where the relaxation of electrons is explored during the first hundreds femtoseconds after the optical excitation.

In our model we consider a low-density regime, where the interaction with phonons dominates the carrier-carrier interaction. Two cases are studied using SALUTE: electron evolution in presence and in absence of electric field. Innovative results for GaAs /gallium arsenide/ material parameters are obtained using the BG01-IPP grid site. The intracollisional field effect is clearly demonstrated as an effective change of the phonon energy, which depends on the field direction and the evolution time (see Figure 4).

The numerical results discussed in Figures 3-4 are obtained for zero temperature and GaAs material parameters: the electron effective mass is 0.063, the optimal phonon energy is 36meV, the static and optical dielectric constants are ε_s = 10.92 and ε_∞ =12.9. The initial condition at t=0 is given by a function which is Gaussian in energy, scaled in a way to ensure, that the peak value is equal to unity. The initial condition is a product of two Gaussian distributions of the energy and space. The k^2_z distribution corresponds to a generating laser pulse with an excess energy of about 150 meV. The z distribution is centered around zero. The side of the wire is chosen to be 10 nanometers. The values of the Wigner function f(z, k_z, t) are estimated in a rectangular domain (-Q_1,Q_1) x (-Q_2,Q_2), where Q_1 =400x10^9 m^{-1} and Q_2 =66x10^7 m^{-1} consisting of 800×260 points. The stochastic error for this case is relatively large. The relative mean squared error is in order of 10^{-3}.

3.2. Grid Implementation

SALUTE solves an NP-hard problem concerning the evolution time, since the complexity is superexponential. On the other hand, SALUTE consists of Monte Carlo algorithms which are inherently parallel. Thus, SALUTE is a very good candidate for grid clusters with MPI support [2, 3, 4,9, 21].

It is proved [16, 17] that the stochastic error has order O($e^{ct}/N^{1/2}$), where t is the evolution time, N is the number of samples of the MC estimator, and c is a constant depending on the kernels of the quantum kinetic equations. This estimate shows that when t is fixed and N $\rightarrow \infty$

the error decreases, but for N fixed and t large the factor for the error is prohibitive. That is why the problem of estimating the electron energy distribution function for long evolution times with small stochastic error requires combining both MC variance reduction techniques and distributed or parallel computations.

By using the grid environment supported by the gLite middleware, we were able to reduce the computing time of Monte Carlo simulations of ultra-fast carrier transport in semiconductors. The simulations are parallelized on the Grid by splitting the underlying random number sequences.

Successful tests of the application were performed at the Bulgarian grid sites using the Resource Broker (WMS). The MPI implementation was MPICH 1.2.6, and the execution is controlled from the Computing Element via the Torque batch system.

These initial tests were performed when the sizes of grid clusters were rather small. However, they already show some limitations, e.g., the sites must have MPI support enabled and the jobs may spend time in the queue waiting for enough resources to be acquired. On the other hand, it is difficult to predict what number of CPUs should be requested, since the grid information system does not provide directly information on MPI job with what size will start immediately.

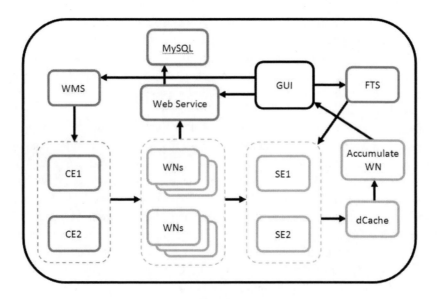

Figure 5. Grid implementation scheme for SALUTE.

Grid Implementation Scheme (Figure 5):

- On the User Interface (UI) computer the scientist launches the Graphical User Interface (GUI) of the application. The job submission, monitoring and analysis of the results is controlled from there. The GUI is written using PyQt, pyopengl and the python bindings for the grid functions (mainly the wmproxymethods module provided by gLite).

- The Web Service computer (WS) provides a grid-enabled secure gateway to the MySQL database, so that no direct mysql commands are ever run by the user or from inside the grid jobs.

- The AMGA (ARDA Metadata Catalog) is used to hold metadata information about the results obtained so far by the user – for example input parameters, number of jobs executed, execution date etc.
- The user selects input parameters and queries the AMGA server to find if data for these parameters are already present or not.
- If a new run is necessary, the user submits request to the WS computer for calculation.
- The user also selects from the GUI the sites that will run the jobs, and how many jobs to be sent to every site. The purpose of this step is to eliminate any known "bad sites", where jobs are simply lost. From the GUI the jobs are sent to the Workload Management System (WMS) and information about them is stored at the MySQL database via WS invocation.
- The WMS sends the job to the selected sites.
- When the job starts, it downloads the executable, which implements the Monte Carlo algorithm, from the dCache storage element. The executable is responsible for obtaining the input parameters from the WS, performing the computations and storing the results in the local Storage Element, which may be of any type. After finishing the store operation, it calls the WS computer in order to register the output and the fact that the run was successful.
- The jobs are monitored from a monitoring thread, started from the GUI, and information about their progress is displayed to the user.
- Another thread run from the GUI is responsible for collecting the output results from the various Storage Elements to the local dCache server. For each output file a request for transfer is sent to the File Transfer Service (FTS) computer.
- The FTS is used in order to limit the number of files that are transferred simultaneously, because of the limited bandwidth available. In this way we also avoid some scalability limitations of the middleware and we try not to overload the Storage Elements. This approach is efficient, because in most cases it will not lead to increase of the total time necessary for completing all transfers, since they compete for the same network resource. Additional benefit of the FTS is that it provides reliable transfer of the files, by retrying the transfers if necessary. This step may be omitted, if the sizes of output files are relatively small or alternative options may be used. For example, the Globus Toolkit provides other means for reliable file transfer.
- After a file has been transferred to the dCache, it is registered in the MySQL database (by WS invocation).
- A special computational job is run at a local WN and it is responsible for gradual accumulation of the outputs of all jobs into one final result. It checks the MySQL database for new results and if they are available at the dCache server, it retrieves them locally and performs the accumulation. At regular intervals the accumulated results are registered to the dCache and made available for the user.
- The User can see how the results accumulate in a window, part of the GUI, and thus decide if perhaps more computations are necessary in order to achieve the desired accuracy. In such case more jobs can be launched.

We utilized several programming languages and technologies: Java and tomcat for the web services, mysql as a database back end, python with the Qt and OpenGL bindings for the GUI, MPI for parallel execution, SPRNG for the random number generation, etc.

This implementation scheme (Figure 5) offers several important advantages:

- Easy to use Graphical User Interface (Figure 6);
- Avoids duplication of effort and fosters collaboration between people, interested in the same problem via the registration of results in the metadata catalog;
- Uses the new improved Application programming interfaces, offered by the gLite middleware;
- Uses powerful yet easy to understand scripting language (python) for the GUI, which simplifies further developments;
- Uses efficient C language code for the heavy computations;
- Fast deployment of the GUI via virtual machines;
- Control of storage and bandwidth utilization via the FTS;
- Fault-tolerance - aborted tasks do not present a problem for achieving the final results.

Figure 7 shows how the number of jobs successfully executed on the grid increases with time, when the new scheme was used for submission of 420 jobs.

Because of the nature of Monte Carlo computations it is not necessary for the user to wait until all jobs are completed. In such case the user can cancel the unnecessary jobs. Normally, the execution times of the jobs at the different sites are similar, and the delay in starting is caused by lack of free Worker Nodes. Thus our new scheme allows the user to achieve the maximum possible throughput.

The SALUTE grid implementation scheme makes heavy use of many different kinds of grid services for solving important scientific problems. In this way bottlenecks and problems of the infrastructure can be revealed and investigated. Because of the fault-tolerance of the scheme these problems are not critical for achieving the desired results.

Alternative schemes for performing such kinds of computations were also developed. The use of AMQP also proved to be effective, simplifying some of the steps, due to the queuing features in the AMQP.

3.3. Implementation Using Hyperthreading and GPUs

We should point out that different kinds of organizations of MPI-enabled Grid clusters are possible. A cluster that is based on Intel CPUs can have the hyperthreading feature enabled or disabled. Since usually enabling hyperthreading does not yield 100% improvement, applications should be carefully tested wether they benefit at all and how they should be launched. In the gLite middleware there is the option to request full worker nodesthrough the wholenodes=yes option. In such case the user can decide how to optimally use the hardware. For example, if there is no benefit from hyperthreading, one can launch with less parallel processes than the number of available logical CPUs.

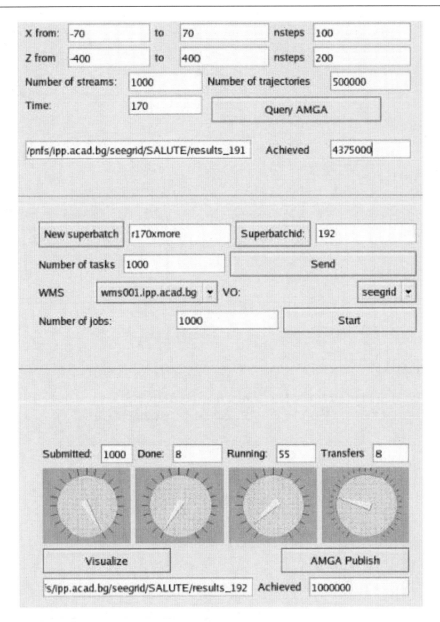

Figure 6. Graphical User Interface (GUI) for submission and monitoring of SALUTE jobs, and accumulation and visualization of their results.

For our test cluster we also measured the performance of the parallel SALUTE code with and without hyperthreading. It is well known that hyperthreading does not always improve the overall speed of calculations, because the floating point units of the processor are shared between the threads and thus if the code is highly intensive in such computations, there is no gain to be made from hyperthreading. Our experience with other applications yields such examples. But for the SALUTE application we found about 30% improvement when hyperthreading is turned on (see Table 1), which should be considered a good result and also shows that our overall code is efficient in the sense that most of it is now floating point computations, unlike some earlier version where the gain from hyperthreading was larger.

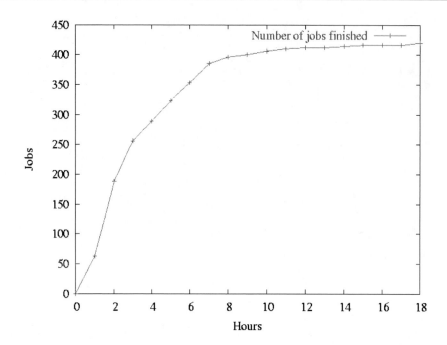

Figure 7. Progress in number of jobs completed after submission of 420 jobs to 21 SEE-GRID sites.

Table 1. CPU times for all 800 × 260 points, the speed-up, and the parallel efficiency for SALUTE execution on MPI-enabled Grid site (BG01-IPP)

Blades/Cores	CPU Time (s)	Speed-up	Parallel Efficiency
1 x 8 = 8	202300	-	-
4 x 8 = 32	50659	3.9937	0.99834
8 x 8 = 64	25423	7.9574	0.99467
16 x 8 = 128	12735	15.8853	0.99283

Blades/Cores/ Hyperthreading	CPU Time (s)	Speed-up	Parallel Efficiency
1 x 8 x 2 = 16	148602	-	-
4 x 8 x 2 = 64	37660	3.94588	0.98647
8 x 8 x 2 =128	18957	7.83889	0.97986
16 x 8 x 2 =256	9552	15.55716	0.97232

The GPGPU computing uses powerful graphics cards for power and cost efficient computations. State-of-the-art graphics cards have large number (even thousands) of cores. For NVIDIA cards one can use CUDA for parallel computations. Parallel processing on such cards is based upon splitting the computations between grid of threads. We use thread size of 256, which is optimal taking into account relatively large number of registers. Generators for the scrambled Sobol sequence and modified Halton sequences have been developed and tested [8, 9]. For Monte Carlo simulation we use CURAND generator. On the grid the use of

GPUs is still not fully supported, but one may first find GPU enabled resources, through the information system, and then launch parallel MPI jobs that request whole worker nodes and then discover and use the GPGPU devices available.

Here we present some results using NVIDIA CUDA version 4. Main target system: two servers HP ProLiant SL390s G7:

- 2 Intel(R) Xeon(R) CPU E5649@ 2.53GHz;
- 96 GB RAM;
- With 16 NVIDIA Tesla M2090cards.

The properties of the M2090 GPU device (Fermi):
- 6 GB GDDR5 ECC RAM, 177 GB/s memory bandwidth;
- 512 GPU threads;
- 665 Gflops in double precision/1331 Gflops in single precision.

Our codes work on devices with support for double precision (devices with capabilities 1.3 and 2.0 used). Observations from running the GPGPU-based version.

- Threadsize of 256 seems optimal;
- Significant number of divergent warps due to logical operators;

Timing results for solving the problem with electric field, for 180 fs, and using same discretization as above show that it takes 67701 seconds on one NVIDIA M2090 card, which means that one card's performance is comparable to that of 3 blades with hyperthreading turned off. We believe that this result can be improved, because there could be some warp divergence due to logical statements in the code. This issue can be mitigated by changes in the way the samples are computed by the threads to make sure that the divergence is limited. We also tested the algorithm when running on several GPU cards in parallel. When 6 Nvidia M2090 cards from the same server were used to compute 107 trajectories, we obtained about 93 % parallel efficiency, achieving better performance than 16 blades of the cluster without hyperthreading and slightly slower than 16 blades with hyperthreading enabled. For such relatively small number of trajectories, the main source of inefficiency is the time spent in the cudaSetDevice call in the beginning of the computations.

Although the advanced kinds of processors like GPGPU devices or Intel Xeon Phi are gradually entering in the Grid environment, we believe that the substantial savings in energy and cost will make them ever more popular.

Conclusion

The Grid environment is a powerful way of aggregating heterogeneous computational resources. There are various strategies for parallel execution and the concrete choice should be made depending on the performance requirements of the application, taking into account practical constraints like the desirable start-up time and requirements for reproducibility or robustness, that should be decided beforehand. The Grids interconnect heterogeneous resources and increasingly adopt modern energy-efficient computing technologies like GPGPU computing and Many Integrated Cores, which motivates the further evolution of the tools, techniques and algorithms.

Acknowledgments

This work was supported by the Bulgarian NSF through grantDVCP02/1 CoE Supper CA++andproject „Development and Investigation of quasi-Monte Carlo Algorithms for Extreme Parallel Computer Systems"(reg. number FNI I-02/48).

References

[1] Al-Ali, R., von Laszewski, G., Amin, K., Hategan, M., Rana, O., Walker, D., Zaluzec, N., (2004). QoS support for high-performance scientific Grid applications, *4th IEEE/ACM International Symposium on Cluster Computing and the Grid,* CCGrid2004, Chicago, Illinois, pp.134-143, http://www.informatik.uni-trier.de/~ley/db/conf/ccgrid/ ccgrid2004.html.

[2] Atanassov, E., Gurov, T., Karaivanova, A., Nedjalkov, M., (2005). *SALUTE: An MPI-GRID Application.* In: Proceeding of the 28th International convention MIPRO 2005, pp. 259-262.

[3] Atanassov, A., Georgieva, R., Gurov, T., Ivanovska, S., Karaivanova, A., Nedjalkov, M., (2007). New algorithms in the Grid Application SALUTE. In: *Proceedings 30thInternational Convention MIPRO 2007, Conference on Hypermedia and Grid Systems,*Opatija, Croatia, May 21–25, pp. 217-222.

[4] Atanassov, E., Gurov, T., Karaivanova, A., (2008).Ultra-fast semiconductor carrier transport simulation on the grid, LSSC 2007, *LNCS* 4818, Springer-Verlag-Berlin-Heidelberg, pp. 461-469.

[5] Atanassov, E., Dimitrov, D. Sl., T. Gurov, T., (2009). SALUTE Grid Application using Massage-Oriented Middleware, *AIP Proc. 1st AMiTaNS'09,* Volume 1186, pp. 183-191.

[6] Atanassov E., Gurov T., Dimitrov D.Sl., *Job Track Service: Architecture and Features,* SEE-GRID-SCI User Forum, 6-11 December 2009, Istanbul, Turkey, pp. 199-202, ISBN: 978-975-403-510-0.

[7] Atanassov, E., Gurov, T., Karaivanova, A., Nedjalkov, M., Vasileska, D., Raleva, K., (2009). Electron-phonon interaction in nanowires: A Monte Carlo study of the effect of the field, *Mathematics and Computers in Simulation,* No: 81, pp. 515-521, 2010, ISSN0378-4754.

[8] Atanassov, E., Karaivanova, A., Gurov, T., Ivanovska S., Durchova M., (2009).*Using Sobol Sequence in Grid Environment,*MIPRO/GVS 2009, ISBN978-953-233-044-1, pp. 290-294.

[9] Atanassov, E., Karaivanova, A., Gurov, T., (2010), Quasi-random approach in the Grid application SALUTE, *Springer LNCS Volume 6068,* Springer-Verlag, pp. 204-213, 2010. ISSN0302-9743.

[10] Atanassov, E., (2013). Development of Grid Services using Erlang, *Proceedings of CSIT2013 Conference,* Yerevan, Armenia, Sept. 23-27, 2013, pp. 286-289.

[11] Brooks, B.R., Bruccoleri, R.E., Olafson, B.D., States, D.J., Swaminathan, S., Karplus, M., (1983). CHARMM: A Program for Macromolecular Energy, Minimization, and Dynamic Calculations, *J. Comp. Chem.*, 4, pp. 187-217.

[12] Czajkowski, K., Fitzgerald, S., Foster, I., Kesselman, C., (2001). Grid Information Services for Distributed Resource Sharing, *Proceedings of the Tenth IEEE International Symposium on High-Performance Distributed Computing*, IEEE publisher, pp. 181-194.

[13] Fischetti, M.V., Laux, S.E., (1988). Monte Carlo Analysis of Electron Transport in Small Semiconductor Devices Including Band-Structure and Space-Charge Effects. *Phys. Rev. B* 38, 9721-9745.

[14] Foster, I., Kesselman, C., (2004). *The grid: blueprint for a new computing infrastructure,* Second Edition, Morgan Kaufmann, pp. 31-32.

[15] Georgiev, D., Atanassov, E., Extensible Framework for Execution of Distributed Genetic Algorithms on Grid Clusters, MIPRO 2014/DC-VIS, *Proceedings of the 37thInternational Convention,* IEEE, pp. 316-321, May, 2014, ISSN: 1847-3938.

[16] Gurov, T.V., Nedjalkov, M., Whitlock, P.A., Kosina, H., Selberherr, S., (2002). Femtosecond Relaxation of Hot Electrons by Phonon Emission in Presence of Electric Field, *Physica B*, vol. 314, pp. 301-304.

[17] Gurov, T.V., Whitlock, P.A., (2002). An Efficient Backward Monte Carlo Estimator for Solving of a Quantum Kinetic Equation with Memory Kernel, *Mathematics and Computers in Simulation*, vol. 60, pp. 85-105, 2002.

[18] Gurov, T., Atanassov, E., Dimov I., Palankovski, V., (2006). Femtosecond Evolution of Spatially Inhomogeneous Carrier Excitations: Part II: Stochastic Approach and GRID Implementation, *Springer LNCS*, 3743, pp. 157-163.

[19] Jacoboni, C., Lugli, P., (1989). The Monte Carlo Methods for Semiconductor Device Simulation, *Computational Microelectronics*, edited by S. Selberherr, Springer-Verlag.

[20] Kalos, M.A., Whitlock, P.A., (2008). Monte Carlo Methods. Second revised and enlarged edition, *WILEY-VCH Verlag GmbH&Co*. KGaA, Meinheim.

[21] Karaivanova, A., Atanassov, E., Gurov, T., Ivanovska S., Durchova, M., (2010). Parallel Quasi-Random Applications on Heterogeneous Grid, *Journal of Scalable Computing: Practice and Experience* (SCPE), Vol. 11, no.1, (March 2010), pp.73-80, ISSN 1895-1767.

[22] Khalili, O., He, J., Olschanowsky, C., Snavely, A., Casanova, H., (2006). Measuring the Performance and Reliability of Production Computational Grids, *Proceedings of the7th IEEE/ACM International Conference on Grid Computing*, pp. 293-300.

[23] Kouvakis, I., Georgatos, F., (2008). A Report on the Effect of Heterogeneity of the Grid Environment on a Grid Job, Proc. LSSC'07, *LNCS 4818*, Springer, pp. 476-483.

[24] Kroese, D.P., Taimre, T., Botev, Z.I., (2011). Handbook of Monte Carlo Methods, *Wiley Series in Probability and Statistics,* John Wiley and Sons, New York.

[25] Li, Y., Mascagni, M., (2005) Grid-based Quasi-Monte Carlo Applications, *Monte Carlo Methods and Appl.*, vol. 11, no. 1, pp. 39-56.

[26] Mascagni, M., Seperley D., Srinivasan, A., (2000), SPRNG: A Scalable Library for Pseudorandom Numbar Generation, *ACM Transactions on Mathematical Software*.

[27] Mikhailov, G.A., (1995). *New Monte Carlo Methods with Estimating Derivatives,* Utrecht, Netherlands.

[28] Miner D., Shook A., (2012), *Map Reduce Design Patterns: Building Effective Algorithms and Analytics for Hadoop and Other Systems,* Published by O'Reilly Media, Inc., 1005 Gravenstein Highway North, Sebastopol, CA 95472.

[29] Misev, A., Atanassov, E., (2008). Performance Analysis of GRID Middleware Using Process Mining, Proc. 8th ICCS'08, *LNCS 5101,* Springer, pp. 203-212.

[30] Misev, A., Atanassov, E., (2010). User Level Grid Quality of Service, Proc. 7th LNCS'09, *LNCS 5910,* Springer, pp. 507-514.

[31] Nedjalkov, M., Kosik, R., Kosina, H., Selberherr, S., (2001). A Wigner Equation for Nanometer and Femtosecond Transport Regime, *Proceedings of the 2001 First IEEE Conference on Nanotechnology,* IEEE, Maui, Hawaii, pp. 277-281.

[32] Nedjalkov, M., Kosina, H., Selberherr, S., Ringhofer, C., Ferry, D.K., (2004). Unified Particle Approach to Wigner-Boltzmann Transport in Small Semiconductor Devices, *Phys. Rev. B*, Vol. 70, pp. 115319-115335.

[33] Nedjalkov, M., Gurov, T., Kosina, H., Vasileska D., Palankovski, V., (2006). Femtosecond Evolution of Spatially Inhomogeneous Carrier Excitations: Part I: Kinetic Approach, *Springer LNCS*, 3743, pp. 149-156.

[34] Ostromsky, T. Z., Zlatev, Z., (2007). Parallel and GRID implementation of a large scale air pollution model, Proc. NM&A'06, *LNCS 4310,* Springer, pp. 475-482.

[35] Pacheco, P.S., *Parallel Programming with MPI,* (1997), Morgan Kaufmann Publishers, Inc, San Francisco, California.

[36] Rathkopf, J. A., (1992). *PMC: A shared short-cut to portable parallel power*, Lawrence Livermore National Laboratory, Livermore, CA, UCRL-112311.

[37] Smith, L., Bull, M., (2001). „Development of mixed mode MPI/OpenMP applications", *Scientific Programming*, series 9 (2/3), pp. 83-98.

[38] Soldatos, J., Polymenakos, L., Kormentzas, G., (2004). Programmable Grids Framework Enabling QoS in an OGSA Context, First International Workshop on Active and Programmable Grids Architectures and Components, *4th International Conference in Computer Science ICCS2004*, Krakow, Poland, June 6-9, 2004, Proceedings, Part III, Volume 3038/2004, pp. 195-201.

[39] *AMQP protocol*: www.amqp.org.

[40] *Erlang language*: http://www.erlang.org.

[41] *European Grid Infrstructure*: http://www.egi.eu/.

[42] *gLite middleware website*: http://www.glite.org.

[43] *Globus Toolkit,* http://toolkit.globus.org/toolkit/.

[44] http://gstat2.grid.sinica.edu.tw/gstat/summary/GRID/EGI/.

[45] https://indico.in2p3.fr/getFile.py/access?contribId=18&sessionId=0&resId=0&materialId=slides&confId=2116.

[46] https://twiki.cern.ch/twiki/bin/view/ArdaGrid/GangaTestingFrameworkGuide.

[47] *LHC experiments:* http://home.web.cern.ch/about/experiments.

[48] *Maui SS Protocol:* http://mauischeduler.sourceforge.net/client-protocol-1.html.

[49] *Monitoring of BG01-IPP site*: http://gstat2.grid.sinica.edu.tw/gstat/site/BG01-IPP/.

[50] *Mono project website:* http://www.mono-project.com/.

[51] *MPICH-G2,* http://toolkit.globus.org/grid_software/computation/mpich-g2.php.

[52] *OpenMP 4.0 Specification Released*, http://openmp.org/wp/2013/07/openmp-40/.

[53] *RabbitMQ broker website:* http://www.rabbitmq.com.

[54] *SEE-GRID-SCI project website:* http://www.see-grid-sci.eu.

[55] *SMP systems,* http://en.wikipedia.org/wiki/Symmetric_multiprocessing.

[56] *SPRNG website,* http://sprng.cs.fsu.edu.

[57] *SQLite,* http://www.tutorialspoint.com/sqlite/.

[58] *Torque batch system,* http://en.wikipedia.org/wiki/TORQUE.

[59] *VOMS documentations:* http://vdt.cs.wisc.edu/VOMS-documentation.html.

[60] *WS-PGRADE portal:* http://guse.hu/about/architecture/ws-pgrade.

[61] *WX Widgets library website:* http://www.wxwidgets.org/.

[62] *XMPP protocol:* http://xmpp.org/rfcs/rfc3921.html.

[63] *ZeroM. Q.,* http://zeromq.org/intro:read-the-manual.

In: Grid Computing: Techniques and Future Prospects   ISBN: 978-1-63117-704-0
Editors: J. G. Barbosa and I. Dutra, pp. 157-186   © 2015 Nova Science Publishers, Inc.

Chapter 6

GRID PROGRAMMING FRAMEWORKS

B. Medeiros, R. Silva and J. L. Sobral[*]
Universidade do Minho, Braga, Portugal

Abstract

Adapting applications for computational grids requires approaches to develop applications that can effectively leverage available computing resources. This chapter surveys current programming frameworks to enable scientific applications to run on grid platforms and discusses the requirements for future programming frameworks that target computational grids. It focuses on how to enable applications to be distributed across multiple computing resources and how to support adaptability to available computing resources. The chapter introduces a programming framework based on the concept of pluggable grid service that provides seamless access to computational grids, using aspect-oriented techniques. Pluggable grid services avoid explicit calls to grid services in scientific codes, localize grid-specific concerns into well-defined modules and can be (un)plugged (into)from scientific codes. In consequence, domain-specific code becomes oblivious of grid issues, allowing scientists to focus on domain-specific issues and to manage grid issues by composing grid-specific modules.

Keywords: Java, grid, multicore, GPU

1. Introduction

Many applications require computational power that is increasingly harder to be provided by a single machine. Computational grids enable the access to virtually unlimited computational power, by aggregating resources provided by multiple organizations [1].

In the latest years, the trend has been on migrating to cloud computing. However, computational grids remain an attractive way to improve the usage of computational resources in organizations, by pooling available resources, thus providing a cost-effective solution.

Grid infrastructures are built upon computing nodes. In recent years there was a shift in the characteristics of those nodes. Computing nodes now include multiple processing cores (i.e., CPUs with many cores) and there is an increasing number of nodes supporting

---

[*]E-mail address: jls@di.uminho.pt

graphics processing units with generic programming capabilities (GPGPU). These units can be used to accelerate the processing time of certain computational tasks within applications. In the future it is expected to see an increasing number of cores per node and a wider variety of units providing special purpose processing capabilities that can accelerate certain tasks within applications.

A grid middleware (e.g., Globus, gLite) is a set of components, services and protocols that enable uniform access to distributed resources in a grid. Grid Programming Frameworks (GPFs) aim to simplify the development of applications that can run on grid infrastructures. These frameworks are built upon the grid middleware in order to automate typical tasks related to the execution of applications in a grid.

Early GPFs targeted parameter sweep applications, where the application was executed several times using different parameters. Thus, early frameworks rely on command line interfaces where the user specifies the parameters for each run, e.g., a Job Description Language [2]. Grid-enabling codes that do not rely on parameter sweep entail an additional burden to decompose the application into a set of independent tasks that can be executed on remote computing nodes. Moreover, parameter sweep may not be appropriate for some kinds of applications because some tasks may depend on others.

This chapter focuses on GPFs supporting the development of desktop-like applications that can be enabled to run on computational grids with minimal programming effort. These exclude frameworks to develop workflow-based applications [3], deploying applications as grid services and command line tools.

GPFs are essential when the usage of grid computing resources entails execution of a massive amount of computational tasks. This contrasts with the early usage of grid resources where users submitted a few tasks, which could be easily managed by a command-line based tool (e.g., a script). Thus, one key functionality of a modern GPF is to help the programmer to coordinate the execution of a massive amount of grid tasks.

This chapter classifies and discusses the functionality provided by a GPF based on two dimensions:

- front-end support for the generation of parallel tasks, by exposing parallelism in the application; this requires the division of the application functionality into independent tasks, along with the data division across those tasks and the collection of the results computed by each task;

- back-end support for execution of parallel tasks into remote resources which is commonly known by job submission; this includes the selection of appropriate grid resources, deploying the executable on those resources, copying the required input data into the selected resources, running the application and copying the resulting data from the remote resources.

Grid computing resources differ from cloud resources in many aspects. One key aspect that may be effectively addressed by a GPF is the grid resources' volatility. Grid resources often cannot be taken for granted during execution. Certain computing resources can become inaccessible during the execution, either due to a fault or due to the necessity to run a higher priority task. Note that in cloud computing normally a service level agreement ensures that the provider delivers the requested computing power during the entire execution time frame.

Designing a GPF requires a trade off among different aspects. On one hand, framework components (e.g, the front-end and back-end) should work in a tightly coupled manner to provide efficient execution. On the other hand, framework components should be used and developed in a loosely coupled manner in order to be able to integrate a large set of services and to make the task of the programmer easier. The most common way to organize the functionality provided by a GPF is to use a classical layered approach (Figure 1): framework services are organized by levels, ranging from hardware level (lower-level) up to application level (upper-level). Within this organization the information flows between levels by using well-defined Application Programming Interfaces (APIs).

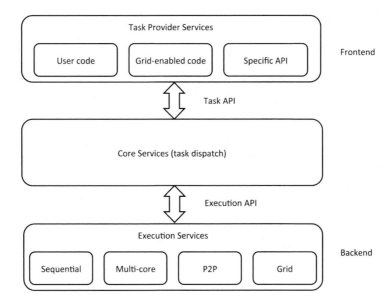

Figure 1. Layered framework.

The classic layered framework organization imposes limitations concerning composition of services and the support of optional services, since requests must go through all layers, even if the layer only passes the information. This chapter also presents a GPF that implements traditional grid functionality through pluggable services, avoiding the explicit use of API calls among layers.

The next section discusses back-end support in GPFs, starting by back-ends for local execution on multi-cores and GPUs, and reviewing several back-ends that support task execution on grid environments. This section also discusses the difficulty in composing services in traditional layered frameworks. Section 3 discusses front-end services and their implementation with pluggable services. Section 4 presents performance results, whereas section 5 discusses related work. Section 6 concludes the chapter.

2.   GPF Back-ends

This section presents various execution back-ends. For illustrative purposes a matrix multiplication case study is presented, where Matrix C = Matrix A x Matrix B. The sequential code is provided in Figure 2. To simplify the discussion and the presented code all matrices are assumed to be square.

```
1   for (int row=0; row<size; row++) {   // for each row of matrix a
2     for (int col=0; col<size; col++) { // for each column of matrix b
3       sum = 0;
4       for (int k=0; k<size; k++)   // dot product of row of A with a column of B
5         sum += matrixA[row][k] * matrixB[k][col];
6       matrixC[row][col] = sum;
7     }
8   }
```

Figure 2. Base code for matrix multiplication.

In this illustrative case, the innermost loop (lines 4 - 5 in Figure 2) computes a dot product of a row of matrix A with a column of matrix B. The *col* loop (line 2) performs this dot product of a row of matrix A with all columns of the matrix B, storing the results into the corresponding row of the matrix C.

In order to effectively use a computational grid, a given program must be decomposed into a set of independent tasks that can be executed in parallel. Hence, the first step in this case study is to identify those tasks. For the illustrative example, it was decided, among many options, to compute each row of the resulting matrix C in parallel. Thus, computing each iteration of the outermost loop in parallel (line 1). In this case, each task generates a row of the matrix C, reads a single row of matrix A and reads the entire matrix B (Figure 3).

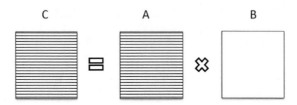

Figure 3. Parallel matrix multiplication.

2.1. Shared Memory Back-ends

After defining the parallel tasks, the next step is to code those tasks into a specific execution back-end. When the target is a shared memory system (e.g., a multi-core system) the matrices A, B and C can be shared among tasks.

One simple approach is to use OpenMP as an execution back-end. In this case, a pragma directive is enough to parallelize the outermost loop (line 1 in Figure 4).

In the case of a Java back-end each task must be encapsulated into a *Runnable* object. Moreover, the parallel execution must be enabled by creating a *Thread* object to run each task (Figure 5).

Lines 01-20 of Figure 5 declare a *Runnable* object that specifies the task. Lines 3-5 relate task specific data: input row of matrix A, matrix B and the resulting row of matrix

```
1  #pragma omp parallel for shared(matrixA,matrixB,matrixC)
2  for (int row=0; row<size; row++) {
3    // .... matrix multiplication code ...
4  }
```

Figure 4. Parallel OpenMP code for matrix multiplication.

```
1   public class MyTask implements Runnable {
2
3     private double[] RowA = null;          // Declaration of instance variables
4     private double[][] MatrixB = null;
5     private double[] RowC = null;
6
7     public MyTask(double[] rowA, double[][] matrixB, double[] rowC) { // constructor
8       this.RowA = rowA;
9       this.MatrixB = matrixB;
10      this.RowC = rowC;
11    }
12    public void run() {
13      for (int col=0; col<size; col++) {
14        double sum = 0;
15        for (int k=0; k<size; k++)
16          sum += RowA[k] * MatrixB[k][col];
17        RowC[col] = sum;
18      }
19    }
20  }
21  // main
22  ...
23  // create a thread to process each task
24  for (int row=0; row<size; row++) {
25    MyTask tk = new MyTask(matrixA[row], matrixB, matrixC[row]);
26    Thread t = new Thread( tk );
27    t.start();
28  }
29  ... // wait for threads to complete
```

Figure 5. Parallel matrix multiplication code with Java Threads.

C to compute. Those parameters are initialized (lines 7-11) at task creation time (line 25). The computation is performed within the *run()* method (lines 12-19) which is executed by the corresponding thread when the *start()* method is invoked (line 27). In this example, threads can share the access to A, B and C so each task will receive a pointer to the input matrix/row and a pointer to the corresponding row in the resulting matrix C (line 25).

In this example each task consists of a single row, which may generate a huge amount of parallel tasks. To obtain the best performance, a trade off between the number of tasks and the available resources is generally required. Therefore, each task should compute several rows of the resulting matrix C. In the previous example it can be addressed by changing the task implementation to compute a set of rows of the matrix C, which requires the insertion of a *row* loop into the *run()* method.

The matrix multiplication example is well suited to illustrate the mapping into a GPU back-end. In a GPU multiple threads execute the same instruction flow in a lock-step (i.e., in a single instruction multiple data fashion). A GPU version of this case study can be derived if a GPU thread is assigned to each task (i.e., to compute a row of matrix C). This chapter illustrates such implementation using the APARAPI [1] back-end, a Java based framework that generates GPU kernels in OpenCL [2] by translating Java bytecode.

Figure 6 shows the APARAPI implementation (note: for simplicity the code in figure uses a matrix syntax, but the APARAPI only supports single dimension arrays). The implementation will execute the kernel with as many threads as the number of rows (line 21). Each GPU thread will execute the kernel *run()* method (lines 9-17), computing a single row of matrix C (line 10). The call *getGlobalId()* returns the current GPU thread id (a number between 0 and *size* -1).

```
1   public class MyGPUTask extends Kernel {
2
3     // ... Declaration of instance variables ...
4
5     public MyGPUTask(double[][] matrixA, double[][] matrixB, double[][] matrixC,
6   int size) {
7       // ... Class constructor ...
8     }
9     public void run() {
10      int row = getGlobalId();
11      for (int col=0; col<size; col++) {
12        double sum = 0;
13        for (int k=0; k<size; k++)
14          sum += MatrixA[row][k] * MatrixB[k][col];
15        MatrixC[row][col] = sum;
16      }
17    }
18  }
19  // main
20  MyGPUTask k = new MyGPUTask(matrixA,matrixB,matrixC,size);
21  k.execute(size);
```

Figure 6. APARAPI code for matrix multiplication.

Current GPUs have a disjoint address space from the CPU. The APARAPI framework is in charge of data copying between these address spaces: before kernel execution, matrix A and B will be copied to the GPU; after the kernel execution the matrix C will be copied from the GPU to CPU.

---

[1] code.google.com/p/aparapi
[2] www.khronos.org/opencl

2.2.   Grid Back-ends

A grid back-end delegates task execution to computational grid infrastructures. This section illustrates the concept of a framework offering a grid back-end with the JPPF framework[3], which is a Java framework that supports application execution into a set of remote machines. Figure 7a illustrates the base JPPF architecture: client entry points provide an API to submit jobs; server(s) receive jobs from clients and dispatch work to nodes; nodes provide the processing capabilities to execute requested tasks. In order to avoid a single point of failure, JPPF also supports a peer-to-peer network of multiple servers, each server managing multiple nodes. In such case, clients can submit jobs to different servers.

Grid back-ends offer the so-called scheduling functionality (Figure 7b): tasks submitted by clients are scheduled into available nodes, which may include the execution of tasks into multiple remote nodes. The framework dispatches each task to an available remote machine (i.e., grid processing node). In order to enable remote execution, the framework must copy the task executable and the required data into the remote machine (stage-in); execute the task remotely and, when the task execution completes, copy the resulting data back to the client machine (i.e., stage-out).

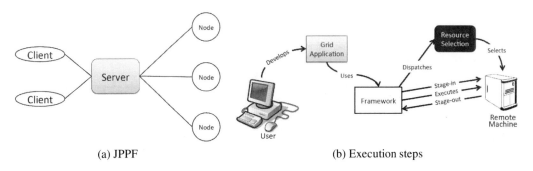

(a) JPPF   (b) Execution steps

Figure 7. GPF architecture and execution mode.

The JPPF framework offers a clean API to execute jobs in a computational grid. The JPPF client API is mainly based on three classes: *Task*, *Job* and *Client* (see Figure 8). A *Job* is a set of tasks, which is submitted for execution using the *Client* interface. A *Task* is a Java class implementing the *Runnable* interface and supporting serialization (i.e., implementing the *Serializable* Java interface). The Java-based approach simplifies three important activities performed by a GPF in order to provide remote execution of tasks: data stage-in and stage-out, executable deployment and remote execution.

To illustrate the use of these classes Figure 9 provides the task implementation of the matrix case study in JPPF. This example is similar to the initial example with Java threads, with a few key differences:

1. the task class now extends a JPPF task (which already implements the Runnable and Serializable interfaces);

2. the memory storage for the computed row is allocated when the task executes (inside the *run* method).

---

[3]www.jppf.org

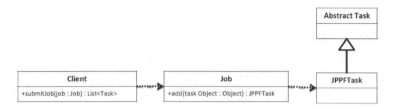

Figure 8. JPPF class diagram.

```
1   public class MyJPPFTask extends JPPFTask {
2
3     // ... Declaration of instance variables ...
4
5     public MyJPPFTask(double[] rowA, double[][] matrixB) {
6       // ... Class constructor ...
7     }
8     public void run() {
9       this.RowC = new double[size];
10      for (int col=0; col<size; col++) {
11        double sum = 0;
12        for (int k=0; k<size; k++)
13          sum += MatrixA[k] * MatrixB[k][col];
14        rowC[col] = sum;
15      }
16    }
17    public double[] getResult() {
18      return RowC;
19    }
20  }
```

Figure 9. JPPF task code for matrix multiplication.

The former (item 1) provides a strategy to automatically define the task's input / output (I/O) data and task executable. Thus, the task is automatically serializable and, using dynamic remote loading of class bytecode, a remote JVM can load the task data (i.e., by deserializing the task object), executing the task (i.e, executing the run method of the loaded bytecode) and saving the resulting data (serializing, again, the task object after execution) in order to send the results back to the client. The latter item (item 2) is particularly important to reduce the sent and received data to/from a remote node. When allocating the *rowC* in the *run* method, only data from *MatrixA* and *MatrixB* is initially transmitted from the client to the remote node.

The task interface provides a clean way to specify the work to be performed within a task and its I/O data. In JPPF, a job consists of a set of tasks and it is submitted for execution using the client API. Figure 10 shows a complete example.

As stated previously, the Java built-in serialization and code/data portability simplifies the programmer's work related to the task definition (including deployment and execution) and task I/O. To illustrate the additional complexity when these mechanisms are not available, it is presented the pseudo-code of the same example in the GMarte framework [4]

```
1    JPPFClient client = new JPPFClient();
2    JPPFJob job = new JPPFJob();
3
4    for (int row=0; row<size; row++) {
5      MyJPPFTask t = new MyJPPFTask(matrixA[row],matrixB);
6      job.add(t);
7    }
8    // blocks until the job has completed
9    List<Task<?>> results = client.submit(job);
10   ... // process result
```

Figure 10. JPPF example code.

(Figure 12). A simplified UML diagram of GMarte classes is presented in Figure 11.

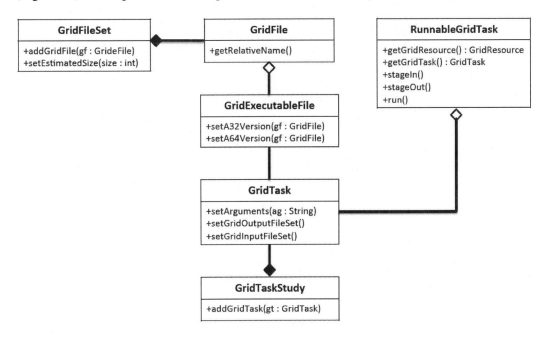

Figure 11. GMarte class diagram.

A job is a *GridTaskStudy* that encapsulates a set of *GridTask* (those are similar to *Job* and *Task* in JPPF). Each task has to specify its *GridExecutableFile* and the set of I/O files. A GMarte task is executed as follows:

1. the application and its dependent input files are transferred via GridFTP from the client to the remote machine;

2. the application is started in the remote machine via the Globus Resource Allocation Manager (GRAM) service;

3. when the execution finishes, the output files generated are transferred to the client machine via GridFTP.

Figure 12 illustrates a simple code that must be generated in GMarte in order to remotely execute a method called *compute*. The code consists in two parts: the client side and the server side code. The client side code is in charge of redirecting the execution of the *compute* method to remote resources by writing the request to a file that is staged-in to the remote resource. The GMarte framework is responsible for staging-in this file, for copying the code of the remote worker (e.g., in this case a jar file), for starting the remote worker and for staging-out the resulting file. The server side code reads the file containing the request, executes the requested method and writes a file with the result of the *compute* call. The GMarte framework is responsible for copying the required I/O files to the resource where the worker is executed. If the target language is not Java (e.g., C) additional problems may arise due to incompatibility between executable and data formats.

```
1    // client code
2           GridTask gt = new GridTask("worker");
3           GridInputFileSet gifs = new GridInputFileSet();
4           gifs.addGridFile("myapp.jar"); // remote executable jar file
5           gifs.addGridFile(/* RPC request file name */);
6           gt.setGridInputFileSet(gifs);
7           GridOutputFileSet gofs = new GridOutputFileSet();
8           gofs.addGridFile(/* result file name */);
9           gt.setGridOutputFileSet(gofs);
10          TestBed tb = new TestBed();
11          Scheduler scheduler = new OrchestratorScheduler(tb, gt);
12          scheduler.start();
13          scheduler.waitUntilFinished();
14          ... // read result from staged-out file
15
16   // server code
17   public static void main(String args[]) { // remote task to execute
18          Object myData = ... // read data from file staged in by GMarte
19          Object result = compute(myData);
20          ... // save result into output file to be staged out by GMarte
21   }
```

Figure 12. GMarte example of code.

2.3.   Composing Back-ends

Traditional approaches to grid-enable applications require a large programming effort. Starting with the example of Figure 2 (base sequential matrix multiplication) the programmer must create *JPPFTask* objects and submit them for remote execution. Moreover, the application becomes grid-dependent by inserting calls to the GPF API into the source code, the application cannot run without the grid framework, e.g., to run the application solely on the client machine.

To run applications on modern grid nodes (e.g., which provide multi-core CPUs or/and GPUs) the burden is heavier, since each task must include also multithreading and/or GPU related code. For instance, to run tasks on remote GPUs, the developer must create a task class that extends the *JPPFTasks* and this task should create a new GPU task that extends the *Kernel* class. This becomes even more complex if the programmer wants to use the computation power of both CPUs and GPUs.

Simultaneously with the coding of tasks, the developer also has to find out how to partition the workload into multiple levels of tasks. In the matrix multiplication case study the original matrix must be initially decomposed into JPPF tasks and each of them must be further decomposed into GPU or multi-core parallel tasks.

3.   GPF Front-ends

A GPF frond-end provides mechanisms to specify potential parallel tasks to execute on a computational grid. Most tools for gridification [5] enforce invasive and non-reversible modifications to applications (e.g., to specify parallel tasks and to execute them on a grid environment) making grid-enabled codes dependent on a grid infrastructure. In addition, decomposing an application into a large set of independent tasks and submitting them to a grid constrains application specific optimizations, such as application-level self-scheduling or fault tolerance. Moreover, current tools focus only on executing applications solely on grids, without taking advantage of the growing number of cores on every computing node.

This section presents a grid-programming framework that is based on the Java language and on the concept of pluggable service in order to simplify the process of migrating base programs into computational grids. The Gaspar framework aims to grid-enable Java applications in a non-invasive manner, through a set of pluggable services [6]. These services can be composed with a given base program in order to meet the requirements of each application/target platform. Current services include parallelization, load-distribution (scheduling), fault-tolerance, remote execution and monitoring.

The framework aims to be a lightweight framework for non-invasive gridification of Java applications. It relies on minimalist interfaces among services that can be extended to match application requirements, through a set of pluggable components. Figure 13 presents an overview of the framework architecture.

The framework is centred on the domain specific code whose functionality can be extended by "plugging" a set of services:

1. the parallelization service is responsible for the generation of a set of independent tasks that can be scheduled into a set of local or remote resources;

2. the load-distribution service performs a more fine-tuned resource selection, based on the specificities of each resource;

3. the fault-tolerance addresses faulty resources by resubmitting a task for execution when it fails;

4. the remote execution service manages task execution on remote nodes, which is currently delegated to JPPF;

5. the monitoring service can manage the progress of tasks execution.

Parallelization service generates tasks to be executed on computational resources, such as applications that are grid-enabled by the approach. However, it is also possible to use

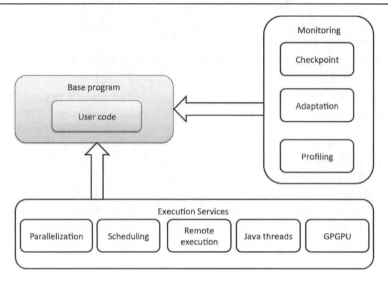

Figure 13. Framework layout.

other task providers, for instance by directly (i.e., invasively) creating tasks within the source code, or by using a skeleton framework [7]. These tasks can be executed on a set of resources provided by execution services.

The Java language was selected since it provides many benefits:

- a large range of applications today are written in Java;

- performance of the JVM has greatly improved in recent years, being very close to other traditionally high-performing languages, such as C and Fortran;

- the language provides automatic object serialization and portability across platforms, both at the level of the data representation and the level of the executables (Java bytecode);

- the language offers many high level features, for instance, bytecode can be transformed at load-time in order to adapt to specific running conditions.

3.1. Pluggable Services

The key strength of the Gaspar framework is the ability to bind services to base programs in a non-invasive manner, making it possible to (un)plug these services into/from programs at any time during and after the gridification process. In addition, connections among services are also performed in a non-invasive manner, minimizing coupling among services. This approach makes it feasible to develop grid-enabled applications that do not depend on a particular:

1. set of services, as services can be plugged only at request to meet certain execution requirements;

2. target platform, as the code can be tuned to meet (some) specific hardware configurations, such as multi-core machines or machines with a GPU.

For instance, to run an application on a local multi-core machine, remote execution and fault-tolerance services are not required. This also presents a performance advantage, since services can be removed from the system build.

Non-invasive composition of services relies on aspect-oriented programming (AOP) [8]. Two fundamental concepts of AOP are quantification and obliviousness [9]. Quantification is the ability of an aspect (or service provided by the framework) to specify a set of execution points where aspect specific behavior can be attached. For instance, a service for remote execution can attach that behavior to certain procedure calls in Java applications. Obliviousness is the ability to apply a mechanism to code that was not specifically prepared for that purpose.

To illustrate these two concepts, consider a pluggable service that prints the name of every method called. The code in Figure 14 specifies how to apply this aspect to all method calls (line 1) and print the method name before its call (lines 3-5). The *thisJoinPoint* construct was used in this case to specify the name of each intercepted execution point (line 4). Both quantification and obliviousness can be observed in this example. First, the set of method calls to intercept is specified in the pointcut construct (quantification). Second, no special adaptations are required to the basic code to attach this feature (obliviousness).

```
1    pointcut events2print() : call(* *.*(..));
2
3    before() : events2print(){
4      System.out.println(thisJoinPoint.getSignature());
5    }
```

Figure 14. Example of an aspect.

3.2. Parallelization Service

Pluggable services avoid making explicit calls to a parallelization API, replacing those calls by coding conventions (e.g., using setter and getter methods for each object field). This brings the benefit of improving the composition of services. After writing the base program following the required coding conventions, multiple services can be "plugged" without further changes to the base program.

The grid parallelization service generates a set of tasks that are executed in parallel using a map/reduce pattern of computation. The idea is to specify *for* loops in the base program that can run in parallel (e.g., each sub-range of the loop iterations becomes a parallel task), identify the input data required for each task and how the tasks outputs are collected (e.g., combined into a single data item).

The coding conventions currently required by the Gaspar framework are:

- task I/O data is stored as object data fields;

- the *for* loop is encapsulated within a method.

The parallelization service requires the specification of a joinpoint that corresponds to a method with a *for* loop and the specification of a scatter and a gather/reduce method. The scatter method specifies how the data of the original object is scattered into independent parts (e.g., when processing an array of data, this method can create several smaller arrays of data; in a simulation it can generate different parameters for each task). The reduce (or gather) specifies how the results are combined after executing the *map* method.

Figure 15 illustrates the coding conventions for the matrix multiplication case study. Matrix A, B and C are stored into three object fields (line 3). The method *compute* performs the actual matrix multiplication, by reading the object field and storing the resulting matrix into another object field.

```
1   public class MMult  {
2
3   // ... Declaration of instance variables ...
4
5   public MMult(double[][] matrixA, double[][] matrixB, double[][] matrixC,
6           int size) {
7           // ... Class constructor ...
8   }
9
10      public void compute() {
11          for (int row=0; row<size; row++) {
12              // .... matrix multiplication code ...
13          }
14      }
15  }
```

Figure 15. Matrix multiplication code.

Figure 16 shows how to plug a parallelization service into this example. The implementation extends the generic service to specify the *map* method (calls to the *compute* method, in this case, line 3); how multiple instances of class *MMult* are created (line 5) and how multiple results are combined (line 7).

```
1   public aspect MMultParallelization extends ParallelizationService {
2
3     pointcut map() : call(void MMult.compute());
4
5     List<MMult> scather(MMult) { ... // create several MMult clones   ... }
6
7     MMult reduce(List<MMult>)  {  ... // merge several MMult objects ... }
8   }
```

Figure 16. Aspect for matrix multiplication.

The base parallelization service (Figure 17) will plug, on each call to the *compute* method in the base program, additional code to call the method *scatter*, invoke the original *compute* method multiple times, one on each object returned by the *scatter* method and combine the multiple results after the execution. The *scatter* method can invoke the method *getNumberOfTasks()* in order to get access to the number of tasks.

```
1   around(Object target) : map() {
2         ArrayList tasks = scatter(target);
3         for(int i=0;i<getNumberOfTasks(); i++)
4                 proceed( tasks.get(i) );
5         target = reduce(tasks);
6   }
```

Figure 17. Parallelization service implementation.

3.3. Execution Services

The framework provides several execution services and can be composed with the parallelization service [10] to map parallel tasks into different execution back-ends. Once that all execution services are "pluggable services" they can be composed with the base program without requiring any further changes.

3.3.1. Remote Execution

The remote execution service dispatches task execution to resources in computational grids. The service is currently implemented on top of the JPPF framework. Thus, when the remote execution service is composed with the parallelization service each generated task will be dispatched to the JPPF framework, which takes care of all steps involved in the execution.

The implementation of the remote execution service is quite simple with AOP-based services and it works as follows (see Figure 18 for a pseudo code of the implementation):

1. the base *MMult* class is transformed into a *JPPFTask*;

2. each call to the *compute* method generated by the parallelization service generates a new task that is added to the current JPPF job; when all tasks have been generated, the job is submitted for execution;

3. the reduce function merges the results from the job submission.

```
1   around(Object target) : map() {
2         currentJob.add(target);
3         currentNumberOfTask++;
4         if (currentNumberOfTask == getNumberOfTasks()) {
5                 client.submit(currentJob);
6                 // ... wait for completion and process tasks ...
7         }
8   }
```

Figure 18. Remote execution on JPPF implementation.

In this case, the JPPF framework will take care of transferring the I/O data required for each task, using the standard Java serialization mechanism.

3.3.2.   CPU/Java Threads

The Java threads execution service dispatches each task to a new local thread (or, alternatively, to a local executor service in order to reduce thread creation overhead). When all tasks have been dispatched the service waits for all threads to complete. Figure 19 shows the pseudo code of this service.

```
1   around(Object target) : map() {
2           currentNumberOfTask++;
3           Thread t = new Thread() {
4                   void run() {
5                           proceed( target);
6                   }
7           };
8           t.start();
9           if (currentNumberOfTask == getNumberOfTasks()) {
10                  // ... wait for completion and process tasks
11          }
12  }
```

Figure 19. Java Threads.

In this case the data can be shared among CPU threads (e.g., matrix A, B and C can be shared among threads to avoid redundant data copies).

3.3.3.   GPU/OpenCL

The GPU execution service dispatches task execution to GPUs, based on the APARAPI framework. The code is similar to the *map*, but it creates a new APARAPI kernel. Moreover, the loop in the base program is rewritten in order for each thread to compute a part of the task. The rewrite of the base program is presented in Figure 20.

```
1   public void compute() {
2     for (int row=threadid; row<size; row+=totalGPUthreads) {
3       // .... matrix multiplication code ...
4     }
5   }
```

Figure 20. GPU mapping.

Each GPU thread will execute iterations of the outer loop in a cyclic fashion. The APARAPI framework will take care of the data copy to/from the GPU memory.

3.3.4.   Hybrid CPU/GPU

In certain cases performance can improve by using both CPU and GPU to execute tasks. However, in such cases, dynamic scheduling is required, since each GPU task can be faster (or slower) than a similar task when executed on a CPU.

To deploy a hybrid CPU/GPU execution with pluggable services it is simply necessary to deploy both CPU and GPU execution services. In such case, CPU thread with id 0 will be in charge of dispatching tasks to the GPU.

Dynamic scheduling between GPU and CPU on a local node is simply obtained by selecting an executor service that dynamically assigns tasks to threads.

3.3.5. Compositions of Services

There are several interesting compositions of services:

1. a local execution on CPU, GPU or Hybrid CPU/GPU, by deploying the parallelization service with the CPU, GPU or both services;

2. remote execution on a single GPU or CPU, by composing the remote execution service and the GPU or CPU service;

3. more complex compositions are possible by composing the parallelization service more than once.

For instance, to deploy remote parallel tasks (e.g., grid tasks where each task is a parallel task) the first level of parallelization generates a set of tasks that are dispatched to remote nodes by the remote execution service and a second level of parallel tasks are executed by local threads.

3.4. Fault-tolerance and Adaptation Services

Migrating scientific applications to computational grids can decrease the execution time. However, as the number of machines increases also the probability of a fault increases. Hence, a system that offers fault-tolerance mechanisms is crucial.

One well-known technique to implement fault-tolerance is checkpoint and restart (CPR). Basically, it consists on periodically saving the application state (checkpointing process), which can be subsequently used for restarting the application state (restart process) in case of fault.

In heterogeneous systems of large dimension, such as computational grids, portability and optimization are two fundamental requirements that must be guaranteed by the fault-tolerance mechanism. In grids, applications should also efficiently deal with the resources volatility, once the resources allocated to a given application can change during its execution (increasing or decreasing). In more extreme cases applications are forced to restart in a completely different set of resources. In order to deal with these problems, and at the same time guarantee portability and efficiency, one should opt for an application level CPR mechanism adding run-time resource adaptation features. Moreover, the files produced by application level CPR mechanism can be used to provide a resource adaptation mechanism. For example, an application may be running on a given machine with 2 cores (e.g., the only machine available at the time), but if later a 24-core machine is released, it can be stopped and restarted on the new machine using the latest checkpoint files.

The Gaspar framework provides an AOP mechanism to support fault-tolerance and adaptation [11]. The state of each task is periodically saved into a safe storage in such a way that it can be restarted later. Thus, it will be not necessary to re-execute the complete task. In order to minimize the overhead, the frequency of checkpoint is selected based on a trade off between the overhead of the checkpointing process and the expected probability of a fault.

One key feature of the Gaspar framework is the ability to checkpoint parallel tasks, which provides an effective mechanism to support adaptation to resources. The basic idea is to use the CPR service for this purpose. During the restart process the number of threads can increase or decrease according to the target system. This is feasible since an application-level CPR is used and all CPR functionalities are provided by pluggable services (i.e., no changes to the base program are required). The CPR package was built based on four requirements:

1. portable among different operating systems;

2. minimize the information saved;

3. functional in multiple environments (sequential/parallel);

4. non-intrusive.

Gaspar uses an application level CPR approach. Such approach avoids modifications to the grid computational middleware along with portable and optimized checkpoint files. Portability is also extensible to parallel applications. The Gaspar CPR also takes advantage of AOP, in order to minimize any modifications to the application source code. Furthermore, the generated code is portable.

Gaspar CPR works as a library that automates checkpoint and restart processes leaving to the programmer the specification of the local, content and frequency of the checkpointing along with the methods that can be ignored during the restart phase. Furthermore, for each of these tasks Gaspar has well defined guidelines to help the programmer throughout this process. Thus, reducing both the time to restart the application and the amount of information that will be saved in disk during the checkpointing. In parallel applications the checkpointing local must be an execution point on the source code where there are no active synchronization mechanisms during the saving of the application state in disk (recovery line). Such local is defined as a safe point, even in sequential applications.

During the checkpointing, along with a recovery line, it is also saved the number of safe points intercepted. During the restart process, in order to reconstruct the stack the library will execute only the methods that cannot be ignored until the number of safe points saved is reached.

In shared memory applications, the checkpointing is performed using a coordinated blocking algorithm, where all threads will call a barrier before and after the master thread saves the application state to disk. The restart process is performed in a sequential manner, where thread constructors are also executed. Every thread calls a barrier while waiting for the master thread to finish loading the recovery line from the disk.

Figure 21 presents a high level overview of the Gaspar CPR packages. The darker rectangles represent aspects whereas the white ones represent classes.

The aspect *CPR Control* will verify, at the begin of each execution, if the last execution terminated successfully. If so the checkpointing process is activated, otherwise the

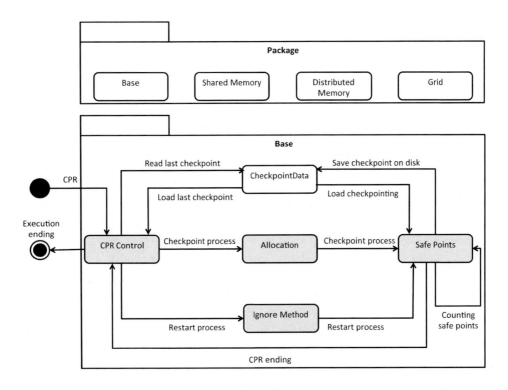

Figure 21. CPR layout.

restart process is initiated. All the data to be saved during the checkpointing is specified in the aspect *Allocation*. The programmer specifies in the *Ignore Method* all the methods that can be skipped during the restart process. The *Safe Points* aspect is responsible for counting the safe points and for verifying the appropriate moment for saving/loading the application state. This moment is determined by the checkpointing frequency defined by the programmer.

In order to extend the CPR mechanism to shared/distributed memory and grid systems, without any modification to the CPR base package, *Shared Memory*, *Distributed Memory* and *Grid* aspects were created. Each one of these aspects adds extra instructions in a non-intrusive manner to the *Base* package aspects.

3.5. Profiling and Monitoring

Monitoring and profiling are two services that have been traditional flagship services of AOP. The Gaspar framework monitors the occurrence of compute methods (e.g., instances of map executions) in order to monitor the application progress. Additionally, it provides an AOP library to profile the execution time of methods specified by the programmer.

4. Evaluation

This section illustrates and evaluates the Gaspar framework with three applications which were grid-enabled using this framework:

1. matrix multiplication;

2. computation of the Mandelbrot set;

3. molecular dynamics simulation based on the Java Grande Forum implementation [12].

The first two case studies were selected as representatives of two extremes of computational properties of grid applications: the matrix multiplication requires a large amount of data, that increases with the number of tasks; the Mandelbrot set requires less data per task, since it performs a large amount of computation per data point. However, it suffers from load balance problems, since each task performs a different amount of work. The third case study corresponds to typical applications of grid environments.

All applications were non-invasively parallelized. The non-invasive nature of the framework implies that no overhead is introduced into the original code, as gridification modules can be plugged at any time during and after the gridification process. Thus, when sequentially executing the code no overhead is observable.

For the benchmarks it was used two different sets of platforms:

1. A small local grid with a client machine (Mac Book Air i5 running at 1.7 Ghz) and two compute nodes, connected by a 100 Mbit network: 1) MacPro with dual Xeon 5130 at 2.0GHz with an ATI HD5770, running OS X 10.6.8; 2) Intel workstation with dual Xeon E5-2603 at 1.8GHz, running Windows 8.1.

2. 4 machines of the Search cluster[4] : 1) 311-1 machine with 8 cores, Intel Xeon CPU E5420 2.50GHz and 6144 KB cache size; 2) 401-1 and 3) 401-2 both with 16 cores each, Intel Xeon CPU E5520 2.27GHz and 8192KB cache size ; 4) 601-1 machine with 24 cores, Intel Xeon CPU X5650 2.67GHz and cache size 12288KB;

All systems used the JPPF 4.2 framework and the OpenJDK 1.7.0. All presented times are the median of 10 executions.

4.1. Matrix Multiplication

The matrix multiplication case study follows the parallelization strategy presented in section 3. Each grid task computes a set of rows of the resulting matrix C, which requires a subset of the rows of matrix A and a complete copy of matrix B. Performance figures were collected with two different matrix sizes: 2000x2000 and 4000x4000. The sequential execution time of the former size is 92 seconds while the latter takes 1084 seconds on a single core of the MacPro machine.

---

[4]http://search.di.uminho.pt

4.1.1. Single Remote Machine

The first test evaluates the execution of the case study on a single remote machine (the MacPro, which has a total of four cores and one GPU). Figure 22 presents four execution times for each matrix size: 1) JPPF - manually creating a single JPPF job with 4 (parallel) tasks; 2) Gaspar CPU - using the Gaspar framework to generate a single JPPF job with a single task which spawns 4 local threads to perform the matrix computation in parallel; 3) Gaspar GPU - using the Gaspar framework to generate a single JPPF job with a single task which performs the matrix computation in the GPU; 4) Gaspar CPU+GPU - using the Gaspar framework to generate a JPPF job with a hybrid CPU/GPU task implementation.

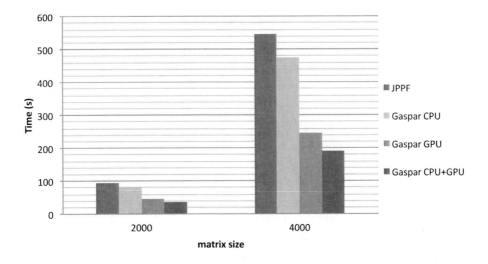

Figure 22. MMult case study on a single remote machine.

The Gaspar CPU implementation presents better performance than the base JPPF implementation since it generates less tasks and consequently less data copies: the matrix B is copied only one time while the base JPPF requires one copy per task. The Gaspar framework also enables the transparent execution on a remote GPU (by using the APARAPI framework), which provides lower execution time. However, the shortest execution is obtained by generating a job that can use all the available resources by running part of the computation on the CPU and another part on the GPU.

4.1.2. Multiple Remote Machines

The second test executes the matrix multiplication case study on two remote machines. These machines together provide 12 computational cores (4 cores on the MacPro plus 8 cores on the Intel workstation). Thus, to effectively use this small computational grid a minimum of 12 tasks should be generated. Since this case study requires a large amount of data, the base JPPF implementation is not feasible in this configuration due to excessive overhead. Thus, this section only provides results for the Gaspar CPU. Moreover, since those machines have different computational capabilities, the best performance might be attained by using the scheduling facility of the JPPF framework, which dynamically assigns tasks to remote machines. In this case a demand driven policy was selected (see Figure 23).

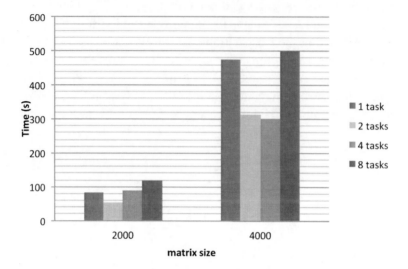

Figure 23. MMult case study on multiple remote machines.

In this case each task in a job spawns a number of Java threads corresponding to the available cores in the remote machine (either 4 or 8). For the smallest data set the best performance is provided by spawning 2 tasks, one per node. For the largest matrix size an additional benefit arises from using 4 tasks since it provides a better load balancing. In both cases using a larger number of tasks is not feasible.

The matrix multiplication is a typical application that provides a low ratio between computation/communication to be feasible for a grid environment. The time to copy the data to a remote machine is 56 and 190 seconds for the smallest and largest data set. Moreover this overhead increases with the number of tasks. This explains the limited gains of this case study.

4.2.   Mandelbrot Set

The second case study is the computation of the Mandelbrot fractal set. This case study differs from the matrix multiplication in two ways:

1. the computation performed per data item is higher;

2. the load per task is highly unbalanced.

Thus, in theory this case study should scale better on a grid environment if the load is well balanced across machines.

The Mandelbrot computation was gridified by computing a set of lines of the resulting image on each task. Each task requires 6 double values that represent the origin point, scale and size of the Mandelbrot space to compute.

Figure 24 provides performance results for the computation of an image of 2000x2000 using a maximum of 50000 iterations per Mandelbrot point on 12 computational cores of the local grid. The X-axis shows the number of generated tasks. In this case there are at most 2000 tasks, since a task computes one or multiple lines of the image. Two performance results are present for the Gaspar framework:

1. Gaspar 1 level - relying solely on the JPPF task scheduling, which generates tasks with 4 or 8 threads, depending on the target machine;

2. Gaspar 2 levels - relying on the Gaspar local node scheduler, which generates tasks on each node with an excess of local threads (in this case twice the number of local cores).

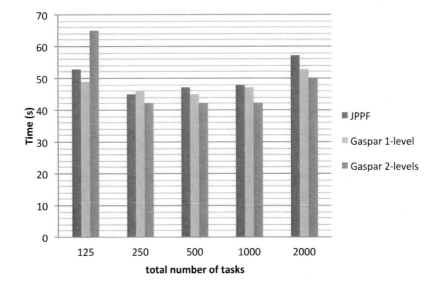

Figure 24. Mandelbrot case study on multiple remote machines.

The base JPPF implementation attains the best performance with 250 tasks (about 20 tasks per core). This is the best trade off between the overhead of tasks (which increases with the number of tasks) and the load balance (which is poorer when using less tasks).

The 1-level Gaspar requires slightly more tasks to attain the best performance since:

1. the task overhead is lower (e.g, there are 4-8 less JPPF tasks in a job);

2. an higher number of JPPF tasks is required for a good load balancing since there are less JPPF tasks per job.

The 2-levels Gaspar provides the best results as it generates less JPPF tasks in a job, and provides a local load balancing: each JPPF task has more threads than the available local cores. Thus, this implementation performs load balancing at two levels:

1. among compute nodes, using the JPPF task scheduler;

2. among cores in a compute node, using the Gaspar local scheduler service.

4.3. Molecular Dynamics Simulation

Molecular dynamics simulation is a popular kind of scientific application. In this kind of application a set of particles (that comprise a molecule and a solvent) interact in a series of time-steps. At each time-step the set of forces acting on each particle is computed and a new particle velocity and position is computed for the next time-step. Most of the computing time is spent on the computation of the forces acting on each particle on the system.

The JGF implementation models the simulation using two base classes:

1. the *MD* class implements the simulation code;

2. the *Particle* class implements the particle representation and the force computation among particles.

For this case study, the performance of the base JGF implementation was improved by changing the particle representation to use a class of arrays instead of the original array of pointers to particles. This provides both an improvement in the sequential execution time (a speed up to 1.3) and better scalability due to a more memory-friendly data layout [13].

```
1   public aspect MDGrid extends ExecutionService {

2

3       pointcut map() : call(void MD.computeForces());

4

5       List<MD> scatter(MD) {
6           ... // create several MD clones
7       }

8

9       MD reduce(List<MD>) {
10          ... // merge the several MD clones
11      }
12  }

13

14  public aspect MDParallelization extends ParallelizationService {
15      pointcut map() : call(void MD.computeForces());
16  }
```

Figure 25. Aspect to grid-enable the JGF MD case study.

Figure 25 illustrates the code required to grid-enable this benchmark. The code in lines 1-12 specificies task execution through the grid back-end:

1. each task will compute a subset of the forces (*map* pointcut in line 3);

2. each task receives a clone of the original *MD* object (the *scatter* method, 5-7);

3. after execution the multiple *MD* instances will be reduced into a single instance (in this case, by summing the forces computed by each task).

The code in lines 14-16 extends the base parallelization service to divide the force computation of each task among several local threads (*map* pointcut). In this case, scatter and gather methods are not required since all threads can work on the same *MD* instance.

Figure 26 compares the execution of the base JPPF implementation (with 19652 particles), by using JPPF sequential tasks against the Gaspar implementation (from Figure 25), which generates parallel tasks, each task spawning a number of threads equal to the number of physical cores in each grid node. The X-axis presents the number of parallel activities generated (i.e., the number of tasks multiplied by the number of threads within each task).

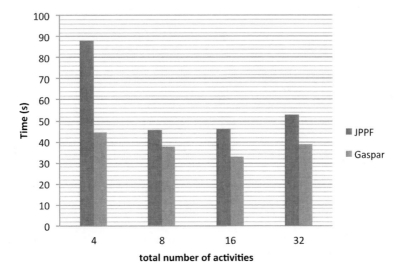

Figure 26. MD case study on multiple remote machines.

The Gaspar attains the best performance since the task overhead is lower (e.g, there are 4-8 less JPPF tasks in a job). In this case, generating a larger number of tasks imposes a higher overhead than in previous case studies, since each task requires a copy of the full set of particles, which is the main source of overhead of the remote task execution process.

4.3.1.   CPR and Adaptation

All the tests shown in this section were performed on the cluster using the 401-1, 401-2, 311-1 and 601-1 machines.

Figure 27 shows the overhead of using the CPR with the aspect approach against intrusively inserting the CPR routines directly on the source code, tested on the 401-1 machine. The aspect's overhead was tested with four different particle sizes, each one of them tested with one checkpoint (1CP) and zero checkpoints (0 CP) per execution. In all the tests the highest overhead was less than 0.52 % corresponding to 0.02 seconds.

Figure 28 shows the benefits of resource adaptation using different machines of the cluster. In this test there were used 500000 particles with only one step of simulation, which takes sequentially around 1700 seconds on the 311-1 machine. The iterations of the force calculation between one particle and the remaining were divided among four different tasks. The first task (task 0) received the first 125000 iterations ([0,125k[), the second task (task 1) received the second 125000 iterations and so on. Each task was executed on a different machine, using a different number of threads: - task 0 on the 401-1 with 8 threads; task 1 on the 401-2 with 16 threads; - the first part of task 2 was executed on the 311-1 with

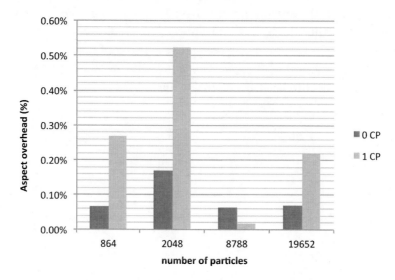

Figure 27. CPR - Overhead of the Aspects.

2 threads while the second part was executed on the 601-1 with 16 threads; Finally, task 3 was executed on the 601-1 machine with 16 threads. For these tests the checkpoint local was the moment after each iteration of the force calculation between one particle and the remaining. Each task saved their application state on file after reaching 62500 safe points, thus performing one checkpointing per task execution. The number of safe points is based on the number of force iterations performed by all the threads within a task.

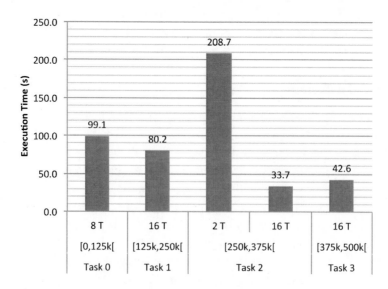

Figure 28. CPR - Grid Adaptation.

As it is possible to see in Figure 28 task 2 was taking by far the longest execution time, once it was being executed in a slower machine with only 2 threads. Therefore, after task 2 finishes to save their state in disk the task was aborted and restarted on a new machine

(601-1) with 16 threads using the checkpoint files from the previous execution. On the new execution, task 2 only had to calculate the force iterations between 315000 and 375000, hence calculating half the iterations with 4 times more threads. Therefore, speed up of 6.2x was obtained.

5. Related Work

There are many systems that implement a grid back-end. The Java GAT [14] is a grid API that aims to provide a simple interface to multiple grid middleware. Gridgain [2] is an open source framework designed specifically to support the development of grid applications, similar to JPPF. Ibis [15], ProActive [16] and HOCs [17] provide a front-end and back-end support to develop parallel applications that can take advantage of grid systems. Grid-enabling applications in these approaches require invasive and non-reversible source code changes. In these approaches grid-enabled scientific applications become dependent of the grid middleware.

GEMLCA [18] and GRASG [19] are two frameworks supporting non-invasive gridification of scientific codes. These approaches perform a coarse grain gridification, by deploying scientific codes as grid services. These approaches lack of support for fined-grained decomposition of the application functionality to take advantage of grids computational power.

Non-invasive fine-grained gridification has been applied to applications that adhere to specific coding conventions. The Pagis system [20] explores the use of reflection techniques to gridify applications structured accordings to the paradigm of process networks. AOP techniques have been previously applied to abstract the remote execution process of Java thread-based applications [21] and to implement the adaptation of a skeleton framework [22] to cluster and grid environments [7]. [23] introduces a bytecode gridifier that is non-invasive. The current implementation provides a connector for acessing grid services through the Satin, which is part of the Ibis GPF.

Montera [24] is a GPF that targets Monte Carlo simulations, which also provides a two-level scheduler. [25] provides a MapReduce framework also based on a two-level scheduler.

There are several Java frameworks that can off-load the execution of certain parts of a Java application into the GPU (see [26] for a recent overview and benchmarks). These frameworks include APARAPI and Rootbeer [27]. These frameworks require the development of both CPU and GPU kernels, since they provide a specific API for GPU. However, they relief the programmer from having to write CUDA or OpenCL specific code, as all code can be written in plain Java. Several works support the transparent execution of applications into GPUs. Java-GPU [28] introduces annotations to off-load certain Java methods into a GPU. It transforms certain loops into GPU kernels in a way similar to the Gaspar framework. None of these works supports computational grids.

The presented framework differs from these previous efforts by supporting non-invasive, fine-grained, gridification of scientific codes, without requiring the source code to adhere to specific API. In addition, gridification services are pluggable, supporting the adaptation of the application to specific running conditions, including the execution on a sequential machine, on multi-core systems and on computational grids composed by multi-core machines with GPUs.

Conclusion

This chapter introduced the current state of the art of grid programming frameworks and presented a framework based on the concept of pluggable service. Computational grids are supported by providing a pluggable service to a lightweight grid framework (JPPF), which can take advantage of desktop grids. The framework is a feasible way to take advantage of the computational power offered by modern machines, which now frequently provide multiple cores as well as programmable graphic processing units.

The presented framework takes advantage of the Java language to promote a seamless usage of grid resources, both at system level and at application level:

1. in order to deploy a computational grid the JPPF framework only requires running a small Java bootstamp program on each computing node and a driver program to coordinate the process of task dispatch to those computing nodes;

2. in order to port a given program to a computational grid, most of the typical burden of the porting process is simplified since Java intrinsically provides object serialization and code/data portability across platforms.

In the future it is expected to see an increasing number of cores per node and a wider variety of units providing special purpose processing capabilities that can accelerate certain tasks within applications. As many of those machines become widely spread across organizations, it will be of critical importance to enable seamless access these heterogeneous resources, preferably requiring the same programming effort as of building traditional desktop applications.

References

[1] I. Foster, C. Kesselman, and S. Tuecke, "The anatomy of the grid: Enabling scalable virtual organizations," *Int. J. High Perform. Comput. Appl.*, vol. 15, pp. 200–222, Aug. 2001.

[2] A. Anjomshoaa, F. Brisard, M. Drescher, D. Fellows, A. Ly, S. McGough, D. Pulsipher, and A. Savva, "Job submission description language (jsdl) specification, version 1.0," in *Open Grid Forum, GFD*, vol. 56, 2005.

[3] J. Yu and R. Buyya, "A taxonomy of workflow management systems for grid computing," *Journal of Grid Computing*, vol. 3, no. 3-4, pp. 171–200, 2005.

[4] J. M. Alonso, V. Hernández, and G. Moltó, "Gmarte: Grid middleware to abstract remote task execution," *Concurrency and Computation: Practice and Experience*, vol. 18, no. 15, pp. 2021–2036, 2006.

[5] C. Mateos, A. Zunino, and M. Campo, "A survey on approaches to gridification," *Software: Practice and Experience*, vol. 38, no. 5, pp. 523–556, 2008.

[6] J. L. Sobral, "Pluggable grid services," in *Grid Computing, 2007 8th IEEE/ACM International Conference on*, pp. 113–120, IEEE, 2007.

[7] J. L. Sobral and A. J. Proenca, "Enabling jaskel skeletons for clusters and computational grids," in *Cluster Computing, 2007 IEEE International Conference on*, pp. 365–371, IEEE, 2007.

[8] G. Kiczales, J. Lamping, A. Mendhekar, C. Maeda, C. Lopes, J. marc Loingtier, and J. Irwin, "Aspect-oriented programming," in *ECOOP*, SpringerVerlag, 1997.

[9] R. E. Filman and D. P. Friedman, "Aspect-oriented programming is quantification and obliviousness," in *Workshop on Advanced separation of Concerns, OOPSLA*, vol. 2000, 2000.

[10] B. Medeiros and J. a. L. Sobral, "Aomplib: An aspect library for large-scale multi-core parallel programming," in *Proceedings of the 2013 42Nd International Conference on Parallel Processing, ICPP '13*, (Washington, DC, USA), pp. 270–279, IEEE Computer Society, 2013.

[11] B. Medeiros and J. L. Sobral, "Checkpoint and run-time adaptation with pluggable parallelisation.," in *ICPP* (G. R. Gao and Y.-C. Tseng, eds.), pp. 434–443, IEEE, 2011.

[12] L. A. Smith, J. M. Bull, and J. Obdrizalek, "A parallel java grande benchmark suite," in *Supercomputing, ACM/IEEE 2001 Conference*, pp. 6–6, IEEE, 2001.

[13] N. Faria, R. Silva, and J. L. Sobral, "Impact of data structure layout on performance," in *Parallel, Distributed and Network-Based Processing (PDP), 2013 21st Euromicro International Conference on*, pp. 116–120, IEEE, 2013.

[14] G. Allen, K. Davis, T. Goodale, A. Hutanu, H. Kaiser, T. Kielmann, A. Merzky, R. van Nieuwpoort, A. Reinefeld, F. Schintke, *et al.*, "The grid application toolkit: toward generic and easy application programming interfaces for the grid," *Proceedings of the IEEE*, vol. 93, no. 3, pp. 534–550, 2005.

[15] R. V. Van Nieuwpoort, J. Maassen, G. Wrzesińska, R. F. Hofman, C. J. Jacobs, T. Kielmann, and H. E. Bal, "Ibis: a flexible and efficient java-based grid programming environment," *Concurrency and Computation: Practice and Experience*, vol. 17, no. 7-8, pp. 1079–1107, 2005.

[16] L. Baduel, F. Baude, D. Caromel, A. Contes, F. Huet, M. Morel, and R. Quilici, "Programming, composing, deploying for the grid," in *Grid Computing: Software Environments and Tools*, pp. 205–229, Springer, 2006.

[17] S. Gorlatch and J. Dünnweber, "From grid middleware to grid applications: Bridging the gap with hocs," in *Future Generation Grids*, pp. 241–261, Springer, 2006.

[18] T. Delaitre, T. Kiss, A. Goyeneche, G. Terstyanszky, S. Winter, and P. Kacsuk, "Gemlca: Running legacy code applications as grid services," *Journal of Grid Computing*, vol. 3, no. 1-2, pp. 75–90, 2005.

[19] Q.-T. Ho, T. Hung, W. Jie, H.-M. Chan, E. Sindhu, G. Subramaniam, T. Zang, and X. Li, "Grasg-a framework for gridifying and running applications on service-oriented grids," in *Proceedings of the Sixth IEEE International Symposium on Cluster Computing and the Grid*, pp. 305–312, IEEE Computer Society, 2006.

[20] D. Webb and A. L. Wendelborn, "The pagis grid application environment," in *Computational Science-ICCS* 2003, pp. 1113–1122, Springer, 2003.

[21] P. H. M. Maia, N. C. Mendonça, V. Furtado, W. Cirne, and K. Saikoski, "A process for separation of crosscutting grid concerns," in *Proceedings of the 2006 ACM symposium on Applied computing*, pp. 1569–1574, ACM, 2006.

[22] J. Ferreira, J. Sobral, and A. Proenca, "Jaskel: A java skeleton-based framework for structured cluster and grid computing," in *Proceedings of the Sixth IEEE International Symposium on Cluster Computing and the Grid*, pp. 301–304, IEEE Computer Society, 2006.

[23] C. Mateos, A. Zunino, M. Hirsch, M. Fernandez, and M. Campo, *"A software tool for semi-automatic gridification of resource-intensive java bytecodes and its application to ray tracing and sequence alignment"*, pp. 172–186, 2011.

[24] M. A. R. Pascual, R. M. Garcia, and I. M. Llorente, "Montera: A framework for efficient execution of monte carlo codes on grid infrastructures.," *Computing and Informatics*, vol. 32, no. 1, pp. 113–144, 2013.

[25] Y. Luo, Z. Guo, Y. Sun, B. Plale, J. Qiu, and W. W. Li, "A hierarchical framework for cross-domain mapreduce execution," in *Proceedings of the Second International Workshop on Emerging Computational Methods for the Life Sciences*, ECMLS '11, (New York, NY, USA), pp. 15–22, ACM, 2011.

[26] J. Docampo, S. Ramos, G. L. Taboada, R. R. Exposito, J. Tourino, and R. Doallo, "Evaluation of java for general purpose gpu computing.," in *AINA Workshops*, pp. 1398–1404, 2013.

[27] P. C. Pratt-Szeliga, J. W. Fawcett, and R. D. Welch, "Rootbeer: Seamlessly using gpus from java.," in *14th IEEE International Conference on High Performance Computing and Communication & 9th IEEE International Conference on Embedded Software and Systems*, HPCC-ICESS 2012, Liverpool, United Kingdom, June 25-27, 2012, pp. 375–380, 2012.

[28] P. Calvert, "Parallelisation of java for graphics processors," *Part II Dissertation, Computer Science Tripos*, University of Cambridge, 2010.

In: Grid Computing: Techniques and Future Prospects ISBN: 978-1-63117-704-0
Editors: J. G. Barbosa and I. Dutra, pp. 187-206 © 2015 Nova Science Publishers, Inc.

Chapter 7

DESKTOP GRID IN THE ERA OF CLOUD COMPUTING

Peter Kacsuk[1,2,*], Zoltan Farkas[1], Jozsef Kovacs[1],
Adam Visegradi[1], Attila Marosi[1], Robert Lovas[1],
Gabor Kecskemeti[1], Zsolt Nemeth[1] and Mark Gergely[1]

[1]MTA SZTAKI, Institute for Computer Science and Control
of the Hungarian Academy of Sciences, Hungary
[2]Centre of Parallel Computing, University of Westminster, UK

Abstract

BOINC desktop grids have been used for more than a decade for running grand challenge applications. In this chapter we show those technologies, and particularly virtualization and cloud solutions, that make BOINC desktop grids more generic and speed up the execution of existing grid-enabled parameter sweep applications without porting them to BOINC and eliminate the tail problem of volunteer BOINC systems. Furthermore, we show a technology by which institutional and public desktop grids can be created in a few minutes in clouds and used without any BOINC knowledge.

Keywords: gLite, BOINC, volunteer computing, desktop grid, cloud

Introduction

Desktop grids (DG) provide the cheapest possible way of building large computing infrastructures for e-science. BOINC became very popular to support grand-challenge scientific applications like climate research, anti-cancer research, etc. However, its mass usage among scientists has not happened so far although, most of the scientific applications are large parameter study simulations where BOINC-like volunteer computing could help a lot. The reason is that porting an application to BOINC is not straightforward. In SZTAKI, we have developed several tools that made the porting much easier, but the real breakthrough

---

* E-mail address: peter.kacsuk@sztaki.mta.hu; Address: 1111 Budapest, Kendestreet 13-17, Hungary. (Corresponding author)

has happened when we introduced virtualization in the BOINC client. We have developed GBAC (Generic BOINC Application Client) [10] based on VirtualBox virtualization technology. As a result, porting does not require any effort and existing applications can be instantly used in BOINC systems without preregistering them on the BOINC server. We have also developed 3GBridge [9] that enables access to BOINC systems via a high level job submission interface, and hence users can exploit BOINC systems even from complex workflow applications. 3GBridge also enables the connection of BOINC to other types of grid middlewares such as gLite [1], ARC [2], and UNICORE [4]. In this way, for example, gLite based middleware can be extended with institutional and volunteer BOINC systems in a transparent way. As a result, gLite users can access larger number of free resources without changing their applications.

Cloud computing [12] opens a new horizon to support the DG systems and hence, can help in many ways to further disseminate the idea of desktop grids and make them easily accessible for researchers. The first aspect in which clouds can assist volunteer desktop grids is the possibility of significantly reducing the tail problem [22] (occurs when failures of unreliable resources accumulate and cause significant delay in the last 10% of batch) by extending a desktop grid with dedicated cloud resources. The number of these resources can be increased and decreased according to the number of tail tasks in the different computations running in the desktop grid. The second issue that prevented researchers from extending their existing grid infrastructure (for example, Globus [3]), with DG systems was the difficulty of creating and installing BOINC systems. Cloud computing solves this problem by providing an extremely easy and fast way to deploy the core BOINC system in a cloud, and then extend it with volunteer resources. We have created such a system to demonstrate the applicability of this technology. This approach can be used in a more generic way to create any kind of architecture in the cloud on demand.

The chapteris organized as follows. First, we shortly summarize the BOINC volunteer desktop grid technology and one of its projects, called EDGeS@home, that was created for EGI (European Grid Infrastructure) user communities. Next we explain how the gLite based VOs (Virtual Organizations) can be extended with BOINC desktop grids, and particularly with EDGeS@home. Afterwards, the chapter introduces the GBAC virtualization technology and its advantages. Then the chapterfocuses on how clouds can be used to eliminate the tail problem in desktop grids. Later, we show examples on how EGI user communities access and use EDGeS@home. Subsequently, the chapter shortly describes the One Click Cloud Orchestrator (OCCO) cloud deployment tool and its usage for quickly creating BOINC desktop grid systems without BOINC knowledge. Finally, we summarize the most important aspects of related research.

EDGeS@home as a Volunteer Desktop Grid

The generic mechanismof BOINC-based volunteer desktop grids can be summarized in the following way. Volunteers join the project by downloading and installing a piece of lightweight software: the BOINC client. First, the client downloads the registered application binaries from the BOINC project. Second, it periodically fetches new input files and parameters for the application in a form of so called workunits. These downloaded tasks are then processed in the background on the volunteer resources.

Any application supported by a desktop grid must be deployed and registered in the project, thus it is not possible to submit and run arbitrary ones. Also, there is no possibility of communication between running tasks, theso called embarrassingly parallel applications are supported only. Therefore, desktop grids are best suited for bag-of-tasks or parameter study type applications, where the applications do not changeoften.

EDGeS@home is a BOINC [5] based volunteer desktop grid project established with the goal to support EGI (European Grid Infrastructure [19]) user communities in executing large parameter sweep applications. Running since 2008, it has beenstarted under the Enabling Desktop Grids for e-Science (EDGeS) EU FP7 project [15]. It was maintained further by the successor of EDGeS, the European Desktop Grid Initiative (EDGI) [8] until late 2012 and is currently maintained by the International Desktop Grid Federation Support Project (IDGF-SP) [16]. EDGeS@home has currently over 13,000 registered volunteers with 21,000 registered hosts.

Traditional desktop grids usually target a single grand-challenge scientific problem. Contrary to the traditional ones, EDGeS@home is running multiple applications, making it an "umbrella" project in order to support as many EGI user communities as possible. Any volunteer has the freedom to select which application(s) he or she wants to support from the deployed ones. This means that applications are usually competing with each other for a given set of resources and each of them can typically use a fraction of the client machines registered for the project. At the time of writing, EDGeS@home hosts 10 applications from different science domains such as physics, logistics or biology, and a framework called Generic BOINC Application Client (GBAC, to be discussed in a later section) [10], which allows running arbitrary applications inside virtual machines.

EDGeS@home is part of the IDGF desktop grid Regional Operations Centre (ROC) in the EGI infrastructure. This centre collects volunteer resources, each of its sites representing a BOINC project. The ROC has been founded with two sites, one of which is EDGeS@home, in order to make the volunteer BOINC projects visible for the EGI user communities as normal gLite resources. The ROC has the same services as normal resource sites have: information system, workloads management system, job submission interface, monitoring and accounting system, and authentication. The EDGeS@home BOINC project is open for EGIscientists for submitting jobs.

EGI user communities typically use ARC [4], gLite [1] and UNICORE [2] middleware based grid systems. They have got used to these grids, and quite oftenthey are not prepared to learn a new type of grid middleware like BOINC. Therefore, if we want to support these communities we have to solve the issue of automatically transferring parameter sweep application jobs from their grid infrastructure into the EDGeS@home BOINC infrastructure. The advantage for the users is accessing hundreds of thousands of resources which is a higher scale than ARC, gLite or UNICORE usually provides. To achieve this goal the EDGI EU FP7 project has extended ARC, gLite and UNICORE with the capability of transferring jobs to BOINC desktop grids. In the next Section, as an example, we describe this solution for gLite. The interested reader can find the description of the ARC and UNICORE integration as well in the deliverables of EDGI project [8].

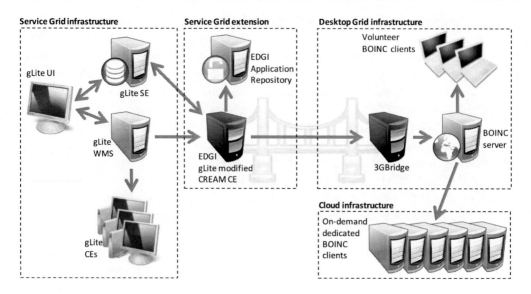

Figure 1. EDGI Infrastructure to bridge gLite jobs to BOINC DGs.

Extending gLite VOs with BOINC Systems

The goal of extending gLite VOs with BOINC systems is to transparently transfer parametric jobs from a gLite VO to one or more supporting BOINC systems, and to distribute large number of job instances of parametric jobs among the large number of BOINC client resources.

In order to extend gLite VOs with BOINC systems we have designed a bridging solution. The key component is the modified Computing Element (mCE; see "EDGI gLite modified CREAM CE" in Figure 1). It extracts the job from the gLite system and transfers it to a remote desktop grid site. On the remote BOINC server a Generic Grid-Grid (3G) Bridge service [17] ("3G Bridge"inFigure 1 is running to receive the incoming jobs and to insert them into the BOINC server. These two components (modified CREAM [1] CE and the 3G Bridge) in the infrastructure represent the two pillars of the bridge.

To control which jobs can be transferred through the bridge, the EDGI application repository [18] ("EDGI Application Repository inFigure 1) has been introduced. This contains those registered applications that are validated for the gLite→BOINC execution.

Concerning the security mechanisms of the two middleware, in gLite, compute resources trust the user who is holding a certificate, and accept any kind of executable from a trusted user. In desktop grids the compute resources (i.e., the clients, or donors, who offer their resources) trust the DG project server, and accept only pre-registered and validated executables. To overcome this conceptual difference we combined the two concepts by restricting the applications that can be passed from the gLitesystem to the particular DG system. This means that the transfer is only realized when a trusted user submits an application that is trusted by the target DG system. Enabling the transfer is done by the central EDGI Application Repository (AR) that stores the validated/trusted applications with all of their executable binaries to be submitted, and with a list of DG systems that trust and has registered this application. Applications are registered by the admins, users can list/query or request new registrations on demand. The EDGI AR [25] distinguishes several platforms (gLite, BOINC, XtremWeb, etc.) for which developers can upload the compatible binaries. In addition to the binaries, the AR stores the description of the application, an example jdl and input files, and all the pieces of information that are necessary to perform a correct job submission. The central EDGI AR also stores the information about which VO the particular application can be submitted from and which computing element (and its queue) will be able to handle the job submission successfully. This information is needed since DG systems are configured for and can be reached through a special CREAM CE queue.

This solution was too complicated for the user communities: it required first the porting of the original grid (ARC, gLite or UNICORE) application to BOINC, then the ported application had to be validated for the various grid and BOINC combinations. In order to avoid all these complexities we have developed the GBAC virtualization framework [10] that has been introduced to enable executing jobs inside virtual machines on the BOINC clients. With the help of the virtualization environment GBAC provides, the mCE becameable to automatically convert non-registered applications into a GBAC workunit. Using virtualization on volunteer resources, untrusted applications can also be executed safely under BOINC. Moreover, gLite users do not need to modify their submission jdl file when changing from normal gLite resources to desktop grid ones.

The last problem that kept grid users from using BOINC was the so-called tail problem [22]. Based on experiences of the BOINC community, the first 80-90% of the jobs belonging to one application are executed according to the expected speed-up of parallel systems but the last 10-20% areexecuted much slower since the unreliable volunteer BOINC clients can cause significant delay in giving back the result of the task they registered for solving. This tail problem can be solved in several ways and we proposed the extension of Desktop Grid infrastructure with on-demand dedicated cloud resources ("On-demand dedicated BOINC clients" in Figure 1) that proved to be a very efficient solution. This cloud extension will be detailed in a later section.

Before giving more detailed description of the cloud-oriented extensions of desktop grids, first we show the two most popular deployment scenarios of creating such a combined infrastructure. In the first case, extending the existing gLite VO with already gathered and maintained volunteer resources is shown, while the second case details setting up the combined infrastructure based on an institutional desktop grid system.

Case Study: Extending a gLite VO by the EDGeS@home Project

There are many gLite VOs around Europe, for which gLite administrators are taking care of the infrastructure, and not willing to take up operating a separate desktop grid site for collecting volunteer resources. EDGI (and later IDGF-SP [16]) eases their work by maintaining and offeringaccess tothe extension services ("Service Grid extension" in Figure 1) and the required volunteer desktop grid project: EDGeS@home with a large number of volunteer desktop grid resources, and cloud resources in addition. In this scenario, the gLite VO admin has nothing to do; EDGI (or IDGF-SP) takes care of the operation of the modified computing element, the 3G Bridge and all the desktop grid related tasks. After the necessary configuration is performed in the Service Grid extension, the gLite mCE appears among the CEs of the supported VO. This experiment is an ongoing and continuous activity performed by the IDGF-SP project in order to support various EGI VOs in accessing EDGeS@home.

Case Study: Extending a gLite VO by Institutional DG Site

BOINC can be usedas an effective solution for aggregating the available compute capacity of desktop computers inside an institute.For example, universities can easily follow this strategy to create a campus-wide desktop grid system to provide large computational capacity for the researchers. University of Westminsteris a good example, where approximately 1800 machines have been collected andutilized by a campus desktop grid and offered for their scientists to run various simulations [20]. Such a newly built campus DG site is a good candidate to be bridged to a gLite VO where the university is a member andto provide a significant capacity increase to that VO. To support this scenario, the IDGF-SP project has consolidated all the necessary software components (gLite mCE, AR, 3G Bridge, GBAC, etc.) and provides them freely for academic institutes. The project set up a website [21] for system administrators on how to setup and operate a combined gLite desktop grid infrastructure. This scenario requires very little effort from the administrators if the required components (BOINC server, 3G Bridge, gLite mCE) of such an infrastructure are deployed in a cloud system. In order to support this easy deployment and maintenance, IDGF-SP provides the necessary cloud images [21] too, as described below in detail in the section about the One Click Orchestrator.

GBAC for Avoiding Application Porting

As mentioned in the previous section, gLite jobs can be transparently transferred to a connected BOINC DG system if the application has been already ported to BOINC. Unfortunately, the porting effort can sometimes be significant, which keepsuser communities from applying desktop grid technologies. SZTAKI has developed the DC-API [7] and GenWrapper [6] tools that significantly reduced the porting effort, but even this was not enough. The communities did not want to invest in any porting effort at all. This is understandable, as they have free access to managed grid resources, i.e., someone else pays for their application execution on the managed grid resources. However, if they have to pay for the resources, as in the case of commercial clouds, this attitude will changesignificantly. Nevertheless, we had to find a solution on how to avoid application porting for BOINC systems.

As a result of searching for such a solution, we developed the Generic BOINC Application Client (GBAC), a virtualization-based wrapper. It is aimed at a generic framework providing virtualized environments for different distributed computing infrastructures (DCIs). GBAC is implemented using the DC-API Meta API [7]and does not rely on any middleware-specific functionalities. Thus, it can be used not only with BOINC, but also on any DCIs that are supported by DC-API. GBAC currently supports VirtualBox as hypervisor. From here on, we refer to the BOINC version of GBAC for demonstrating its concepts and internals.

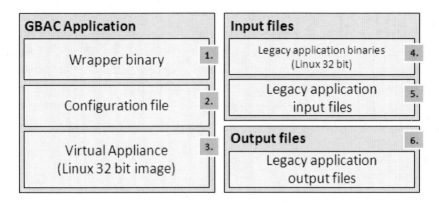

Figure 2. GBAC: application, inputs and outputs.

As shown in Figure 2, the GBAC wrapper consists of the following components. First, the wrapper binary itself is a BOINC enabled DC-API application that contains all BOINC related parts and handles communication with the BOINC client.

Its task is to set up the client execution environment and manage the virtual machine on the client machine. Second, a user-supplied XML based configuration file is used to set the parameters of the virtual machine: (i) the operating system type (e.g., Linux 64bit); (ii) the size of the allocated memory for the virtual machine; (iii) whether the machine should have network access; (iv) which virtual appliance to use; (v) whether to enable a shared directory between the host and the guest (the virtual machine); and (vi) whether to enable network for the guest. The third component is a compressed virtual appliance that contains the operating systems and libraries for the virtual machine. By default it contains a 32bit Linux installation with the Guest Toolscomponent of GBAC installed. However, arbitrary Linux distributions, both 32bit and 64bit, can be used instead. The Guest Tools, which is the fourth and final component, is deployed in the virtual appliance, and handles the interaction between the GBAC wrapper and the application inside the virtual machine. It acts as an agent of the wrapper, sets up a sandboxed environment for the application, executes it, performs logging, and returns the outputs. More details about GBAC can be found in [10].

Contrary to the normal BOINC use case, where the available applications are registered at the project, GBAC provides two use cases. First, a single-purpose mode, in which GBAC is registered with a single legacy application. This conforms to the normal BOINC use case with the following additions: (a) the legacy application does not require any BOINC related porting; (b) the legacy application will be run in a homogeneous environment based on the same virtual applicance (VA) regardless of the software and hardware characteristics of the donor machines; and (c) as a consequence, only a single binary of the applicationcompatible with the guest VM under GBACis required. The second use case is the multipurpose mode. Here, GBAC is deployed on BOINC without any legacy applications, and arbitrary ones can be submitted as inputs for GBAC. In this case, both the legacy application binaries and theirinputs are inputs of GBAC. This allows, on top of the previous additions ((a)-(c)), to overcome the limitation BOINC imposes on applications. Namely, that each of them must be deployed and registered before use, and only these trusted ones are available to the users. GBAC allows delegating this trust and, instead of the legacy application, the submitting user is trusted. As a result, beyond avoiding the application porting effort, there is another advantage of using the GBAC concept. It eliminates the need of using the EDGI Application

Repository (which filters the applications to be executed). In the case when the target BOINC server is equipped with the GBAC virtualization framework, the modified Computing Element recognizes this situation and skips the AR checking procedure, and submits the incoming job wrapped as a GBAC-jobto the BOINC server. All is done automatically, no user interaction is needed for the bridging. In this case, the BOINC clients trust the GBAC application, which safely encapsulates the original job by running it inside a virtual machine.

Cloud for Tail Elimination

EDGeS@home has over 21,000 registered volunteer hosts. However, the active number of hosts is always lower and varies over time depending on the volunteers' usage pattern; e.g., some volunteers only run BOINC when their computer is idle, but some turn off completely their computers when they are about to be idle for longer periods of time. Hardware failures on volunteer resources cannot be neglected either. The consequence of these is that the task failure and completion deadline-miss ratios can be high. In case of batches of tasks, a single delayed task is going to affect the completion time of the whole batch, resulting in the so-calledtail problem [22].

There are different methods available for improving task completion times: (i) redundant computing, (ii) reliability and availability based scheduling, and (iii) resubmission. Redundancy (i) means that multiple copies of the same task are distributed to clients with the expectation that at least a single one is going to finish in time. Reliability and availability based scheduling (ii) means that the system will prioritize the reliable resources over less reliable and less available. Finally, resubmission (iii) identifies problematic tasks and submits them again, e.g., in case of a batch the last 10% uncompleted tasks can be resubmitted trying to avoid the tail effect. Each of these methods on its own will improve the completion time to some extent; however, usually a combination of these is used. The problem is always twofold. First, the set of resources that is considered highly available and reliable must be determined. Second, a redirection mechanism is required for the tasks. Determining reliability and availability is a challenge itself; however, there are already good mechanisms implemented, e.g., for BOINC, that can be used as a foundation [23].

One of the goals of EDGI was adding certain Quality of Service (QoS) capabilities to desktop grids to improve task completion times. The project investigated different alternatives like redundancy with resubmission [24], however the final method chosen was resubmission with reliability based scheduling. BOINC provides information about reliability and availability of the connected (volunteer) resources that can be used to determine the most reliable resources.

These resources can be used as complementary ones, but primarily resources from private Infrastructure-as-a-Service (IaaS) clouds provided by the consortium members were utilized, with the option to scale out to public providers, like Amazon Web Services. It has been designed as a non-interactive solution, meaning that the system automates the process of task redirection for the users without any interaction from the users. Table 1 describes the available IaaS cloud resources for EDGeS@home. These are single virtual core resources, thus each resource provides a worker with a single core CPU. Each resource runs a special Virtual Appliance that contains the BOINC Client. These instances run 64 bit version Debian

Linux 6.0 and have at least 2GB free space for BOINC tasks. The instances are instructed via contextualization data to attach to a given BOINC project with given user credentials.

As Table 1shows (in its 3rd column) each private cloud has a dedicated user at EDGeS@home. The dedicated users are used to group together the resources coming from the different clouds for the reliability based scheduling. Also, the profiles of these users are public, i.e., their performance can be checked on the website of EDGeS@home.

As shown in Figure 3, the cloud resources are managed from a dedicated virtual machine ("EDGI Cloud Management") from the LPDS cloud. This management VM instructs all configured clouds. It uses an enhanced version of the solution described in [10]. The management node is responsible for starting and stopping instances as required. It is able to interact with different IaaS cloud middleware, namely OpenNebula, OpenStack, Eucalyptus and Amazon Web Services using the de facto standard Amazon EC2 interface.

Table 1. IaaS cloud resources available for EDGeS@home

Cloud Acronym	Cloud Provider	EDGeS@home User	Middleware	Number of Resources (up to)
CICA	Centro Informático Científico de Andalucía	CloudCICA	OpenNebula	100
LPDS	MTA SZTAKI LPDS	CloudLPDS	OpenNebula	64
UniMainz	University of Mainz	CloudMAINZ	OpenStack	32
UNIZAR	University of Zaragoza	CloudUNIZAR	OpenStack	50
UoW	University of Westminster	UoW	OpenStack	52
EC2	Amazon EC2	CloudAmazon	Amazon WS	∞
Total				300 +

When a new worker is requested, the URL of the BOINC project and a specific authenticator unique to each configured cloud is used as contextualization. This allows them to connect to the BOINC project. The instances remain attached to the BOINC project and continue processing tasks until they are terminated by the manager.

This way, the different configured private clouds contribute reliable resources for EDGeS@home. However, this solves only the first part of the problem. For the second part, EDGI developed a complementary Scheduler component for BOINC that reassigns problematic tasks to multiple sets of resources. This component assigns the oldest non-finished tasks in the system to one of the configured reliable resource group. In this case, a resource group is the set of resources made available from each connected private cloud.

The scheduler keeps track of the number of assigned tasks for each resource group and assigns new tasks based on the number of resources available in that group. It also provides an interface extending the administrator interface of BOINC for querying the status of assignments as showninFigure 4. It allows filtering the jobs based on the different configured clouds (e.g., "LPDS", "UNIZAR")according toFigure 4 and applications (e.g., "DSP" in the figure) or all tasks ("All" in our figure). Reassignment is performed in round-robin order, where each configured cloud has a weight and capacity assigned and a global limit for the assignments total. The Scheduler keeps track of the total number of assigned jobs and the currently processed ones for each resource group. It continuously keeps the number of assignments at the global limit while removing finished assignments and adding new ones based on the group limit and prioritizing between resources based on the group weights.

Utilization of EDGeS@home by EGI User Communities

After the technical solutions shownin the previous sections every obstacle of using the desktop grid technology has been eliminated and indeed EGI user communities have started to use the EDGeS@home volunteer desktop grid more and more intensively. Furthermore, these communities use EDGeS@home via different interfaces, demonstrating that the user interface flexibility we provide is indeed an important feature of supporting the user communities. There are three ways of accessing the services of EDGeS@home as shown in Figure 5.

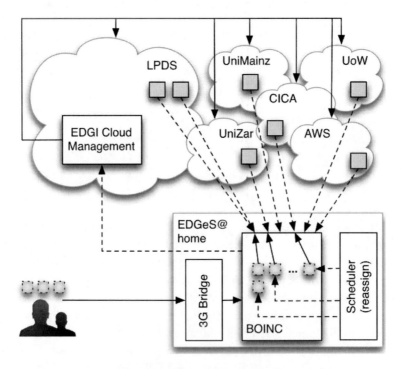

Figure 3. Task reassignment in the non-interactive QoS process.

	LPDS	UNIZAR	CICA	MAINZ	UOW	Amazon EC2
Jobs on Clouds	MetaJobs	Assignments Log				
Over	All | DSP	All | DSP	All | DSP	All | DSP	All | DSP	All | DSP
In-progress	All | DSP	All | DSP	All | DSP	All | DSP	All | DSP	All | DSP

Figure 4. Information interface for querying the different desktop grid tasks (by application) assigned to the configured clouds.

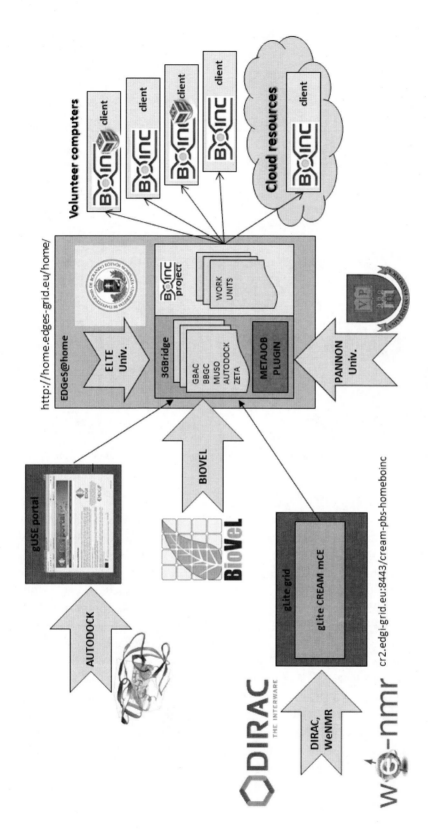

Figure 5. Overview of various access modes of EDGeS@home volunteer resources.

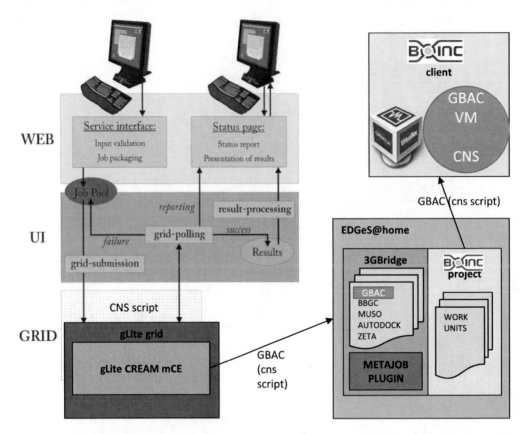

Figure 6. WeNMR HADDOCK portal: modeling of biomolecular complexes, and its connection to EDGeS@home.

One possibility of accessing EDGeS@homeis from a gLite VO as we introducedbefore. This interface is applied by the WeNMR project [30]. They use the WeNMR HADDOCK portal for modeling of biomolecular complexes by submitting their jobs to the WeNMR VO. This VO is extended with the gLite CREAM mCE provided by the IDGF-SP project. So, the transfer of the WeNMR jobs to EDGeS@home is transparent for the WeNMR gateway users. Currently the WeNMR VO decided to send every 10th job to EDGeS@home to utilise volunteer resources beyond their own infrastructure. Notice that the utilisation of volunteer resources did not require any application porting, or any Windows version development since most of the applications are written for Linux OS, but most of the volunteer resources are MS Windows based. The architecture of supporting the execution of WeNMR jobs in EDGeS@home is shown in Figure 6.

The second option to access EDGeS@home is from a gateway that is directly connected to the 3G Bridge component of EDGeS@home. This interface possibility is used by the AUTODOCK gateway of the SCI-BUS project that was set up jointly by MTA SZTAKI and the University of Westminster. Biologists and chemists can easily do docking experiments via this gateway that is tailored for this application type. All the docking jobs defined by the users of the gateway are directly sent to the 3G Bridge component of EDGeS@home and results returned by EDGeS@home are directly shown on the gateway.

The third possible access mode to EDGeS@home is via the 3G Bridge API. This approach has been used by three projects: the EU FP7 BioVEL project [31], the Riemann zeta research project of the Eötvös Loránd University (ELTE, Budapest) [36] and the Optimiser for Linear Programming project of the Pannon University Veszprem[37]. The first one searches for values of t on the critical line, where the Riemannzeta function Z(t) is larger than a predetermined threshold, in order to get a better understanding of the behavior of the distribution of primes. In the second one they are trying to find optimal values for system solvers of Linear Programming problems by doing parameter sweep of a large number of runtime parameters. Due to the lack of space, these projects are not detailed here. The interested reader can find their descriptions in the following literature [36, 37].

Cloud for Automatic Deployment of Desktop Grids

As described beforehand, grid VOs can easily be extended with new institutional desktop grids. Institutional desktop grids have the advantage to use resources that are already available in the institutes and hence, without investment of new hardware significant computing resources can be put together. However, to set up such institutional desktop grid requires BOINC knowledge that is usually not available in universities and other academic institutes. In order to overcome this problem we have developed a new tool called as One Click Cloud Orchestrator (OCCO) and a web-based cloud installation environment that enables for institutes and universities to quickly (in several minutes) set up their own desktop grid in a cloud without any BOINC knowledge.

One Click Cloud Orchestrator (OCCO)

Here we give a short overview of the OCCO architecture and components (see Figure 7) that allows the prompt creation of various infrastructures in the cloud including the required BOINC infrastructure, too. OCCO has the following components:(i) Automated Infrastructure Maintenance, (ii) Infrastructure Processor, (iii) Cloud Handler, (iv) VM Reshaper, and (v) Information Dispatcher. We have defined the Automated Infrastructure Maintenance component as the one responsible to understand the customized deployment descriptors. But this component does not only provide the descriptor processing capabilities but it also offers dependency resolution (so the nodes of the particular instantiated infrastructures are instantiated in a natural order), scalability and error resilience rule evaluation and enactment (so the end user does not have to intervene in its infrastructure's internal operations). The Infrastructure Processor component of OCCO is used to ensure that the definitions of the infrastructure nodes are propagated to the VM Reshaper (which allows runtime reconfiguration of a virtual machine to meet a particular node description). In addition, the Infrastructure Processor sends such virtual machine requests to the Cloud Handler that ensures the intended role of the virtual machines after their creation. Next, the Cloud Handler is responsible for selecting a cloud infrastructure that will host a particular virtual machine, and interfacing with the infrastructure provider in a unified manner. Finally, the Information Dispatcher allows the Automated Infrastructure Maintenance component to determine the current state of the infrastructure to be used during the scaling and error resolution rule evaluation process.

In order to enable the creation of a BOINC infrastructure in a cloud we have to provide the Infrastructure Deployment Descriptor (IDD) of the target BOINC infrastructure for OCCO. The preparation of such an IDD requires some expertise and therefore we have created the required IDD. We have also created a web based UI through which user community or university representatives can initiate the creation of their BOINC infrastructure. The current version of the BOINC infrastructure we provide through this web interface is a demonstration infrastructure that connects the Autodock gateway of SCI-BUS to a BOINC infrastructure via the 3G Bridge as shown in Figure 8. As an extra functionality, the BOINC project is associated with a public IP address; therefore, the user can attach his/her own BOINC client to the server. Using automatically deployed and configured BOINC clients in virtual machines, computational resources are automatically attached to this BOINC project. Our descriptor template allows the customization of the number of computational resources. Computing jobs arrive to the BOINC project as work units with the help of the WS-PGRADE/gUSE science gateway (also automatically deployed as a node of the virtual infrastructure). Overall, the prototype shows how a complete gateway plus DCI with resources can be deployed by OCCO and how the components attach to each other. Detailed description of a similar infrastructure is shown at http://doc.desktopgrid.hu/doku.php?id=scenario:unidg with a different application.

In the prototype's welcome- and request submission page (see Figure 9) the user is not only requested to fill in the list of customization options, but he/she must also provide some details about him/her for identification and for justification. After a request is submitted, the prototype first asks for approval by the SZTAKI cloud administrators then initiates the infrastructure's creation with the Automated Infrastructure Maintenance component. Once the infrastructure is created, the notification service generates an email with all the authentication and access details to the new infrastructure (e.g., url of the science gateway and of the BOINC project plus user/password for login). With these details, users just need to login to the gateway, submit a scientific workflow (implementing molecule docking simulation based on the autodock tool) with their inputs and inspect the operation (i.e., how the jobs are flowing through the infrastructure and processed by the BOINC clients). To prevent SZTAKI's IaaS from overloading the OCCO created virtual infrastructures have a limited lifetime. Our notification service sends an email to the infrastrucure's user before the shutdown procedure is initiated. Limitation for the lifetime of the infrastructure is only applied for the demonstration infrastructure.

Notice that this service is used just for demonstration and trial purposes but the same technology can be used to set up real BOINC infrastructures with generic purpose WS-PGRADE/gUSE gateways in the cloud to which the user has access. The created BOINC infrastructure is using the GBAC technology and, as a result, no application porting is needed: the gateway/BOINC infrastructure created can immediately be used by the university or other user communities to submit and run applications in the created BOINC system.

Related Work

SpeQuloS [22] aims to shorten the completion time of a batch (collection of jobs) running on a desktop grid by redirecting the workunits to cloud resources. This is similar to our proposed solution however, it requires user interaction as users must explicitly request the speed-up of their batches and must pay for it by virtual credits that can be earned by volunteering their own machine for the target desktop grid site. The more capacity they offer, the more credit they collect. The more credit they have, the more jobs can be redirected to cloud resources and the less completion time the batch will reach.

Another work targeting the elimination of the tail-effect has been introduced by the University of Westminster. The system introduced in [26] is similar to the one presented in this chapter; however, they use a different batch system (PBS) for executing the replicas of the delayed workunits in BOINC. Therefore, the delayed jobs are not handled in the frame of BOINC, but resubmitted to a separate PBS cluster that is set up on-demand when a tail has to be handled. Another difference is that they use an institutional BOINC system,not volunteer resources.

Lei Ni and Aaron Harwood [27] propose the "next generation Volunteer Computing systems on top of well studied Peer-to-Peer techniques to fully take advantage of its decentralized characteristic and its very large, shared data storage capacity". Their proposed system is based on a P2P-Tuple system where the execution of a job is done by a kind of cooperation of the peers. The paper proposes to handle the tail effect by peers pushing unfinished jobs to each other. Based on this, completion time of a job can be much lower than in a normal BOINC system.

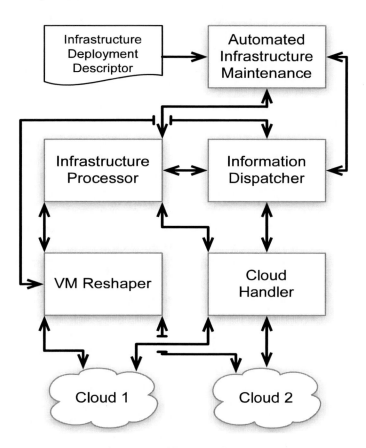

Figure 7. Architecture of OCCO.

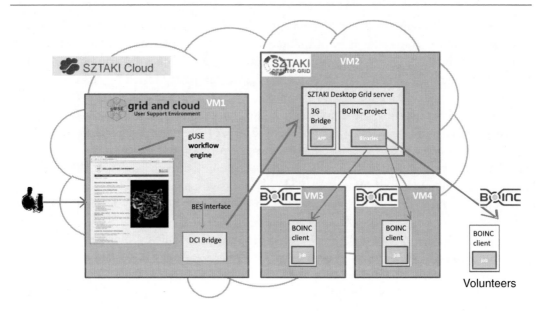

Figure 8. Infrastructure created by OCCO.

Various pilot systems like DIRAC [28] or Diane [29] are widely used by scientists these days. In these systems, a single pilot job is submitted through gLite, as a placeholder, to a given CE. The pilot job pulls real jobs from the pilot system's job repository for execution on the CE, and transfers information and results back. Pulling jobs and all communication are executed bypassing the gLite infrastructure, reducing the overhead of job submission from linear to constant time. This is also a way of decreasing the overhead of the gLite system; however, it is not targeted to use volunteer resources, and hence the number of accessible resources will be much smaller than in a volunteer system.

The notion of dynamic resource provisioning/orchestration and automatic deployment similar to the OCCO concept appears in other works, too. These solutions are general and are not aimed at supporting or extending desktop grids particularly. Chen et al. [32] present Sulcata, an on-line virtual cluster provisioning. They assume a pool of various physical resources that act as VM containers. Upon an user's request the system deploys a virtual cluster on-the-fly involving VM image preparation, VM creation and configuration and VM reboot. They solve basic functionalities of dynamic infrastructure provisioning; furthermore, the solution largely focuses on minimizing the overhead of VM image handling and deployment and proposes a resource mapping scheme. These solutions are general and are not aimed at supporting or extending desktop grids particularly.

Dörnemann et al. [33] introduced an on-demand on-the-fly deployment scheme to avoid peak loads. In a later work [34], this solution was advanced to support workflows and eliminate some shortcomings with respect to throughput and cost. To find a trade-off between task based scheduling (imprecise) and graph based scheduling (complex) of workflows, they propose a critical path based scheduling where the graph is annotated with information on anticipated run times and data transfers to calculate the makespan. Possible allocations for critical paths are predicted by genetic algorithms and the process is iterated until a mapping with minimalestimated runtime is reached. As it can be seen, in this case the goalis improving the quality of experience (as opposed to general resource provisioning in our case) by deployingservices on the flywith focus on workflows (as opposed to embarrassingly parallel applications in our case).

Vukojevic et al. [35] present a similar solution to OCCO in a service oriented scenario to support simulation workflows. Their aim is to provide and redeem services on-demand according to the progress of the workflow. The core of the solution is dynamic binding with software stack provisioning. Their aims are similar to ours, the technical realization is entirely different due to the service oriented approach.

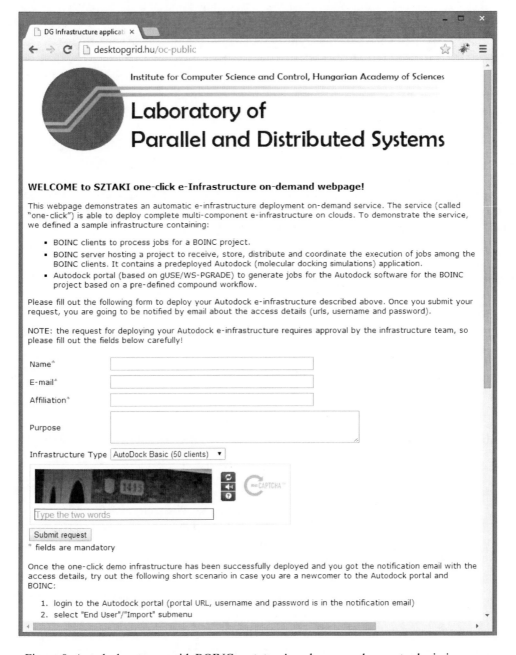

Figure 9. Autodock gateway with BOINC prototype's welcome- and request submission page.

Conclusion

BOINC-based desktop grid systems are excellent in collecting large number of volunteer resources worldwide. Despite their cost-effectiveness, there were several problems that prevented their widespread use in e-science environments. Recent innovations in virtualization and cloud technology helped us to overcome these major problems. Overall, we can claim that all the major obstacles witnessed in the former use of BOINC systemshave been eliminated. Our GBAC technology eliminates the need of porting applications to BOINC and the integration of clouds with BOINC systems solves the tail problem in volunteer desktop grids. As a result, more and more user communities start to use the EDGeS@home BOINC desktop grid either via a gLite VO (e.g., WeNMR), or via a gateway (e.g., biologists and chemists using autodock), or directly (e.g., BioVEL project). We expect more radical increase in use of BOINC systems in the near future, when the recently introduced one-click creation method of BOINC systems in clouds will be widely applied by scientists.

Acknowledgment

The research leading to these results has received funding from the European Union Seventh Framework Programme (FP7/2007-2013) under grant agreement no 261556 (EDGI), no. 283481 (SCI-BUS) and under grant agreement no 312297 (IDGF-SP).

References

[1] Cristina Aiftimiei, Paolo Andreetto, Sara Bertocco, Simone Dalla Fina, Alvise Dorigo, Eric Frizziero, Alessio Gianelle, Moreno Marzolla, Mirco Mazzucato, Massimo Sgaravatto, Sergio Traldi, Luigi Zangrando, *Design and implementation of the gLiteCREAM job management service,* Future Generation Computer Systems, Volume 26, Issue 4, April 2010, Pages 654-667, ISSN 0167-739X, 10.1016/j.future.2009.12.006.

[2] Streit, P. Bala, A. Beck-Ratzka, K. Benedyczak et al., *Unicore 6:Recent and future advancements,* Berichte des Forschungszentrums Julich, vol. 65, 2010.

[3] Globus Toolkit Version 4: Software for Service-Oriented Systems. I. Foster. *IFIP International Conference on Network and Parallel Computing,* Springer-Verlag LNCS 3779, pp 2-13, 2006.

[4] M. Ellert, M. Grønager, A. Konstantinov, B. Konya, J. Lindemann, I. Livenson, J. Nielsen, M. Niinimaki, O. Smirnova and A. Waananen, *Advanced resource connector middle ware for lightweight computational grids,* Future Generation Computer Systems, vol. 23, no. 2, pp. 219-240, 2007.

[5] David P. Anderson 2004. BOINC: A System for Public-Resource Computing and Storage. In *Proceedings of the 5th IEEE/ACM International Workshop on Grid Computing (GRID '04).* IEEE Computer Society, Washington, DC, USA, 4-10. DOI=10.1109/GRID.2004.14 http://dx.doi.org/10.1109/GRID.2004.14.

[6] A. C. Marosi, Z. Balaton & P. Kacsuk (2009). Gen Wrapper: A generic wrapper for running legacy applications on desktop grids. In *2009 IEEE International Symposiumon Parallel & Distributed Processing* (pp. 1-6). IEEE. doi:10.1109/IPDPS.2009.5161136.

[7]   C. Marosi, G. Gombás, Z. Balaton & P. Kacsuk. (2008). *Enabling Java applications for BOINC with DC-API.* In P. Kacsuk, R. Lovas, & Z. Németh (Eds.), Distributed and Parallel Systems SE-1 (pp. 3-12). Springer US. doi:10.1007/978-0-387-79448-8_1.

[8]   *The EDGI EU FP7 project:* http://edgi-project.eu.

[9]   P. Kacsuk, J. Kovacs, Z. Farkas, A. Marosiand Z. Balaton, Towards a powerful european DCI based on desktop grids. *Journal of Grid Computing,* 9:219-239, 2011.

[10]   Attila Marosi, József Kovács, Peter Kacsuk, *Towards a volunteer cloud system, Future Generation Computer Systems,* Volume 29, Issue 6, Pages: 1442-1451, 2013, ISSN 0167-739X, http://www.sciencedirect.com/science/article/pii/S0167739X12000660, 10.1016/j.future.2012.03.013.

[11]   Ádám Visegrádi, József Kovács, Peter Kacsuk: *Efficient extension of gLite VOs with BOINC based desktop grids,* Future Generation Computer Systems, Volume 32, March 2014, Pages 13-23, ISSN 0167-739X, http://dx.doi.org/10.1016/j.future.2013.10.012, (http://www.sciencedirect.com/science/article/pii/S0167739X1300229X).

[12]   Rajkumar Buyya, Chee Shin Yeo, Srikumar Venugopal, James Broberg, Ivona Brandic, Cloud computing and emerging IT platforms: Vision, hype, and reality for delivering computing as the 5th utility. *Future Generation Comp. Syst.* 25(6): 599-616 (2009).

[13]   C.U. Soettrup, A. Waananen, J. Kovacs, Transparent execution of ARC jobs on Desktop Grid resources, MIPRO 2012, *Proceedings of the 35th International Convention IEEE Conference Publications Croatian Society for Information and Communication Technology, Electronics and Microelectronics,* MIPRO Rijeka, Croatia 2012 pp. 271-276, ISBN: 978-953-233-072-4.

[14]   M. Keller, J.Kovacs, A.BrinkmannDesktop Grids Opening up to UNICORE, *Proceedings of UNICORE Summit 2011,* IAS Series 09, Forschungszentrum Jülich GmbH Zentralbibliothek, Verlag, Torun, Poland 2011 pp. 67-76 ISBN: 978-3-89336-750-4.

[15]   *The EDGeS EU FP7 project:* http://edges-grid.eu.

[16]   *The IDGF-SP EU FP7 project:*http://idgf-sp.eu.

[17]   Z. Farkas, P.Kacsuk, Z.Balaton, G.Gombás, *Interoperability of BOINC and EGEE, Future Generation Computer Systems,* Volume 26, Issue 8, October 2010, Pages 1092-1103, ISSN 0167-739X, 10.1016/j.future.2010.05.009. (http://www.sciencedirect.com/science/article/pii/S0167739X10000890).

[18]   Gabor Terstyanszky, Tamas Kiss, Tamas Kukla, Zsolt Lichtenberger, Stephen Winter Pamela Greenwell, and Sharron McEldowney and Hans Heindl (2012) Application repository and science gateway for running molecular docking and dynamics simulations. Healthgrid applications and technologies meet science gateways for life sciences. *Studies in health technology and informatics* (175). IOS Press, pp. 152-161. ISBN 9781614990536.

[19]   *The European Grid Initiative,* http://www.egi.eu.

[20]   *WMIN DG:*http://wgrass.wmin.ac.uk/index.php/Desktop_Grid:Westminster_Local_DG.

[21]   *The online documentation site:* http://doc.desktopgrid.hu.

[22]   Simon Delamare, Gilles Fedak, Derrick Kondo, Oleg Lodygensky, SpeQuloS. A QoS Service for BoT Applications Using Best Effort Distributed Computing Infrastructures, in *International Symposium on High Performance Distributed Computing (HPDC'2012),* Delft, Nederlands, 2012.

[23]   Javadi, B., Kondo, D., Vincent, J.-M., Anderson, D.P., Discovering Statistical Modelsof Availability in Large Distributed Systems: An Empirical Study of SETI@home,

Parallel and Distributed Systems, IEEE Transactions on, vol. 22, no. 11, pp. 1896-1903, Nov. 2011. doi: 10.1109/TPDS.2011.50.

[24] Pataki, M., Marosi, A. C. (2012). Searching for Translated Plagiarism with the Help of Desktop Grids. *Journal of Grid Computing*, 1-18. http://dx.doi.org/10.1007/s10723-012-9224-5.

[25] Gabor Terstyanszky, Tamas Kiss, Tamas Kukla, Zsolt Lichtenberger, Stephen Winter, Pamela Greenwell, Sharron McEldowneyand Hans Heindl, Application Repository and Science Gateway for Running Molecular Docking and Dynamics Simulations, in Sandra Gesing etal.,*Editors HealthGrid Applications and Technologies Meet Science Gateways for Life Sciences, Studies* in Health Technology and Informatics, Vol. 175, pp. 152-161, IOS Press, 2012, ISSN 0926-9630 (print), ISSN 1897-8365.

[26] Reynolds, C.J., Winter, S., Terstyanszky, G.Z., Kiss, T., Greenwell, P., Acs, S., Kacsuk, P., Scientific Workflow Makespan Reduction through Cloud Augmented Desktop Grids, Cloud Computing Technology and Science (CloudCom), 2011 *IEEE Third International Conference* on, pp. 18-23, Nov. 29 2011-Dec. 1 2011, doi: 10.1109/CloudCom.2011.13.

[27] Lei Ni, Aaron Harwood, P2P-Tuple: Towards a Robust Volunteer Computing Platform pdcat, *International Conference on Parallel and Distributed Computing*, Applications and Technologies, 2009, pp.217-223.

[28] Tsaregorodtsev et al., DIRAC: a community grid solution, *J. Phys. Conf. Ser.* 119 (2008) 062048.

[29] Vladimir V.Korkhov, Jakub T.Moscickiand Valeria V.Krzhizhanovskaya, 2009. *Dynamic workload balancing of parallel applications with user-level scheduling on the Grid. Future Gener. Comput. Syst.* 25, 1 (January 2009), 28-34. DOI=10.1016/j.future.2008.07.001 http://dx.doi.org/10.1016/j.future.2008.07.001.

[30] *The WeNMR community,* https://www.wenmr.eu.

[31] *The BIOVEL community,*http://www.biovel.eu.

[32] Yang Chen, Tianyu Woand Jianxin Li. An efficient resource management system for on-line virtual clusterprovision. *In IEEE CLOUD,* pages 72-79, 2009.

[33] Tim Dörnemann, Ernst Juhnkeand Bernd Freisleben. On-demand resource provisioningfor bpel workflows using amazon'selastic compute cloud. In *IEEE/ACM Int. Symp. on Cluster Computing and the Grid (CCGrid),* pages 140-147, 2009.

[34] Tim Dörnemann, Ernst Juhnke, Thomas Noll, Dominik Seilerand Bernd Freisleben. Data flow driven scheduling of bpel workflows using cloud resources. *In IEEE CLOUD*, pp. 196-203, 2010.

[35] Karolina Vukojevic-Haupt, Dimka Karastoyanova, Frank Leymann., On-demand Provisioning of Infrastructure, Middleware and Services for Simulation Workflows. *SOCA* 2013: 91-98.

[36] http://riemann-siegel.com/.

[37] Péter Tar, IstvánMaros, Parameter sweep of a linear programming solver on distributed computing infrastructures, presented at: *17th Spring Wind Conference,* Debrecen, 2014. March 21-23.

INDEX